Essential Clinical Social Work Series

Series Editor

Carol Tosone, New York University, New York, USA

More information about this series at http://www.springer.com/series/8115

Terry B. Northcut
Editor

Cultivating Mindfulness in Clinical Social Work

Narratives from Practice

Springer

Editor
Terry B. Northcut
School of Social Work
Loyola University of Chicago
Chicago, IL
USA

ISSN 2520-1611 ISSN 2520-162X (electronic)
Essential Clinical Social Work Series
ISBN 978-3-319-43840-5 ISBN 978-3-319-43842-9 (eBook)
DOI 10.1007/978-3-319-43842-9

Library of Congress Control Number: 2017931340

Printed on acid-free paper

This Springer imprint is published by Springer Nature
The registered company is Springer International Publishing AG
The registered company address is: Gewerbestrasse 11, 6330 Cham, Switzerland

To my mother, Mary Jean Blythe Brumley
(1925–2011), for emphasizing religion
and spirituality as an essential part of life

Acknowledgments

The writing and editing of this book has been challenging as well as rewarding. I want to thank each of the authors who contributed their personal and professional wisdom and experiences with mindfulness. Several colleagues and graduate students also helped with any number of important and much needed tasks: Amelia Joseph contributed early ideas and professional research; Merretta Dickerson found numerous needles in the proverbial haystack as well as edited all the chapters; Mindy Wilkerson enthusiastically investigated idiosyncratic topics; Rebecca Strauss provided essential motivation, opinions, and feedback; and Siddhesh Mukerji thoughtfully reviewed and discussed selected chapters. This text would not have been written if not for Carol Tosone's encouragement, support, and ability to detect unresolved ambivalence with the subject matter. I appreciate my colleagues at Loyola University of Chicago School of Social Work for continuing to provide an environment that stimulates and supports my scholarship and teaching.

My family has tolerated the endless hours of my sitting at the computer and distracted attention as I tried to read, study, write, and practice mindfulness. They appreciated the irony with very good humor. Blythe and Sam continue to provide enormous inspiration and unequivocal support for wherever my academic and personal interests take me. My husband Greg has the ability to find the right article or resource I need even before I know I need it; his love and devotion has spanned three continents of travel. My sister Beth continues to provide essential humor and pragmatism on a daily basis as she saves my sanity from the absurdities of life.

Contents

Contributors

Natalie Beck Institute for Clinical Social Work, Chicago, USA

Robin Carnes Warriors at Ease, Silver Spring, MD, USA

Susan Grossman School of Social Work, Loyola University Chicago, Chicago, IL, USA

Susan A. Lord Department of Social Work, University of New Hampshire, Durham, USA

Terry B. Northcut School of Social Work, Loyola University of Chicago, Chicago, IL, USA

Corinne Peterson iRest® Yoga Nidra Meditation, Therapeutic Yoga and Massage, Chicago, IL, USA

Michael Rogan LCSW, Psychotherapist and Neuroscientist, New York, USA

Connie Sheehan Department of Social Work, DePaul University, Chicago, IL, USA

Rebecca Strauss Turning Point Behavioral Health Care Center, Skokie, IL, USA

Jenifer Talley Psychology Department, The New School for Social Research, New York, USA; The Center for Optimal Living, New York, USA

Amy Zajakowski Uhll Chicago Center for Integration and Healing, Chicago, IL, USA

Chapter 1
Introduction: The Tincture of Time

Terry B. Northcut

There can be no health without mental health.
World Health Organization.

Why does the world need another book on mindfulness? There are currently at least two million books on practicing mindfulness, teaching mindfulness, the philosophy of mindfulness, and applying mindfulness to any situation, illness, work environment, or daily activity. There is even a book with 108 metaphors for mindfulness (Kozak 2009). Frankly, the idea of adding anything to this body of literature seems presumptuous, and even grandiose. After hundreds of years of practice and focus, what can be said that has not been said before? While it is true that there seems to be "nothing new under the sun," it is still worthwhile to revisit the concept of mindfulness for the practicing clinical social worker or mental health professional today. One aspect that has tugged at the "collective minds" of the authors included in this text is an exploration of the implications of integrating mindfulness into our professional practice and work. We have moved to a model of practice that takes into account the internal world and the external world and the dynamic interplay between the two, albeit, not without controversy or snags in our implementation and understanding. However, what is less clear is what place mindfulness holds in the process of "helping" and how does it change the professional dialogue about how people change, develop, and cope with the complicated, multidimensional world in which we live and practice.

Acknowledging and accepting mindfulness into clinical social work compels us to think about the implications for our understanding of human behavior, our social systems, our educational structures, our understanding of health and mental health, and our approach to clinical research. What happens if we reintegrate an understanding of mind and body that builds on current perspectives of functioning, rather than relying on the seemingly primitive, preindustrial perspectives popular in the Middle Ages, that considered mind and body intertwined? Sweet (2012) compared

T.B. Northcut (✉)
School of Social Work, Loyola University of Chicago, Chicago, IL, USA
e-mail: tnorthc@luc.edu

T.B. Northcut (ed.), *Cultivating Mindfulness in Clinical Social Work*,
Essential Clinical Social Work Series, DOI 10.1007/978-3-319-43842-9_1

the attitude about the human body in the twelfth century with medical practice today, in her book *God's Hotel*. Using the twelfth century perspective of a mystic, healer, and nun, Sweet describes the human body as a "garden to be tended." She became convinced that the physical body needed ways to reawaken its capacity for growth in a world where the practice of medicine had morphed into the "delivery of health care" (Ofri 2013). Beginning with the practice of medieval medicine, which supplied "regular meals, clean linens, cheerful surroundings, and the opportunity for careful observation," Sweet struggled to provide health care that made "efficient use of its inefficiency" in a hospital setting on the verge of converting to managed care (Zuger 2012). NY Times writer Abigail Zuger questioned the sensibility of Sweet's work at attempting to change our current healthcare methodology comparing the experience to interrupting "cowboys in the midst of a stampede" (2012). Practitioners have been choking on the dust of the stampede in our society's rush to make everything cost-effective and accountable. To some degree, the practice of mindfulness has been folded into that stampede towards efficiency—classes on mindfulness have been relegated to five-minute sound bites that can be accessed by a phone app for the busy executive or carpool driving parent—which is not necessarily a bad advancement. However, we should take the time to consider the implications of seemingly contradictory applications, i.e., a quick way to be mindful.

One of the legacies of the industrial age is the perspective of the human body as a machine and human behavior as mechanical; a metaphor that has worn thin with time, experience, and research (Sederer 2013). Neuroscience continues to validate our professional social work experience which has consistently emphasized that relationships matter (Siegel 2007; Cozolino 2013; etc.). Whether it is in the therapeutic relationship or the teaching role, we have empirically validated what we have long known, that "relationships exist at the intersection of mind-body. They are the precursor to learning" (Hammond 2015, p. 45).

Postmodernism and qualitative research has also confirmed that we are limited in our learning if we only look at observable behavior. However, we do not yet know how to apply the "tincture of time" as Sweet would call it, to allow us to reconsider what we can learn from our evolving understanding of our minds and our experiences in healing. Certainly acute care is still needed; a bone needs to be reset, discrimination still needs to be eradicated, and healthcare disparities need to be neutralized and equalized. However, we have learned much about good care necessary for healthy development, to be professionally mindful about what constitutes good mental and physical health and how to facilitate that healing process. Sweet championed the motto that "sick people need time….and their doctors do too."

The application of mindfulness to clinical social work practice needs time and study as well. It is worthwhile to hesitate before declaring mindfulness a panacea for all that ails us as individuals, families, and societies. A businessman and software engineer, Schmidt (2013), stated in a radio interview, "Countries that have the Internet already are not going to turn it off. And so the power of freedom, the power of ideas will spread, and it will change those societies in very dramatic ways." We cannot turn back the clock to some imaginary ideal when things were simpler, nor would we want to. Technology and medical research are two areas that have brought us immeasurable benefits. Nevertheless, as we have learned from years of medical and mental health practice, some things cannot be hurried. In the meantime there can be treatments, practices, activities, facilitating environments, therapy, etc., that can be helpful during the process of mindfully engaging clients. This text proposes to take that time and effort to examine mindfulness with critical optimism and its implications for practice now, and in the near future.

The perspectives of authors included here vary in the populations they work with and the type of social work provided. For the purposes of the collection of applications in this text, each author will discuss the relevant research into mindfulness within his or her subject area, rather than have one chapter summarizing the preponderance of quantitative and qualitative results supporting its usefulness in health and mental health care. In the past many mindfulness-based treatment program evaluations were focused on Jon Kabat Zinn's Mindfulness-Based Stress Reduction (MBSR) which emphasizes mindfulness in daily living (Lazar 2005). Research on the benefits and applications of MBSR continue, however, programs evaluating physiological and cognitive changes associated with other forms of mindfulness increase each year, as well as the benefits of mindfulness when combined with physical movement (e.g., yoga or qigong), (Lazar 2005; NIH 2016; Pigeon et al. 2015; Rhodes et al. 2016; Stoller et al. 2012; Williams 2016). The positive results associated with the practice of mindfulness will likely continue as it offers a sustainable way that individuals can enhance physical and mental health at very little cost. Undoubtedly, the emphasis in the United States will also be on the effectiveness in brief treatment models. Research also continues on using mindfulness as an intervention with nondominant cultural and/or marginalized backgrounds (Fuchs et al. 2013; Thurnauer 2016).

Just as there are diverse populations benefitting from mindfulness, there are diverse ways to incorporate mindfulness and diverse ways of how we talk about mindfulness. One difficulty that quickly surfaces when preparing and reviewing these chapters is the ambiguity of terms that the mindful practitioner may intuitively know and understand, but for a beginner may sound vague and almost without meaning. What does it mean to be "open" or "soften the breath"? I am reminded of Stern's (1985) work on infancy when he characterized the first stage of the self as "coming into being," so essential for creativity and the integration of physical and emotional aspects of each of us, yet extremely vague when trying to explain it. This vagueness is also common with concepts associated with religion or spirituality, although those beliefs or practices are not necessarily a requirement in order to practice mindfulness, as some of these authors will attest to.

Another important characteristic common in the written work of colleagues in this text is the inclusion of personal experiences in tandem with the reporting of professional experiences. It is vital that a clinical social worker or other mental health professional not introduces mindfulness to clients without having been trained sufficiently, and without having developed extensive personal experience. Each author will discuss how they make use of their personal experiences, both good and bad, in their work with clients. Despite the understanding that mindfulness can be helpful in training the mind, it does not mean that the process of getting there is without trials and tribulations. As with therapy, there are times of smooth progression but there are also times of stress and remembrance of pain, anxiety, and stress. If a practitioner is familiar with the terrain of the journey to mindfulness, he or she can help clients prepare for and negotiate the more difficult times. Often in our Western society, there is an assumption that we should enter or achieve a new "state of being" without suffering. We cling to the medical model still prevalent today that suffering can be or should be cured. However, as anyone who has been through personal therapy knows, a good and helpful treatment does not equate to cure, nor to a smooth transition to "healthy" functioning. Rather, we learn to recognize when we are in the same cul-de-sacs of experience, but we cannot completely escape from ever entering the well-worn dysfunctional pre-established pathways. Consequently, it is important that the authors in this text include their personal experiences incorporating personal mindfulness in their clinical work with clients and colleagues or when they brought in an expert.

Chapter 2 begins our timely examination of the current context of mind–body medicine. Using Harrington's (2009) ideas of narrative themes, we can see how the remnants of each still impacts health and mental health practice today. While the world has continued to evolve with medical and technological advances, we do not yet know how to reintegrate the mind and body in our treatment methodologies, economic systems, and theoretical frameworks.

Chapter 3 reviews the terms and origins of mindfulness in order to clarify and differentiate the many similar but not equal practices. As with any clinical intervention, the introduction of a "technique" should be based on a clear understanding of the contraindications and pitfalls that can occur when practicing or utilizing mindfulness with clients. When relevant, authors in each of the subsequent chapters also discuss potential problems that can or have occurred when integrating mindfulness into clinical work.

Natalie Beck begins Chap. 4 describing her work in an intensive outpatient program with substance abusing clients who have confounding serious comorbidity issues as well. Given the difficulty one group of clients had with tolerating and/or numbing affective states, she brought in a therapist specializing in mindfulness. Impressed with how effective mindfulness practices were in allowing clients and herself to manage the overwhelming affect often present in the group, Natalie became curious about what exactly happens in the brain and body when experiencing mindfulness. Consequently, her doctoral work and research interests have allowed her to explore more clearly how the neurophysiological changes via mindfulness, facilitate and enhance therapeutic experiences for both clients and clinicians.

Chapter 5 demonstrates that our professional and personal selves overlap as we move across the lifespan and into different mindful work. Corrine Peterson, Susan Grossman, and Amy Zajakowski Uhll built on prior connections through their work in yoga nidra and mindfulness within different contexts to describe the overlap despite wearing different professional "hats." As a yoga instructor and a social service provider and administrator, Corinne speaks from her experience teaching many social workers and allied mental health professionals mindfulness as they cope with the stresses of clinical work. As a marital and family therapist, Amy Zajakowski Uhll discusses and illustrates how yoga nidra and mindfulness enhance her work with an individual client in and out of a therapy session. As a social work researcher, policy specialist, and administrator of a social work program, Susan Grossman reflects on her career and how her effectiveness increases when implementing the strategies learned with Corrinne and other specialists. The three authors weave together their stories to demonstrate how mindful yoga nidra facilitates self-care for professional social workers and their clients, students, or colleagues.

Michael Rogan shares his extensive background in Buddhism and in mental health in Chap. 6 as he demonstrates how he teaches clinicians to use mindfulness personally and with clients. One of my greatest concerns about writing and editing works on mindfulness has been about the tendency for clinical practitioners of all kinds, to profess expertise with mindfulness, perhaps with the best intentions, with minimal training and experience. We have all seen clients trying something new based on trends and information from social media that have resulted in decreased psychosocial functioning. Practicing mindfulness can, in fact, be quite disruptive to one's current functioning and clinicians need to know how to plan for and respond to difficulties as they occur. Michael provides numerous examples in which he attends to the individual context of each of his students and clients.

Research is in the early stages of documenting contraindications for mindfulness, however, the apparent universal aspect is also part of the appeal. The critical feature is how mindful teachers and clinicians must be very careful when working with trauma and/or clients with difficult and often unpredictable mental health symptoms. Robin Carnes and I wrote about her work in founding the Warriors at Ease (WAE) program with veterans suffering from PTSD in Chap. 7. Robin's story is a very personal one reflecting how opportunities in her life led to the type of practice that she conducts today. She utilizes the first person perspective to highlight each step that led her to appreciate the task of the student and teacher to "reconcile opposites" as they come to terms with experiencing their own body within the context of a "welcoming" attitude and relationship with mindfulness.

Chapater 8, authored by Susan Lord, describes her extensive experience with providing couples' treatment and negotiating the often harsh and critical environment that can predominate in this kind of systemic work. Her work on meditative dialogue facilitates couples' ability to provide compassion and empathy for themselves and each other in order to develop a relationship that can be rewarding for both. Susan's chapter shows her dedication to hearing each of the clients' voices by demonstrating compassion, and empowering them to accept themselves and their significant partners. Through her use of mindfulness with couples, she is able to show how more effective communication within the triadic relationship of the therapist and couple enhances the couple's level of intimacy.

Sometimes clients come to therapy because they are very clear that there is an identifiable problem they feel is out of control. Very often, other confounding issues surface complicating the symptom picture. Chapter 9 tackles the issue of substance use and misuse as one of the most difficult behaviors to contend with given the potential for deadly results. Historically, there has been focus on "blaming the victim" as an explanation for substance abuse as we learn in the mind/body narratives discussed in this chapter. The AA model has had significant success, although its anonymity makes it difficult to have clear quantifiable data. However, there are clients who do not find success with that model or are not able to completely abstain from substance use. Harm reduction therapy has become an important treatment focus to help manage substance misuse. Jenifer Talley describes how she has incorporated mindfulness in the treatment with substance misuse in her work at The Center for Optimal Living in New York City with Andrew Tatarsky. A harm reduction focus acknowledges the complexity and multiple personal and social meanings and functions of substance use while not requiring a commitment to abstinence as a starting point in treatment (Tatarsky 2002). Mindfulness is uniquely suited to this approach as it allows for a nonjudgmental observation of the patterns associated with substance misuse such as wishing to escape from harsh self-critical thoughts, an inability to tolerate frustration or discomfort, or as a habitual response to cravings. The integration of mindfulness with harm reduction empowers clients to make choices about the relationship they wish to have with a certain substance or problematic behavior without a presumption that abstinence is the ideal or only acceptable outcome.

Rebecca Strauss has creatively turned the concept of "learned helplessness" into "**learned helpfulness**" as she provides group work for clients with serious mental illness. She beautifully demonstrates in Chap. 10, the ebbs and flows of ongoing practice with clients having a chronic condition. Each day is different and consequently each practice of mindfulness is unique. By accepting the fluctuations of their physical states, clients are also able to find commonality with each other and acceptance despite often debilitating symptoms.

As part of a Religion and Spirituality in Clinical Social Work course that I teach at Loyola University of Chicago, I have been fortunate to have Connie Sheehan lead my classes in "talking circles" to demonstrate the use of mindfulness in Restorative Justice in situations where there has been a conflict and/or personal violation. She discusses her journey to using talking circles in a variety of settings, particularly within the criminal justice system in Chap. 11. Blending what she has learned about micro, mezzo, and macro practice, Connie is able to intervene with populations not ordinarily placed together in a group, in ways that empowers group participants by accepting each point of view and context of the focal experience.

Chapter 12 entitled "On the road to mindfulness" describes common themes from each of the chapters including understanding the personal context of each participant, tailoring mindfulness to the current context of the individual, and the underlying assumptions about health and resiliency in the theoretical and philosophy of mindfulness. The title of this chapter speaks to the importance of understanding "cultivating mindfulness" as a process rather than an end result with many unexpected turns and twists critical to the process. It is my hope that you will approach this text not as a definitive resource on mindfulness, but rather a collection of some of the important facets necessary to understand the application in practice. The focus is on pragmatism; whenever possible illustrations are given as to how, when, and where mindfulness has been found to be useful to this selection of social workers and clinicians in their professional and personal development. Authors represent professionals at many different levels of their careers each committed to finding mindful ways to empower and enhance the lives of others.

References

Cozolino, L. (2013). *The social neuroscience of education: Optimizing attachment and learning in the classroom*. NY: W. W. Norton.

Fuchs, C., Lee, J. K., Roemer, L., & Orsillo, S. M. (2013). Using mindfulness- and acceptance-based treatments with clients from nondominent cultural and/or marginalized backgrounds: Clinical considerations, meta-analysis findings, and introduction to the special series. *Cognitive and Behavioral Practice, 20*(1), 1–12.

Hammond, Z. (2015). *Culturally responsive teaching and the brain: Promoting Authentic engagement and rigor among culturally and linguistically diverse students*. CA: Corwin/Sage.

Harrington, A. (2009). *The cure within: A history of mind-body medicine*. NY: W. W. Norton & Company.

Kozak, A. (2009). *Wild chickens and petty tyrants: 108 metaphors for mindfulness*. Somerset, MA: Wisdom publishing.

Lazar, S. (2005). Mindfulness research. In C. Germer, R. D. Siegel, & P. R. Fulton (Eds.), *Mindfulness and psychotherapy*. NY: Guilford.

National Institute of Health. (2016). Study finds mindfulness meditation offers relief for low-back pain (news release). Retrieved from http://www.nih.gov/news-events/news-releases/study-finds-mindfulness-meditation-offers-relief-low-back-pain

Ofri, D. (2013). 'God's hotel.' by Victoria Sweet: Review. *SFGATE* 9/20/13. http://www.sfgate.com/books/article/God-s-Hotel-by-Victoria-Sweet-review-3498879.php

Pigeon, W., Allen, C., Possemato, K., Bergen-Cico, D., & Treatman, S. (2015). Feasibility and acceptability of a brief mindfulness program for veterans in primary care with posttraumatic stress disorder. *Mindfulness, 6,* 986–995.

Rhodes, A. M., Spinazzola, J., & van der Kolk, B. (2016). Yoga for adult women with chronic PTSD: A long-term follow-up study. *Journal of Alternative and Complementary Medicine, 22*(3), 189–196.

Schmidt, E. (2013). NPR interview. Retrieved 9/8/2016 http://www.npr.org/sections/alltech considered/2013/04/23/178620215/google-execs-say-the-power-of-information-is-underrated

Sederer, L. I. (2013). 'God's Hotel.' by Victoria Sweet: Review. *Huffington Post.* 7/22/13. http://www.huffingtonpost.com/lloyd-i-sederer-md/book-review_b_3624307.html

Siegel, D. J. (2007). *The mindful brain: Reflection and attunement in the cultivation of well-being*. NY: Norton.

Stern, D. (1985). *The interpersonal world of the infant*. NY: Basic Books.

Stoller, C. C., Greuel, J. H., Cimini, L. S., Fowler, M. S., & Koomar, J. A. (2012). Effects of sensory-enhanced yoga on symptoms of combat stress in deployed military personnel. *American Journal of Occupational Therapy, 66*(1), 59–68.

Sweet, V. (2012). *God's hotel: A doctor, a hospital, and a pilgrimage to the heart of medicine*. NY: Riverhead Books/Penguin.

Tatarsky, A. (2002). *Harm reduction psychotherapy: A new treatment for drug and alcohol problems*. NY: Jason Aronson/Rowman & Littlefield.

Thurnauer, E. (2016). *Cultural competence and mindfulness-based treatment with Asian Americans: A literature review*. Unpublished manuscript. New York University Silver School of Social Work DSW Student.

Williams, M. E. (2016). Why every mind needs mindfulness. *Time special edition: Mindfulness the new science of health and happiness*. NY: Time Inc. Books.

Zuger, A. (2013). A hospital that gave its patients time to heal. *New York Times* 5/28/12. http://www.nytimes.com/2012/05/29/health/29zuger.html?_r=0

Chapter 2
Beginning with the Context: The Mind–Body Conundrum

Terry B. Northcut

> *In fact 'connection' understates the case: in the yoga tradition [and Āyurveda] the mind is said to be the most subtle aspect of the body, and body the most tangible aspect of mind. They exist on a continuum*
>
> Wallis (2016).

Understanding what is meant by the term "mind" is dependent on who you ask and during which period in history. In current times, Siegel (2007) speaks of the mind in terms of "an embodied and relational process that regulates the flow of energy and information" (p. 5). As an interpersonal neurologist, he views the mind as encompassing more than what the brain does. What we think of as that the mind cannot be separated from the body despite our Cartesian heritage. "Mindfulness is a process of self-inquiry directed at what is happening in the moment, often focused on how the body feels, on how we *embody* this moment…without inner commentary, judgment, or storytelling" (Kozak 2009, p. 2). Conceptualizing mindfulness as a whole body experience rejoins the mind and the body in a way that the western world has historically had difficulty reconciling and operationalizing. The current medical, economic, and political environment reflects that mis-attunement. Too often our pattern in America has been that of segregated health care:

> In a hospital, the body is divided into departments. One department for the ear, nose and throat, one for the eyes, one for the stomach and the intestines, one for the sexual organs, one for heart and blood vessels, and one for the soul, which is treated in the psychiatric wards (Knausgaard 2014).

However, research has shown that the tendency to separate the mind and body leads to missing vital information which then leads to "poorer outcomes and higher costs in the care of patients" (Petterson et al. 2008, p. 1). In order to better understand the relevance of mindfulness for clinical practice, it is important to first consider the context of health and mental health care in the United States today.

T.B. Northcut (✉)
School of Social Work, Loyola University of Chicago, Chicago, IL, USA
e-mail: northc@luc.edu

T.B. Northcut (ed.), *Cultivating Mindfulness in Clinical Social Work*,
Essential Clinical Social Work Series, DOI 10.1007/978-3-319-43842-9_2

Clinical social workers, physicians, and healers in many if not all cultures recognize that our bodies can be understood as conduits or carriers of messages if we listen carefully. However, this holistic approach to health has not been consistently understood or appreciated. Harrington (2008) proposes that the relationship between mind and body in medicine represents a complex myriad of stories woven together across time. Such narratives are formed, edited, and influenced by scientific and humanistic disciplines, as well as economic, political, religious, secular, and historical factors. Consequently, we must look at results of empirical study and the narratives surrounding the study of both mind and body to gain a more complete understanding of how to best intervene clinically.

Gay (2010) suggests in his analysis of the contrasts between progress in science versus progress in the humanities that science has advanced by examining objects under study with greater and greater magnification.[1] In contrast, understanding advances in the humanities requires an examination of individuals and the contexts in which they lived, which cannot be made more meaningful by simple magnification of the object under study.[2] In a similar way, to better understand mindfulness and how it can be used with clients in western culture at this point in time, we should examine some of the narratives that have shaped our scientific and humanistic advances and not just elucidate the steps to becoming more mindful. As with progress in the field of humanities, we are in essence trying to understand the "intellectual ecology" shaping our study of the mind and body by looking at the persuasive narratives surrounding health and mental health (Gay 2010).

What then have been some of the more predominant narratives influencing our current understanding of mind and body? Harrington (2008) suggests six important narratives beginning around what was known in Europe as the Renaissance period: the Power of Suggestion; the Body that Speaks; the Power of Positive Thinking; Broken by Modern Life; Healing Ties; and Eastward Journeys. She resists confining these narratives to particular dates and times because with any narrative there is not a strict beginning and end for when the stories are true (White 2007). In epigenetic fashion, each narrative builds on the prior, continuing to exert influence even as new narratives take shape and dominate. As the protagonist in Bernhard Schlink's novel *The Reader* states, "the tectonic layers of our lives rest so tightly one on top of the other that we always come up against earlier events in later ones, not as matter that has been fully formed and pushed aside, but absolutely present and alive" (Schlink 1995, p. 217). There cannot be a linear exposition of narratives as they cycle forward and backwards in ever widening circles. It is also important to emphasize that covering a few of the historical narratives relevant to mind–body medicine, inevitably leaves out innumerable other narratives and influences. The authors and significant figures and events mentioned in this chapter are a

[1]e.g., the discovery of cells under a microscope advancing to examination of these same cells under greater magnification for the presence of DNA and even genetic markers.

[2]e.g., poems or paintings lose their beauty and value if appreciation and understanding is restricted to a dissection of each word or brush stroke.

microcosm of the many important contributions to the ongoing narratives that have impacted each of us in how we conceptualize good health. A biographer, reports Oates (1987), often feels a "tapping on the shoulder" leading him or her to choose a particular subject (Hart 2014, p. 787). While not writing a biographical narrative, I did find particular scholars more compelling perhaps based on a curiosity about why I had not heard them mentioned before in many historical accountings of mental health. In an effort to change what has unfortunately been a "white man's history" so common in the medical and psychological fields, I have tried to include voices not often heard, which of course reflects my own personal narrative. There cannot be one scientific reality or an equitable balance or fair representation of the impact of each historical event, professional discipline, scholarly researcher or theoretician. However, I have tried to include some of the more obvious influences as well as voices that have been perhaps marginalized in usual discussions of mind and body medicine. We begin where Harrington does, with **The Power of Suggestion**.

The impact of religious and political environments is evident in the first narrative of **The Power of Suggestion** (Harrington 2008). Mental illness was viewed as representing demonic possession requiring a form of exorcism by a special person consecrated by God. That legacy of the importance of someone other than ourselves as necessary to facilitate healing of another continues today. Centuries ago this "essential other" was only able to heal the other when appropriately endowed with religious or spiritual powers. This paradigm of the Power of Suggestion dominated many developed countries at least as far back as the 1600s when Pope Paul V affirmed the existence of demons and laid out the process for exorcism of these demons.[3] All through centuries in the United States, many religious beliefs and practices have immigrated to form a powerful rubric that influences how we understood any form of dysfunction—physical or psychological. These dysfunctions in the 1600–1700s were not yet viewed as having a sociological source. Rather, they were believed to stem from an external force inhabiting the person against their will, requiring another person to force the possession to leave the patient. An "other" could assess and determine whether someone was ill, why they became ill, and how and if they could be cured.

By the 1700s, a general skepticism about the likelihood of possession took hold with some recognition that perhaps there was an investment by ruling parties in supporting the power of the "healers". The political philosopher Thomas Hobbes living in a time of economic, political, military, and religious turmoil in England, questioned what he saw as the inappropriateness of blending religion and public policy (Williams, n.d.). Hobbes was grappling with the dominance of civil conflict and trying to figure out how human beings can live together peacefully. While Descartes is credited (or blamed) with the Cartesian dualism of separating mind and

[3]The procedures for exorcism by priests "remained on the books" until 1999 when the "rules for the millennium" were changed as part of the liturgical reform (Harrington 2008, p. 37, and endnote on p. 260).

body, it is Hobbes who promulgated the mechanistic view of the human body as an alternative to the view in which mind and body were able to be influenced by those in power at the time. Hobbes' influence on the separation of the material world from the spiritual world relied on his belief that human judgment was inherently flawed and should not be trusted as authority. Science needed to have a much more powerful role in decisions affecting the public domain in his view, to separate civil discourse from emotional and passionate ideology that interfered with peaceful coexistence. He believed men were "vehemently in love with their own new opinions…and obstinately bent to maintain them" (*Leviathan*, vii. 4). The emerging scientific method challenged the belief in the ability of another human being to exorcize demons and the apparent magical ability of one person to cure another. In contrast to Foucault's twentieth century views on the use of scientific knowledge as a form of social control (Chambon et al. 2009), Hobbes ushered in what he saw as the need for scientific knowledge to combat the power of the ruling class to use their religious knowledge to control public and private behavior. The social world, influenced by Hobbes, was no longer willing to accept changes in the human body by faith alone. As historian Ellenberger eloquently states, "It is not enough to cure the sick; you have to cure them with methods accepted by the community" (1970, p. 57 as cited in Harrington 2008). The "power of suggestion" narrative was ushered out by skepticism of the power of religious confessional rituals and replaced by a narrative of **The Body That Speaks** (Harrington 2008).

Darwin's research supporting natural selection (that species evolved in order to adapt to the environments around them) and the theory of evolution reinforced how helpful science could be in explaining human behavior. Guided by the need to be considered scientific and therefore valid, Freud, as well as other European psychosomatic scientists examining the effects of WWI (and subsequently WWII), viewed the mind as having depth warranting excavation and exploration. There was an attempt to examine the body as a scientific object—one capable of being understood by magnification, as Gay (2010) would suggest. As a detective is confronted with a mystery, the body became the subject to investigate to decipher the message being conveyed through symptoms. Healing was believed possible when messages the body sends were decoded. The mind–body narrative shifted to **The Body that Speaks** as a result. It was believed, if we could find a way to listen appropriately, we could find a more effective way to intervene therapeutically.

Freud and other European scientists were dominant influences during this time period. Many texts and websites have recounted and analyzed that history.[4] However, we need to look further than just European Freudians, to understand what was happening in the United States. For example, social work became a part of the mental hygiene movement in America during the early twentieth century, as the profession combined efforts on casework stemming from work in the settlement

[4](e.g., Freud's texts, Jones 1955; Mitchell and Black 1996; Berzoff et al. 2016; Heller and Gitterman 2011; http://www.dualdiagnosis.org/mental-health-and-addiction/history; http://www.mentalhealthamerica.net/our-history, etc.).

houses with the scientific method attempted by psychoanalysis. Mary Jarrett was a welfare worker in the Children's Aid Society and was trained in the casework method. She was hired by Dr. E.E. Southard at Boston Psychiatric Hospital to help engineer the clinical approach that became the hallmark of psychiatric social work. In 1918, they began what would become one of the earliest schools for social work, Smith College School for Social Work to address the growing needs of World War I veterans suffering from shell shock. They thought soldiers' reactions to stress were parallel to civilian's response to high stress situations. Their emphasis was on trying to understand the relationship between emotions and symptoms as psychiatry shifted focus from a moral to a physiological one (Rubin 2009).

A female voice not often referred to in mental health literature is that of Helen Flanders Dunbar. She notably tried to bridge the mind, body, and spirit and was an important advocate of physicians and clergy cooperating in their efforts to care for the sick. Dunbar received degrees in mathematics, psychology, theology, philosophy, and medicine. The founder of the American Psychosomatic Society and its professional journal *Psychosomatic Medicine*, she explicitly focused on the mind–body connection during her short life (1902–1959). Influenced by philosophers such as Alfred North Whitehead, William James and the American School of Psychiatry, Dunbar and her colleagues "saw patients first as human beings who were dynamically involved in an environment in which they were formed and transformed…. And her concern with seeing patients and disease in terms of a patterned, organic whole anticipates what came to be formally called by the 1960s the 'biopsychosocial model'" (Hart 2014, p. 784). The patient began to be viewed as a combination of the psych and soma, body and soul. Dunbar was also interested in trying to link certain diseases with certain personality types related to her observation of 1300 patients and seeing their varying inhibitions or unregulated expression of emotion.[5]

Franz Alexander, a Hungarian psychoanalyst arriving in the United States in the 1920s, emphasized Freudian theories about the physiology of emotions. Similar to Dunbar, Alexander also believed that repressed emotional conflicts led to certain diseases by "chronically stimulating or activating different specific vegetative organs in one's body…until they finally begin to malfunction" (Harrington 2008, p. 91). The implication that the body held secrets that could make us ill had important ramifications: who then knew what the secrets were and what they meant?

Feminists became concerned about men in positions of power assuming the role of telling women what their bodies needed. While women were struggling to ratify the 19th amendment in 1920 to allow their right to vote, it took almost 50 more years before women used their voice to reclaim the right to know their own bodies. It was not until the late 1960s that a women's health movement in Boston attempted to

---

[5]Dunbar foreshadowed current work on emotional regulation as being one of the cornerstones in understanding personality syndromes considered for DSM5 and further research (e.g., Bradley et al. 2011; Carpenter and Trull 2013; Cole et al. 1994; Hoermann et al. 2013; etc.).

dispel the mysteries popularized by the paradigm of the body speaking, by organizing to publish *Our Bodies, Ourselves* (Boston Women's Health Book Collective and Norsigian 2011; Our Bodies, Ourselves (2016). Women wanted to take ownership over their own bodies and to prevent being at the mercy of a significant other, medical or personal, usually male, who claimed to know what was best for them. They decided to put their knowledge into an accessible format that could be shared and would serve as a model for women who want to learn about themselves, communicate their findings with doctors, and challenge the medical establishment to change and improve the care that women receive. Scientific gains were filtered with the sociological and psychological ramifications of those discoveries.

It was not only that the body had secrets or communicated via its symptoms that was important. With Darwin's understanding of the human body adapting to the needs of the environment over generations, we began to recognize that the body has self-righting, evolutionary guidelines that react to external traumatic events. Walter Cannon believed the body could, would, and should experience a severe reaction when confronted with danger. In 1923, he published his empirical findings related to how trauma impacted the body. Traumatic shock was caused by blood being drained into the dilated capillary region, a phenomenon for which he coined the term exemia. The treatment of shock, he argued, should concentrate on reinstating normal circulation. His observations also convinced him that the living body always strives toward a harmonious equilibrium—a state which Cannon called "homeostasis" in his book, *Wisdom of the Body* (Harrington 2008). Cannon is also responsible for the term "flight or fight" to represent how the body responds to fear and anxiety (Massey 2015). One of his investigations as early as the 1930s showed that when cats were upset by the presence of an enemy (a barking dog), their peristaltic activity was inhibited. Excitation and fear were producing an increase in blood pressure, blood sugar, pupil dilations, and piloerection (hair standing on end) (Harrington 2008, p. 146). We now had scientific proof that the body was directly impacted by the immediate physical environment in ways that would be evident in physiological measures. The physiological impact became even more critical to understand when trying to discover methodology of appropriate treatment. *What interventions could be introduced to patients experiencing the effects of trauma that would cause their bodies to recalibrate and return to normal functioning?*

Traumatic experiences increased with the impacts of both WWI and WWII. America experienced two world wars that stimulated an essential positive sense of unity and pride in the country. The victory with WWII brought a new optimism, which in turn impacted the mind–body narrative as it evolved into "**The Power of Positive Thinking**" (Harrington 2008). Norman Vincent Peale's (1952) positivism was popular with the majority white middle class as evidenced by subscription rates to his popular *Guideposts* religious magazine exceeding 4.5 million (Harrington 2008). As veterans reestablished themselves in their "victorious" homeland, there was a great emphasis on the belief in the ability to achieve the American Dream of economic success and prosperity. It was believed we could do anything we set our minds to. However, with men returning from war, they returned to jobs that women held during their absence. It was considered patriotic for women to leave their positions for the men and return to care for the home and children. The economy flourished after years in postdepression stagnation. Veterans had access to the GI bill for their respected service to the country to help train and educate them for the new frontier of the business and technological world, with less emphasis on manual labor. However, minorities had limited voice and power in setting public policy, consequently a robust economy was seen as a result of the hard work of the majority, not as a combination with optimal privileges setting the stage for optimal development.

Despite the scientific "proof" that the body can be ill for a variety of reasons, the mind was viewed as very powerful and capable of overruling any symptoms or difficulties. This was a popular American message of the Christian gospel as well; healing could occur with the appropriate level and kind of faith. As William James predicted in his philosophical text *The Varieties of Religious Experience*, "the greatest discovery of my generation is that man (sic) can alter his life simply by altering his attitude of mind" (Harrington 2008, p. 117; James 1905, p. 95). Research caught up to ideology espoused by earlier philosophers by proving the power of placebos in effecting change, which translated into the power of the mind to cure. The double-edged sword of the scientific research supporting the ability of placebos to effect positive change was that if the mind could heal, then it could also make us sick.

Ehrenreich's (2009) timely book *Bright-Sided: How Positive Thinking is Undermining America* challenged the scientific argument for cheerfulness during her personal experience of breast cancer. The predominant message she received was that a positive attitude could reduce the risk of cancer or its return. During the 1980s Bernie Siegel published his book *Love, Medicine and Miracles* which proposed that a healthy, vigorous, immune system could overcome cancer. In addition to Siegel's work, many other physicians, psychiatrists, and life coaches began to emphasize that not only could a positive attitude facilitate better health, but that sickness was a gift that could help realign someone's priorities. Ehrenreich challenged the extremism evident in some of these simplistic conclusions when she described the content of many motivational speakers and her response:

> If you want to improve your life – both materially and subjectively – you need to upgrade your attitude, revise your emotional responses, and focus your mind. One could think of other possible means of self-improvement – through education, for example, to acquire new "hard" skills or by working for social changes that would benefit all. But in the world of positive thinking, the challenges are all interior and easily overcome through an effort of the will (Ehrenreich 2009, p. 51).

In Ehrenreich's experience and in emerging scientific results, the pressure to be positive was proving to be exhausting and not delivering physical cures or stress relief. As one example, sociologist Hochschild (1983) published results of her study with flight attendants who were exhausted by the work requirement of cheerfulness to passengers at all times. At its extreme, the push for optimism resulted in the imperative to get rid of not only negative thoughts and emotions, but also the negative people in our lives.

Another major impact of the power of positive thinking narrative is the belief that you can manipulate external reality through your thoughts and feelings. Visualization of what you wanted could bring it to you via positive energy. If you do not receive what you are wanting then it is because of your faulty vision. "External conditions such as failure and unemployment were projections of one's inner sense of well-being" (Ehrenreich 2008, p. 61). A paradoxical result of that kind of mentality was the Calvinistic need to work harder to be happy. Overwork became a virtue and an admirable trait. Workplaces became "reprogrammed" into new age motivational environments that needed to overcome negativity. Positive thinking had become an obligation and the mind shifted to be a focus of observation. If we could just train our minds, we could also have the power to change our circumstances.

Despite the positivity movement, there were still large economic and demographic changes brought about by war such as the population increase with baby boomers. However, all was not positive; research on the negative impact of military experience on bomber pilots continued. Hans Selye, an endocrinologist contemporary of Cannon, had continued to study how negative emotions impacted body chemistry. While popular writers and speakers such as Norman Vincent Peale in the 1950s and physician Norman Cousins in the 1970s focused on positive emotions, there was still simultaneous research continuing on the impact of "stress entering our bodies not as a disease, but as a human experience" (Harrington 2008, p. 145). Unfortunately at that time, pilots who experienced negative reactions to their experiences in war were viewed as having preexisting character weaknesses. Selye and other colleagues were able to convince military researchers that their study of stress had some bearing on military personnel which helped to reduce the moral bias against stressed based reactions. However, that moral bias still exists in the public as many mental health and health difficulties are still viewed as being the personal failure of the politician, sports figure, entertainer, or neighbor next door (Drexler 2016; Sundararaman 2009).

Health problems escalated despite the discoveries and emphasis on the power of the mind to heal. Cancers and other illnesses defied attempts to be cured by positive thinking. At this point, "stress" developed as a separate focus and we moved into the narrative of **Broken by Modern Life**, according to Harrington (2008). Stress as a concept or entity for study helped us make sense of postwar anxieties and what appeared to be the cost of prosperity. Heart disease was on the increase and the Type A personality emerged—a tragic yet admired figure evident in Western culture. The dialectic of admiration and yet concern led to the uniquely American individualistic approach of biofeedback which asked how can we systematically and individually cope with the consequences of modern life. We cycled back to listening to the body to determine the slightest physiological response in brainwaves, heart rate and pain perception utilizing our new technological advances. The goal was to harness the mind to change thoughts, emotions, and behavior in order to improve health (Association for Applied Psychophysiology and Biofeedback 2011).

The 1950s also saw the rise and plateau of behaviorism. According to Miller (2003), Pavlov and B.F. Skinner argued that mental events were not observable and consequently not sufficiently scientific. Using behaviorism as the gold standard, psychology attempted to become an objective science.[6] Fortunately, a first revolution of cognitive theorists and researchers realized that there were problems with a strict behaviorist approach:

> Behaviorism was an exciting adventure for experimental psychology but by the mid-1950s it had become apparent that it could not succeed. As Chomsky remarked, defining psychology as the science of behavior was like defining physics as the science of meter reading. If scientific psychology were to succeed, mentalistic concepts would have to integrate and explain the behavioral data. We were still reluctant to use such terms as 'mentalism' to describe what was needed, so we talked about cognition instead. Whatever we called it, the cognitive counter-revolution (against behaviorism) in psychology brought the mind back into experimental psychology (Miller 2003, p. 142).[7]

The fields of psychology, anthropology and linguistics began to connect with the emerging fields of artificial intelligence, computer science, and neuroscience. American theorists drew strength and ideas from psychologists in other countries, namely Piaget in Switzerland (cognitions in children), Luria in the Soviet Union (connections between brain and mind), and Bartlett in the United Kingdom (memory and thinking) (Miller 2003). The work of Albert Ellis and Aaron T. Beck focused on irrational and automatic thoughts, respectively. Many publications have documented the history of the movement and the empirical results supporting the premise that modifying thoughts could alter behavior.[8] By the 1970s, Beck's work with colleagues was demonstrating that cognitive therapy was effective in treating depression in randomized controlled studies by helping patients solve problems, become behaviorally activated, and "identify, evaluate, and respond to their depressed thinking, especially to negative thoughts about themselves, their worlds, and their future" (Beck 2011, p. 6).[9] Therapeutic work on anxiety followed with shifting the focus to assessing risk, evaluating internal and external resources, and testing negative predictions via behavioral exercises (Beck 1976).

Modern life also included numerous traumas, whether it was the lingering effects of war or the increasing visibility of physical and sexual traumas. Herman (1992) became known for her distinctive contributions to the understanding of trauma and its survivors. She was able to shed light on the impact of single-incident traumas and complex or repeated traumas such as Complex Post-Traumatic Stress Disorder. Bessel A. van der Kolk M.D., another clinician, researcher and teacher in the area

---

[6]Alfred North Whitehead challenged Skinner to "account for utterances that allude to stimuli conspicuously absent from the environment of the speaker and that therefore appear to require conceptual tools unavailable to the behaviorists" (Palmer 2006, p. 253). Ultimately Skinner wrote *Verbal Persuasion* (1957) to try to demonstrate that all verbal and nonverbal behavior could be explained by the conceptual tools of behaviorism.

[7]For a full discussion of Chomsky's critique of behaviorism, see Palmer (2006).

[8](See Beck 1976; Messer and Gurman 2011; Turner 2011; Northcut et al. 2016; etc.).

[9]However, Jacobson et al. (1996) provide a critique of the theory of change proposed by Beck and associates by breaking down the treatment into its specific components (i.e., behavioral activation, modifying automatic thoughts, or the full cognitive therapy treatment protocol).

of posttraumatic stress and its effects, worked (and continues) to work to integrate developmental, biological, psychodynamic, and interpersonal aspects of the impact of trauma and its treatment (van der Kolk 1984, 1987, 2014). The quest was to find a way to reunite mind and body based on the results of research in a variety of disciplines studying trauma.

While depression and anxiety may have resulted from the stresses of everyday living postindustrial society, the AIDS epidemic exposed the power and vulnerability of the immune system. The nervous system could lead to more illness if stress taxed the immune systems of vulnerable individuals. Focus then turned to how resistance and resilience could be built within our immune systems and what kind of stressors tax the body. Minority groups, LGBTQ in particular, began to speak out about the effects of being marginalized by society as they had been pre- and post AIDS epidemic. The western bias of individualism at all costs, even down to our own individual cognitive distortions, began to also consider how groups might serve as a form of social protection and treatment for what ails us and isolates us.

Consequently, a narrative of **Healing Ties** ushered in nostalgia for an ideal of life before modernity which had a greater sense of community and intimacy (Harrington 2008). Post World War II also led the psychiatric profession to transform care from asylum-based mental health care to community-oriented therapeutic approaches. Despite the attempts of the mental hygiene movement to visualize a whole community as the patient (Bertolote 2008), it had not been effective in achieving great strides with the care and prevention of mental illness. The deinstitutionalization movement focused on social integration of the mentally ill and emphasized prevention and rehabilitation (Novella 2010). Massive funding supported studies that showed how social support could alleviate the symptoms or behaviors considered unhealthy or pathological. One of the consequences of our technological advances had been the creation of social isolation, and rather than abandon those advances, technology was utilized to address an ironic sense of disconnection. Social media advanced rapidly and created the means for contact that could transcend geographic and time limitations.

The baby boomer generation produced children that were considered "digital natives" or at the very least able to possess "digital wisdom" (Prensky 2001, 2012). The first social networks and blogs surfaced by the turn of the millennium making it possible to communicate in real time around the world (Palfrey and Gasser 2008). Platforms such as Facebook still in use by "digital immigrants" (parents of digital natives) (Prensky 2001), made way for ephemeral social media that displays shared content for a limited period of time such as Snapchat and Instant Messaging (Bayer et al. 2015). While concerns about the effects of social media on intimacy and brain wiring continue, there is preliminary evidence that with our new ways of relating and gathering information, we are less likely to feel intimacy despite extensive self-disclosures on Facebook, or less likely to think in deep and contemplative ways as a result of endless surfing with short message bytes (Carr 2010; Dakin 2014). Interestingly enough, teens seem to have moved away from Facebook in favor of the newer apps such as Snapchat or Instagram in order to feel a closer connection with a more limited number of closer friends. However, Snapchat interactions do not necessarily correlate with higher rates of social support. In contrast, Snapchat is associated with lower social support, albeit with higher positive affect (Bayer et al. 2015). Heavy social media users report higher levels of anxiety because of what is called FOMO—Fear of Missing Out. Despite feeling that their heavy social media use has "brought stronger relationships, more effective goal setting, ability to seek help through social media as well as feeling part of a global community" (Bayer et al. 2015, p. 1), teens report fears their friends are having more fun and rewarding experiences than they are, which is leading to greater anxiety (Fuller 2015).

While the rapid growth of social media has produced increased communication around the world, it has not necessarily reduced the stress associated with modern life. If anything, modern life, with its greater technological advances, has brought its own set of stressors associated with always being available electronically 24 hours a day, 7 days a week. In addition, we are immersed in a positive psychology movement, an outgrowth of the positive thinking paradigm despite efforts of that movement to distance them from pop psychology.

Martin Seligman is generally credited with being the founder of the positive psychology movement with the goal of leading a good life. A life is considered good if we use our unique strengths every day to produce happiness and gratification (Seligman 2002, 2009). The Positive Psychology Institute's website suggests:

> Positive Psychology is grounded in the belief that people want to lead meaningful and fulfilling lives, to cultivate what is best within them, and to enhance their experiences of love, work, and play…The field is intended to complement, not to replace traditional psychology. It does not seek to deny the importance of studying how things go wrong, but rather to emphasize the importance of using the scientific method to determine how things go right (Positive Psychology Institute 2012).

While the attempt to balance a mind–body narrative that has become too focused on pathology and dysfunction has been critical, it has raised a number of problems as identified by Held (1995, 2001, 2002; Held and Bohart 2002) and other humanist psychologists. For example, Aspinwall and Staudinger (2003) stated:

> …a call for the scientific study of…positive states…should not be misunderstood as a call to ignore negative aspects of human experience. That is, a psychology of human strengths should not be the study of how negative experience may be avoided or ignored, but rather how positive and negative experience may be interrelated….Indeed, some philosophical perspectives suggest that the positive and negative are by definition dependent on each other, that is, human existence seems to be constituted by basic dialectics (Aspinwall and Staudinger 2003, pp. 14–15; Held 2004, p. 13).

A balance or integration of good and bad or positive and negative feelings and thoughts has been the focus of theories of human behavior for decades although more common in the eastern religions.[10] **Healing Ties** segued into another important narrative **Eastward Journeys** (Harrington 2008). This evolving narrative

---

[10]For example, Zen focuses on the need to move beyond or not to be confined by the basic dialectics.

epitomized the western fantasy that other societies had a better way to heal than through just developing or expanding social communities. This exoticism approach focused on ancient Eastern cultures that have not traditionally had a strong influence in this country. There has been a longstanding orientalist (Said 1978) tendency in western culture to consider the East as a foil to our own Western values and lifestyles—generally to the West's advantage. We were superior because we had moved from the scientific revolution to a social world that emphasized efficiency, rationality, and self-control. However we were victims of our own success. We could draw on the wisdom of the other to learn from, but not forsake any of our progress. The American perspective of "West is Best" had to make way to appreciate that the East had lessons to teach us about morality and medicine.

This process of changing the narrative was built on several other historical phenomena as well. Novelists and poets of the Beat generation in the 1950s paved the way for musicians and actors to search for wisdom in Buddhism in the 1960s. Drug use and anti-Vietnam sentiment brought about a countercultural movement. Maharashi and Transcendental Meditation (TM) took the country by storm during the 60s and 70s with the emphasis on mantras and spiritual regeneration (fees not included). Celebrities proved fickle in their interest, however, scientists began to debate the relationship between Eastern mysticism and quantum physics. Fortunately, Robert Keith Wallace studied the physiological effects of meditating college students in Los Angeles and found not only changes in oxygen consumption, heart rate, and skin resistance, but also the occurrence of newly identified brain activity: an altered consciousness. It was not until Harvard psychologist Herbert Benson attempted to determine the connection between stress and heart disease that a potential opportunity presented itself to incorporate the effects of transcendental meditation into medical research. Benson used operant conditioning and biofeedback to alter the blood pressure in monkeys and human subjects. Young TM practitioners offered to be guinea pigs simply by allowing Benson to study the effects on them during routine meditation practice. Even though he was nervous about admitting to the world that he was combining medicine and TM, once Benson learned of Wallace's work, collaboration began. By 1972 they were clear: regardless of the original purpose, "TM and all the other ancient meditative techniques central to faith traditions around the world also acted as technologies for turning off the stress response" (Harrington 2008, p. 217). Though Benson renamed the use of meditation as relaxation and published the New York Times bestseller *The Relaxation Response*, he "domesticated and medicalized meditation" in the 1970s (Harrington 2008, p. 219). Benson articulated its universal appeal in this way: "Even though it (the relaxation response) has been evoked in the religions of both East and West for most of recorded history, you don't have to engage in any rites or esoteric practices to bring it forth" (Benson 1975, p. 117).

Meanwhile in China, efforts to reduce economic and ideological dependence on the Soviet Union contributed to Mao Tse-Tung's celebration of traditional Chinese medicine as the socialist wave of the future. In addition, the United States reopened diplomatic relations with China in the 1970s under the Nixon administration. Acupuncture was publicized as helpful in overcoming postoperative complications.

The reopening of diplomatic relations encouraged more cultural exchange including the Chinese practice of qigong:

> Qigong is an ancient Chinese health care system that integrates physical postures, breathing techniques and focused intention. The word Qigong (Chi Kung) is made up of two Chinese words. Qi is pronounced *chee* and is usually translated to mean the life force or vital-energy that flows through all things in the universe. The second word, Gong, pronounced *gung*, means accomplishment, or skill that is cultivated through steady practice. Together, Qigong (Chi Kung) means cultivating energy, it is a system practiced for health maintenance, healing and increasing vitality (NQA 2016).

In 1990, Jon Kabat Zinn published the renowned book *Full Catastrophe Living: Using the Wisdom of Your Body and Mind to Face Stress, Pain, and Illness*, based on his work from the previous ten years. He had a degree from MIT in molecular biology and taught Buddhist meditation and yoga. With the support of the University of Massachusetts Medical Center in Worcester, he designed and implemented a program to help patients utilize mindfulness in order to cope with chronic pain and suffering. The course itself was not stress-free; it was a demanding, intense eight-week course. But by couching the terminology as stress reduction, Kabat-Zinn had successfully introduced a nonthreatening way for the medical establishment and the public to try a consistent, meditative practice and document the results. Mindfulness-based stress reduction (MBSR) proved to be successful and began to be replicated around the country (Kabat-Zinn 2013).

The twenty-first century brought even more scientific research focused on the health benefits of Buddhism.[11] However, what is sometimes forgotten is the fact that meditation was not designed to alleviate stress. Rather it was a spiritual technology that had an ethical and moral imperative about how we live with and treat each other. The Dalai Lama's investment in the results of scientific research into the relationship between the spiritual practices of his Tibetan community and physiology was based in part on his political concerns. Traditionally, a Buddhist religious leader would not expose his followers to any kind of study or potential interference. However, out of concern about the Chinese occupation of Tibet, Dalai Lama agreed to afford the opportunity of access to Harvard researcher Herbert Benson (Harrington 2008). Although part of the proliferation of mindfulness practices in a variety of disciplines and settings stems from its positive results, the nonsectarian nature makes it easier and user-friendly for reluctant participants to engage in.

While research in this country may have begun studying meditation from a place of trying to obtain relief from stress, achieve health benefits, or even reach a state of higher consciousness, there remains several related pragmatic questions. Hobbes was asking how we can live together and negotiate civil conflict when he pushed for reliance on the scientific method to inform public policy. Theoreticians, researchers, and practitioners since then have tried to use science to prove what treatment methods improve individual functioning. Our lingering narrative about utilizing an

[11] This research will be discussed in subsequent chapters when relevant.

"other" to persuade our bodies to cooperate into health, has led us to look to other cultures and charismatic figures to provide answers. We do know the body expresses many experiences, positive and negative, and seeks to restore itself to cope with the demands our current environment places upon it. The challenge currently is how to find a way to reintegrate the mind and body in a manner that allows us to "knit together domains of experience that we struggle otherwise to relate: the medical and the moral, the biological and the biographical, the natural and the cultural" (Harrington 2008, p. 255). The need for greater integration in mind and body reflects our historical conundrum about how to do so. It appears we have reached a point in health and mental health care when we can perhaps balance the many narratives we have in order to appreciate that mind and body are not separate, have never been, and philosophically and pragmatically exist on a continuum. "This happy marriage of objective science and subjective patient experiences may be the aspect of modern medicine that allows for a deeper understanding of the mind-body connection, and ultimately creates a culture of medicine that reserves a space for the soul" (Mokrycke and Li 2015, p. 21). The inclusion of mindfulness in clinical social work is one attempt to do so.

References

Association for Applied Psychophysiology and Biofeedback, Inc. (2011). Retrieved from http://www.aapb.org/i4a/pages/index.cfm?pageid=1.

Aspinwall, L. G., & Staudinger, U. M. (2003). A psychology of human strengths: Some central issues of an emerging field. In L. G. Aspinwall & U. M. Staudinger (Eds.), *A psychology of human strengths: Fundamental questions and future directions for a positive psychology* (pp. 9–22). Washington, D. C.: American Psychological Association.

Bayer, J. B., Ellison, N. B., Schoenebeck, S. Y., & Falk, E. B. (2015). Sharing the small moments: Ephemeral social interaction on Snapchat. Retrieved from http://dx.doi.org/10.1080/1369118X.2015.1084349.

Beck, A. T. (1976). *Cognitive therapy and the emotional disorders*. NY: International Universities Press.

Beck, J. S. (2011). *Cognitive behavior therapy: Basics and beyond* (2nd ed.). NY: Guilford.

Benson, H. (1975). *The relaxation response*. NY: Avon Books.

Bertolote, J. M. (2008). The roots of the concept of mental health. *World Psychiatry, 7,* 113–116.

Berzoff, J., Flanagan, L. M., & Hertz, P. (Eds.). (2016). *Inside out and outside in* (4th ed.). NY: Rowman & Littlefield.

Boston Women's Health Book Collective, & Norsigian, J. (2011). *Our bodies, ourselves*. NY: Touchstone.

Bradley, B., DeFife, J. A., Guarnaccia, C., Phifer, J., Fani, N., Ressler, K. J., et al. (2011). Emotion dysregulation and negative affect: Association with psychiatric symptoms. *Journal of Clinical Psychiatry, 72*(5), 685–691. doi:10.4088/JCP.10m06409blu.

Carpenter, R. W., & Trull, T. J. (2013). Components of emotion dysregulation in borderline personality disorder: A review. *Current Psychiatry Report, 15*(1), 335. doi:10.1007/s11920-012-0335-2.

Carr, N. (2010). *The shallows: What the internet is doing to our brains*. NY: W. W. Norton & Company.

Chambon, A. S., Irving, A., & Epstein, L. (Eds.). (2009). *Reading foucault for social work*. NY: Columbia Universities Press.

Cole, P. M., Michel, M. K., & Teti, L. O. (1994). The development of emotion regulation and dysregulation: A clinical perspective. *Monographs of the Society for Research in Child Development, 59,* 73–102. doi:10.1111/j.1540-5834.1994.tb01278.x.

Dakin, P. (2014, February 24). Social media affecting teen's concepts of friendship, intimacy. *CBS News*. Retrieved from http://www.cbc.ca/news/health/social-media-affecting-teensoncepts-of-friendship-intimacy-1.2543158.

Drexler, P. (2016, February 12). The political and the psychological: What politicians are not saying about mental health. *Huffington Post*. Retrieved from http://www.huffingtonpost.com/peggy-drexler/the-political-and-the-psy_b_9218626.html.

Ellenberger, H. (1970). *The discovery of the unconscious: The history and evolution of dynamic psychiatry*. NY: Basic Books.

Ehrenreich, B. (2009). *Bright-sided: How positive thinking is undermining America*. NY: Picador.

Fuller, A. (2015, November 8). 'FOMO': Heavy social media use leading to depression among teens. *SBS*. Retrieved from http://www.sbs.com.au/news/article/2015/11/08/fomo-heavy-social-media-use-leading-depression-among-teens.

Gay, V. (2010). *Progress and values in the humanities: Comparing culture and science*. NY: Columbia University Press.

Harrington, A. (2006, March 28). Minds, bodies & stories. *The Paula Gordon Show*. Recording retrieved from http://www.paulagordon.com/shows/harrington/index.html.

Harrington, A. (2008). *The cure within: A history of mind-body medicine*. NY: W. W. Norton.

Hart, C. W. (2014). Biography as an art form: The story of Helen Flanders Dunbar, M.D., Ph.D., B. D., and Med. Sci.D. *Journal of Religion and Health, 53,* 778–788. doi:10.1007/s10943-013-9818-7.

Held, B. (1995). *Back to reality: A critique of postmodern theory in psychotherapy*. NY: Norton.

Herman, J. (1992). *Trauma and Recovery: The Aftermath of Violence—From Domestic Abuse to Political Terror*. NY: Basic Books.

Held, B. (2001). *Stop smiling, start kvetching*. NY: St. Martin's Griffin.

Held, B. (2002). The tyranny of the positive attitude in America: Observation and speculation. *Journal of Clinical Psychology, 58,* 965–991.

Held, B. (2004). The negative side of positive psychology. *Journal of Humanistic Psychology, 44* (1), 9–46.

Held, B. S., & Bohart, A. C. (2002). Introduction: The (overlooked) virtues of "unvirtuous" attitudes and behavior: Reconsidering negativity, complaining, pessimism and "false" hope. *Journal of Clinical Psychology, 58,* 961–964.

Heller, N. R. & Gitterman, A. (2011). *Mental health and social problems: A social work perspective*. NY: Routledge, Taylor & Francis.

Hochschild, A. R. (1983). *The managed heart: Commercialization of human feeling*. Berkeley: University of California Press.

Hoermann, S., Zupanick, C. E., & Dombeck, M. (2013, December 5). Defining features of personality disorders: Problematic emotional response patterns. *MentalHelp.net*. Retrieved from https://www.mentalhelp.net/articles/defining-features-of-personality-disorders-problematic-emotional-response-patterns.

Jacobson, N. S., Dobson, K. S., Truax, P. A., Addis, M. E., Koerner, K., Gollan, J. K., et al. (1996). A component analysis of cognitive-behavioral treatment for depression. *Journal of Consulting and Clinical Psychology, 64*(2), 295–304.

Jones, E. (1955). *The life and work of Sigmund Freud, vol. 2: Years of maturity, 1902–1919*. NY: Basic Books.

Kabet-Zinn, J. (1990; 2013 revised). Full catastrophe living: Using the wisdom of your mind to face stress, pain, and illness. New York: Dell.

Knausgaard, K. O. (2014, May 28). The other side of the face [blog post]. *The Paris Review*. Retrieved from http://www.theparisreview.org/blog/2014/05/28/the-other-side-of-the-face/.
Massey, J. (2015, June 1). Mind-body medicine its history and evolution. *Naturopathic Doctor News and Review*. Retrieved from http://ndnr.com/mindbody/mind-body-medicine-its-history-evolution/.
Messer, S., & Gurman, A. S. (Eds.). (2011). *Essential psychotherapies: Theory and practice* (3rd ed.). NY: Guilford.
Miller, G. A. (2003). The cognitive revolution: A historical perspective. *TRENDS in Cognitive Science, 7*(3), 141–144.
Mitchell, S., & Black, M. J. (1996). *Freud and beyond*. NY: Basic Books.
Mokrycke, S. & Li, H. (2015, Winter). Separation and reunion: A short history of mind-body dualism. *The University of Western Ontario Medical Journal*. 20–21.
National Qigong Association (NQA). (2016). What is qigong? Retrieved from http://nqa.org/about-nqa/what-is-qigong/.
Northcut, T., Heller, N., & Kumaria, S. (2016). Integrating psychodynamic theory and practice with cognitive-behavioral interventions. In J. Berzoff, L. Flanagan, & P. Hertz (Eds.), *Inside out and outside in* (4th ed.). Lanham, MD: Rowman and Littlefield.
Novella, E. J. (2010). Mental health care and the politics of inclusion: A social systems account of psychiatric deinstitutionalization. *Theoretical Medicine and Bioethics, 31,* 411–427.
Oates, S. B. (1987). *William Faulkner: Man and artist*. NY: HarperCollins.
Our Bodies, Ourselves. (2016). History. Retrieved from http://www.ourbodiesourselves.org/history/.
Palfrey, J., & Gasser, U. (2008). *Born digital: Understanding the first generation of digital natives*. NY: Perseus Books.
Palmer, D. C. (2006). On Chomsky's appraisal of Skinner's verbal behavior: A half century of misunderstanding. *The Behavior Analyst, 29,* 253–267.
Peale, N. V. (1952). *The power of positive thinking*. NY: Prentice-Hall.
Petterson, S., Phillips, B., Bazemore, A., Dodoo, M., Zhang, X., & Green, L. A. (2008, March 15). Why there must be room for mental health in the medical home. *American Academy of Family Physicians*. Retrieved from http://www.graham-center.org/rgc/publications-reports/publications/one-pagers/mental-health-medical-home-2008.html.
Positive Psychology Institute. (2012). *What is positive psychology*. Retrieved from http://www.positivepsychologyinstitute.com.au/what_is_positive_psychology.html.
Prensky, Marc. (2001). Digital natives, digital immigrants. *On the Horizon., 9*(5), 1–6.
Prensky, Marc. (2012). *From digital natives to digital wisdom: Hopeful essays on education in the 21st century*. Thousand Oaks, CA: Corwin.
Rubin, D. B. (2009). From private demons to public problems: The work of Mary Cromwell Jarrett. *Affilia: Journal of Women and Social Work. 24*(4), 417–423.
Said, E. (1978). *Orientalism*. NY: Pantheon Books.
Schlink, B. (1995). *The reader*. Translation by C. B. Janeway. NY: Vintage Books.
Seligman, M. E. P. (2002). *Authentic happiness: Using the new positive psychology to realize your potential for lasting fulfillment*. NY: Free Press.
Seligman, M. E. P. (2009). *Authentic happiness*. New York: Free Press.
Siegel, D. J. (2007). *The mindful brain: Reflection and attunement in the cultivation of well-being*. NY: Norton.
Sundararaman, R. (2009, April 21). The U.S. mental health delivery system infrastructure: A primer. Retrieved from https://www.fas.org/sgp/crs/misc/R40536.pdf.
Turner, F. J. (2011). *Social work treatment: Interlocking theoretical approaches* (5th ed.). NY: Oxford University Press.
van der Kolk, B. A. (Ed.). (1984). *Post-traumatic stress disorder: Psychological and biological sequelae*. Washington DC: American Psychiatric Press.

van der Kolk, B. A. (1987). *Psychological trauma.* Washington DC: American Psychiatric Press.

van der Kolk, B. A. (2014). *The body keeps the score: Brain, mind, and body in the healing of trauma.* NY: Viking.

Wallis, C. (2016, July 25). How yoga can turn a jerk into an even bigger jerk [blog post]. Retrieved from http://www.tantrikstudies.org/blog/2016/7/25/does-the-practice-of-yoga-automatically-make-you-a-better-person.

White, M. (2007). *Maps of narrative practice.* NY: Norton.

Chapter 3
Beginning with the Concept: The Meanings of Mindfulness

Terry B. Northcut

The mind is active and dynamic, and sometimes represents an unruly world. In its simplest terms, mindfulness suggests an ability to harness, channel, or engage the mind in a way that allows us to ride the waves of thoughts and experiences, without being pulled into their undertow. Perhaps the briefest and the best known definition of mindfulness in the western world is Jon Kabat–Zinn's: "intentional awareness with acceptance" (1990). Implicit in Kabat–Zinn's definition is that mindfulness is not purely a cognitive experience. With awareness comes feelings and sensations that are not always expected; consequently the purpose of mindfulness is to recognize those experiences and accept them with compassion (Fulton 2005, 2014).

Mindfulness can have many connotations. For the novice clinician or a mental health practitioner unfamiliar with including eastern philosophy, spirituality, or any associated tool into their practice, mindfulness can seem mysterious, intimidating, or even too simplistic to be an effective adjunct to treatment. For the experienced Buddhist, however, it may be inconceivable to imagine mindfulness as an "adjunct" rather than as a way of life. There are many ways in which mindfulness can be included in practice that are both simple and complicated to do. As with the mind and body relationship, mindfulness has an essential humanistic aspect as well as a scientific component. It is similar to psychotherapy in this regard, manifest through art and science. The apparent paradox of studying something that can be as elusive as art yet also grounded in observational science is befitting for a practice that has been around over 2600 years and continues to offer rich avenues of potential healing (Shapiro and Carlson 2009). Just as clinical social work values the biopsychosocialspiritual perspective of human development and functioning, Kabat–Zinn suggest the teaching of mindfulness "requires that each individual client, patient, or participant be seen as a whole human being and be accorded the

T.B. Northcut (✉)
School of Social Work, Loyola University of Chicago, Chicago, IL, USA
e-mail: tnorthc@luc.edu

T.B. Northcut (ed.), *Cultivating Mindfulness in Clinical Social Work*,
Essential Clinical Social Work Series, DOI 10.1007/978-3-319-43842-9_3

dignity and sovereignty that are intrinsic to being human" (Shapiro and Carlson 2009, ix).

Despite the popular and deceptive idea that mindfulness is strictly a solitary activity, engaging a client mindfully requires an embodied relational experience. *This is not something to recommend to a client that he or she go home and practice without understanding what is personally involved in the practice and without knowing a client's reactions to changing emotional and physiological states.* The practice of mindfulness has always included the importance of a spiritual guide or teacher as well as a community or Sangha to facilitate and monitor a student's progress. Likewise, utilizing mindfulness as a treatment intervention needs careful and purposeful feedback throughout the process. This chapter will explore the concepts of mindfulness, the mechanisms of action that make it important for clinicians and clients, the similarities and differences with psychotherapy, and the contraindications or pitfalls inherent in the process of mindfulness.

What Is Mindfulness?

One of the more confusing aspects of mindfulness is that it represents both a process (mindful practice) and an outcome (mindful awareness) in some spiritual paths. Shapiro and Carlson (2009) explain mindfulness as including a process variable as well as an outcome of this practice. Mindfulness is one path to accept all that is present in each moment, not passively, but with clarity and insight about what is true. Shapiro and Carlson (2009) describe this process as "re-perceiving" what is currently in conscious awareness. Doing so enables the practitioner to accept and evaluate how wholesome[1] the thoughts are (i.e., whether they are causing suffering by wishing for what is not in the present).

When speaking about mindfulness it is important to remember that while Buddhism is the most common association with mindfulness, many religious traditions have historically utilized and advocated some version of mindfulness, e.g., Hinduism, Judaism, and Christianity. Nevertheless, for many practicing meditation in the United States, mindfulness has been stripped of its Hindu and Buddhist traditions.

> Unlike the dominant Western religions, which are grounded in a historical story line and come equipped with specific belief systems, Buddhism and its contemporaries were much more agnostic on matters of metaphysical revelation and focused instead upon the practitioner's inner experience (Olendzki 2005, p. 242).

When mindfulness is removed from its historical legacy however, the richness is also absent. For example, the contextual world view that frames Buddhism emphasizes that change is continuous and multidetermined, and that causality

[1]Buddhism teaches thoughts are wholesome or unwholesome rather than healthy or unhealthy or good or bad (Olendzki 2005). Acceptance and Commitment Therapy (ACT) emphasizes the recontextualizing and accepting all emotions and thoughts which will be discussed later.

depends on the context and multiple "universe of causes" at a particular point in time (Olendzki 2005, p. 242). Buddhist philosophy also emphasizes that pain is an inevitable part of life, but suffering can be managed as it comes from not accepting the present state. The challenge, of course, is in differentiating pain from suffering which requires ongoing conscious awareness. Buddha was understood to have been human, not a God, albeit more of a physician dedicated to alleviating psychological and existential suffering (Olendzki 2005). Despite being focused on the importance of an individual having a personal experience along his or her own unique path, there were guidelines offered depending on the spiritual levels of students of Buddhism. For example, Buddhist mindfulness is just one of seven "factors of awakening" on the path to wisdom which also includes investigation, energy, joy, tranquility, concentration, and equanimity that are paradoxically separate but yet inseparable. Each of these factors forms the scaffold supporting the next in development (Olendzki 2005). As is expected, there is vast literature exploring and explaining these paths and stages (see for example, Nanamoli and Bodhi 1995 for a translated reading; Olendzki 2005, etc.) Authors in the current text direct the reader to resources for this information when relevant. In addition, Appendix A also includes references for further study. For the beginning meditator trying to develop mindfulness, understanding the philosophy or theology behind his or her practice may provide an important rationale to explain what is happening during their practice, and normalize those feelings. The framework can also help differentiate what is pain versus, what is suffering by showing the transitory nature of our emotional states. For some clients that may not be necessary to achieve therapeutic benefits, but for others it may help them persevere during the process of "not knowing" when feelings may seem as if they will last forever.

Meditation to facilitate mindfulness can be divided into at least two types: concentrative (samatha) or non-concentrative (vipassana) (Olendzki 2005; Steinberg and Eisner 2015). Concentrative meditation employs the use of a mantra or other focus for attention such as a candle, breath, etc. When attention veers from the focus point, attention is redirected back to the object of concentration in order to bring about a state of peace and relaxation. Concentrative meditation is particularly useful with reducing physiological arousal common with trauma survivors (Lang et al. 2012). The continual redirection has a calming effect which is also why it is helpful to utilize at bedtime in order relax or unwind before sleeping.

In contrast with concentrative, non-centrative is the type of meditation that intends to train the mind to be aware and accept all mental events leading to insight. "The goal is to observe moment-to-moment shifts in internal experiences without judging their content" (Steinberg and Eisner 2015, p. 11; Strauss et al. 2011). For example, in Acceptance and Commitment Therapy (ACT) the exercise of "Leaves in the Stream" directs clients to close their eyes and imagine leaves floating downstream. As their thoughts surface, they "place" thoughts on leaves and watch them float away (Hicks 2009). This type of non-concentrative exercise facilitates the process of recognizing the changing nature of thoughts and feelings as well as accepting whatever comes to mind. As thoughts are identified, they are recontextualized which decreases their emotional power. Enhanced moment to moment awareness and acceptance ultimately leads to less self-criticism and judgment. Many intervention programs combine concentrative and nonconcentrative aspects to provide benefits of each for the practitioners.

What Are the Mechanisms of Action Inherent in the Process of Meditation as Identified in Western Practices?

There is enormous depth and variety written about the state and process of mindfulness, yet there are also some essential common themes, particularly in practices in the western world. For example, Bishop et al. (2004) specifies that mindfulness includes three characteristics: "a self-regulation of attention; a recognition of mental events occurring in the moment; and a particular orientation toward one's experiences in the present moment that is characterized by curiosity, openness, and acceptance" (p. 232). Vujanovic et al. (2011) also considers awareness and acceptance as the key components of mindfulness. Three concepts are discussed here as being relevant for clinical social work practice: attention, exposure, and acceptance. Again, Appendix A lists other helpful resources that describe these mechanisms in more detail.

Attention requires an experience of "optimal presence" and evenly hovering attention that is reminiscent of Freud's instructions on psychoanalytic technique (Pstein 1984). Karen Horney believed Zen training would help develop this ability in therapists (1952). Research has consistently found that mindfulness leads to a greater ability to develop and sustain attention (Jha et al. 2007; Shapiro and Carlson 2009; Slagter et al. 2007, etc.). One explanation for this may be found in neurobiology. A study conducted by Lazar et al. (2005) showed greater cortical thickening in areas of the brain associated with sustained attention and awareness (the right prefrontal cortex and right anterior insula) in experienced mindfulness meditation practitioners compared with nonmeditating control participants. Clinically, we know that being able to direct and maintain attention is essential for clinical social workers in quickly processing subtle and more direct information from clients as well as separating their own thoughts and reactions in the moment. Likewise, utilizing Demos' (1996) "tracking the trigger" component in either psychodynamic or cognitive-behavioral therapy requires helping clients (and clinicians) develop an "observing ego" that observes their thoughts and feelings prior to acting on them. Attention to the existing internal experience is an essential step in mindfulness and in clinical work.

Exposure to the thoughts and feelings that emerge during focused attention, leads to an increased ability to experience these fluctuations. While exposure therapy is replete with therapeutic interventions geared to build up clients' tolerance for anxiety around feared objects or situations (including PTSD), a common feature is the need to first have experiences that stimulate these different affective states. When mindfulness is practiced, the focused attention provides an evenly hovering perspective from which to observe the thoughts and feelings that surface and/or pass through consciousness (e.g., "leaves in a stream" exercise described above). In measured doses, participants can strengthen their ability to use their mind to experience all that is present in a particular moment. From a clinical perspective, the subjective experience in a session is different when both client and therapist are grounded in the present moment (e.g., see Chap. 8 in this text). Although this clinical presence is hard to empirically study and duplicate, one effort was the "experiencing scale" developed by Klein et al. (1969) years ago to assess language used by clients during a therapeutic session.

> The Dimension of Experiencing… refers to the quality of an individual's experiencing of himself as revealed in his verbal communications; it ranges from impersonal, superficial, or abstract-intellectual content at low levels, progresses through intermediate stages where bodily feelings and experiencing are revealed in fuller descriptive detail, to more advanced stages where feelings are purposefully explored and emergent levels of experiencing serve as referents for problem resolution and understanding. Its association with independent evaluations of therapeutic success is established in a number of studies with different patient populations (pp. 56–63).

Likewise, Bucci's (1982, 1984, 1985, etc.) work on referential activity attempts to indicate a type of linguistic usage that reflects different brain activity as it relates to subjective experiences in therapy. Other therapeutic research has tried to capture therapeutic process variables extensively because understanding what transpires within the clinical relationship in the present moment is the best exposure or example to "live" dynamics that may be problematic outside the therapeutic relationship (see Crits-Christoph et al. 2013 for a full discussion of this research).

We can see that a therapeutic relationship can be a type of "exposure-therapy" with clients, increasing their ability to experience and re-experience an interpersonal empathic relationship between themselves and the therapist (Borden 2016). Mindfulness offers the chance to exercise and increase the tolerance of affect through attention and intention without necessarily requiring the verbal dexterity that is relied upon in psychotherapy. Mindful practice allows clients to re-perceive their thoughts and feelings in the present moment. Ogden (2009) uses a form of this, "directed mindfulness" as one way to guide clients' attention and awareness toward those aspects of the present moment that support therapeutic goals and target procedural memory.[2] This type of sensorimotor therapy is also a way to utilize the mechanisms of action of mindfulness in a specified physical way that can complement and enhance clinical work.

Acceptance of thoughts and feelings as they occur, rather than getting stuck on particular states of being, brings enormous relief from psychological suffering. When we engage in the process of mindfulness we keep turning our attention to the focal object (concentrative) or to the action of observing whatever comes into awareness (nonconcentrative). The purpose is simply observing and mentally recording what we notice without resisting. This form of observation is the "muscle" that needs developing—to simply observe and/or redirect without turning away from the thoughts or the feelings. Chögyam Trungpa describes our human

[2]I.e., including negative early attachment experiences and unresolved trauma impacting the body's physical characteristics.

tendency to avoid what is painful as "negative negativity," or reacting against what seems unbearable and trying to escape it (Chodron 1999). The act of continually attending and observing without turning away also brings acceptance. Kabat Zinn (1990) describes this process as a form of "uncoupling" the sensory, emotional, and cognitive/conceptual dimensions of an experience in order that we can recognize each dimension independently of the other. The process of attending to, allowing, and observing the present moment lets us experience the continually shifting states which, in turn, allow us to see that we are more than just our feelings or our thoughts. For many people this acceptance of thoughts and feelings is one of the most difficult aspects of the mindful experience.

Unfortunately many individuals who try mindfulness tend to be extremely critical of their own efforts, believing they are failing at being mindful, thus leading to a cycle of self-sabotage. Brach (2003) states that for some reason western practitioners tend to have a "trance of unworthiness". The Dalai Lama (1997) also observed that Western meditation students seem to possess a low self-esteem that is not usually present in Eastern students. This phenomenon may result from a combination of the relentless focus on individuality at all costs, the need to feel good in a culture of capitalism that profits from never reaching that goal, a historical religious belief built on the concept of original sin, and the need for positive thinking in American culture as discussed in Chap. 2. A great deal of pressure is placed on the individual to "get right" whatever he or she is attempting to do, including seeking happiness or mindfulness. While acceptance is a critical component of mindfulness, it is sometimes necessary to begin of visualizing others for whom we have positive feelings in order to begin to experience the sense of acceptance toward oneself. Difficulties inevitably arise any time we engage in mindfulness practice, however, we can increasingly feel acceptance and compassion to a broader range of individuals, including ourselves over time. The process of accepting whatever thoughts, feelings, and physical sensations that emerge in the present leads to the development of compassion. Some programs emphasize the role of compassion for ourselves and others more predominantly (e.g., ACT, Compassion Focused Therapy, etc.) as it is an integral part of the process of mindfulness.

What Are the Implications for Clinical Practice?

Our clinical role usually involves some degree of helping clients develop self-awareness which includes recognition of the thoughts and feelings that they may have not acknowledged or were not aware of. This self-awareness has to be titrated, however, based on the available internal, interpersonal, and social supports as well as the therapeutic goals. Awareness of what may be thought of as "negative" feelings can interfere with acceptance, if they bring with them a sense of shame that overwhelms clients' personal resources available at that point in time. One of our essential clinical skills is to continually assess and evaluate clients' current emotional and environmental state from moment to moment to help anticipate upcoming and past stressors that may intrude on the present. This dynamic process is unique to our role as clinical social workers, distinct from being in the role of a spiritual guide or pastoral counselor.[3] We are monitoring clients' functioning so that important subjective states are not crowded out to "forgive and forget" or achieve other spiritual goals prior to the exploration of present conscious and preconscious feelings and thoughts. Clients may, however, move to the point of forgiveness and acceptance more easily as a result of the therapeutic process.

When conducted with a helpful teacher or trained clinician, mindfulness can facilitate and support a healing process as well. Hahn (1998) states, "our suffering is us, and we need to treat it with kindness and nonviolence. We need to embrace our fear, hatred, anguish, and anger." (Szczygil 2016, p. 29). As always, developing an ability to "radically accept" where we are in each moment must be balanced with the challenge to "feel and function" in the nontherapeutic space (Brach 2003, p. 245; Linehan 1993). Knowledge of self is not more important than being able to operate on a day-to-day basis for clients or clinicians. However, accepting all that is part of us and feeling compassion for ourselves and consequently for others, too, is the desired result and process of mindfulness practice.

Compassion and Equanimity in Mindfulness and Clinical Work

Development is rarely linear with any growth process. Each component of mindfulness, attention, exposure, and acceptance circles back to enhance and reinforce each other. In addition, mindfulness represents a systemic process, i.e., the whole is greater and different than the simple addition of its parts. However, other conditions develop as a result of the process of mindfulness. For example, as mentioned above compassion is a related quality that has been shown to surface over time with mindfulness and hopefully can emerge in a therapeutic relationship as well. We may recognize compassion for oneself in clinical work for example, when a client is able to internalize the therapist's unconditional positive regard and respond kindly to him- or herself. The seeds of compassion for others can be seen when a client formerly angry and hurt by a loved one, recalls something positive or insightful about the significant other without diminishing his or her own personal experiences. In mindfulness, compassion for others is a critical component that varies in emphasis depending on the practitioner (Lang et al. 2012; Steinberg and Eisner 2015). Unfortunately, the process of developing compassion gets overshadowed when mindfulness is reduced to a soundbyte designed to be done quickly and efficiently. The objective is to guide participants toward the goal of being able to wish others happiness and a life free of suffering, but not to skip over the part of

---

[3] Although some clinicians view moments of presence within the therapeutic process as a form of spirituality.

experiencing and understanding individual subjective experiences. Too often when practicing on our own, we forget that there are intrapersonal as well as interpersonal aspects in our zeal to excel at mindfulness.

Experiencing compassion in meditation can be facilitated with an experienced meditator. When therapeutically relevant, this process can be added to developing skills through visualizing a caring person in the participant's history or current life. As the ability to visualize that person increases and positive feelings are regularly generated, the focus of the visualizations gradually move from the caring person, to neutral persons (perhaps seen in daily life but without a close personal relationship), to finally being able to visualize a person that causes more discomfort or negative feelings (Morgan and Morgan 2005). This compassion form of meditation should follow a careful screening and assessment by the clinician to ensure that sufficient emotional and mental resources are available for the participant to draw strength from, before trying to visualize someone with more negative feelings. For clients with a traumatic background, this is not a process that should be introduced, hurried, or circumvented without careful collaboration and clinical experience.

The additional and crucial emphasis on compassion can be a slippery slope for clinicians wanting to emphasize the role of positive emotions in clients' lives. Szczygiel (2016) explains that compassion should emerge within the context of healthy interdependency that attempts to balance individuality with relational universality. Introspection and management of an unruly mind lead to openness to others and a commitment to facilitating a mindful understanding and interaction in the world. In a similar way, psychotherapy has the goal of improved mood and effective behavior, but should not stop with a focus on self-referential intrapsychic changes (e.g., ego functioning related to impulse control, mastery, judgment, defenses, etc.). There should also be an outward manifestation of therapeutic gains including an ability to have positive relationships outside the therapy office or the therapeutic relationship; as Freud was reported to have emphasized the goal was to love and to work.

This connection between self and others has been obscured in the Western world by a psychoanalytic focus on "psychological man, self-maximization, not participation in the polis" (Rubin 1997, p. 81). An autonomous self-centered subjectivity has been the therapeutic goal with any nonself-focused experiences often being interpreted as dysfunctional regression or psychosis. Feminists as well as intersubjective theorists have attempted to correct this egocentrism (Jordan et al. 1991; Storolow and Atwood 1992; Mitchell 2003, etc.). Rubin (1997) discusses a "nonself-centered subjectivity" as part of psychological development[4] that may prove to be similar to the desired outcome of mindfulness.

> In nonself-centric states of being there is a nonpathological, dedifferentiation of boundaries between self and world: a self-empowering sense of connection between self and world that results in a lack of self-preoccupation, a sense of timelessness, efficacy, and peace. Moment of nonself-centricity – whether surrendering, merging, yielding, letting go – seem to be part of most spiritual traditions. (p. 84)

[4]Similar to Loewald's (1978) description of these kind of nonself-centered manifestations.

The practice of mindfulness facilitates the process of de-centering a sense of self, so that the meditator can experience his or her shift between "self as content… to self as context" (Hayes et al. 1999 cited in Shapiro and Carlson 2009, p. 97). In the act of observing the content of our thoughts, we shift to experiencing the act of observing and realizing that our self is a psychological construction. We are much more than just what we think we are at this present moment or what we are feeling in this space in time. This is very different from the western prioritizing the role of the ego or the self and their importance in psychological functioning. For example, a goal in Buddhism is not to eliminate the ego or a self per se; rather it is to develop the awareness that the self does not really exist in the way we think of as something constant and consistent (Epstein 1988). Mindfulness enlists a "therapeutic split in the ego" (Engler 1983; Sterba 1934; as cited in Epstein 1988) dividing the ego into both subject and object. "This capacity for observing the dynamic flow of psychic events is very much a synthetic function, maintaining equilibrium in the face of incessant change" (Epstein 1988, p. 66).

When initially anticipating the possibility of any kind of split in the perception of the self, clinicians often worry that this process is similar to the psychological phenomenon of splitting, which can be very alarming if clients are vulnerable to regression or psychosis. Likewise the Buddhist concept of no-self is not the same thing as a loss of self that we may associate with a loss of cohesion in self psychology. This type of split or no-self is not the type of fragmentation that Kohut is referring to (Kohut and Wolf 1978); quite the contrary. There are indeed moments of fragmentation when practicing at an advanced level of insight meditation, but those experiences can be synthesized and a "re-equilibration rather than a progression beyond an outmoded structure" (Kohut and Wolf, p. 67) can occur. These are not dissociative or regressive experiences that result in psychosis. Fortunately others have discussed this process and concept at length. For example, Epstein (2013) describes a period of time when he was struggling with why he did not understand "no-self". After a period of walking when he did not feel he was "mindfully walking," he recalled a diagram in medical school explaining the process of how the brain converts images into what we see. He remembered that the brain does not perfectly reflect the outside world.

> The brain actually creates our reality…it does not just mirror it. Sensory data enter the brain as raw material not finished images. The eye perceives angles and edges, not objects or backgrounds. It's up to the brain to make reality coherent, building it up out of the raw information our organs of sight, smell, touch, taste, hearing and memory feed it. (p. 132) No-self was not a state to be achieved, it was a testament to my embedded nature. No self apart from the world. (Epstein 2013, p. 133)

Mindfulness is a pathway to connect people to their own humanity that they share with others; not to retrieve a "self" that has been hidden and buried. For clinicians interested in Buddhism or in including elements of mindfulness in their personal or professional lives it would be important to study these concepts with a more skillful practitioner (as discussed in Chaps. 5 and 6). There are also many resources available that discuss the Buddhist concept of no-self in detail beyond what can be explored here and in addition to those listed in Appendix A (Epstein 1988, 1995; Rubin 1997, etc.).

In addition to compassion toward one's self and toward others, equanimity is an essential part of acceptance that occurs during mindfulness and can develop in psychotherapy; equanimity about our own limitations, the impermanence of feelings and thoughts, and receptivity to what is happening in the present. We can see more clearly what is a mental construction that paradoxically also instills a more realistic sense of confidence in what we can do as well. As one client triumphantly described to me years ago, "I can be ambivalent—I don't have to be limited to what I am feeling." Mindfulness can facilitate the change in one's relationship to the thoughts, rather than trying to alter the content of the thoughts, which is the more common goal in cognitive-behavioral therapy (Thurnauer 2016). This "reperceiving" does not mean that "detachment" follows, which implies a lack of connection to what is being experienced. While there is greater clarity which is a type of distancing, there is not apathy, numbness, dissociation, or disconnection. Instead "a deep, penetrative, nonconceptual seeing into the nature of the mind and world" results (Kabat-Zinn 2003, p. 146). A person can experience what is happening without a commentary about what is happening or a need to react, which is more the norm in everyday functioning. Another client describes this continuous internal monologue as "my mind is always judging, comparing, evaluating, so that I never get to experience what is happening at the moment". By focusing on the present moment in a nonjudgmental manner, one can systematically explore and refine one's own awareness (Bishop et al. 2004; Shapiro et al. 2006). This awareness leads to compassion toward oneself and ultimately toward others (Bruce et al. 2010; Greeson 2009). Research is ongoing that demonstrates the impact of mindfulness on therapists in training and their increased ability to facilitate the common factors deemed critical to positive outcomes with clients (Shapiro and Carlson 2009). Beck, in the next chapter of this text, explains the neurobiological process that transpires in mindfulness that facilitates the development of empathy between client and clinician.

What Are the Contraindications and Pitfalls of Mindfulness?

While mindfulness does not have any inherent drawbacks, there are several caveats that emerge when reviewing reports of personal or professional experiences, and empirically informed research. When clients or patients have experienced trauma and are experiencing flashbacks of any kind, care is essential to understand and predict how and when those flashbacks can be triggered, prolonged, or experienced by patients. In a group setting (as discussed in Chap. 10 by Strauss), a thorough knowledge of group dynamics is essential to understand how group members may influence each other, stimulate dependency issues, experience problems with group affiliation, and likely instigate therapeutic transference and countertransference issues (Steinberg and Eisner 2015).

It is not clear whether particular kinds of mindfulness or meditation practices are most suited to clients with certain kinds of disorders (Lazar et al. 2005). However, many interventions have been designed with a particular population in mind. The key seems to be the leader (or guide or therapist) must have personal and professional experience with mindfulness and clinical work in order to understand that particular population and help convey to clients what to expect and how to manage those feelings. It is critical that participants be trained with the "tincture of time" so that trauma histories and compulsive thoughts or images are not triggered without some tools to negotiate the rough waters.

A common practice in mental health care in the United States is the combination of mindfulness with other treatment modalities, such as CBT, pharmacotherapy, and psychoeducation. There are any number of approaches currently in practice with impressive demonstrated efficacy including Acceptance and Commitment Therapy (ACT) (Hayes et al. 1999), Dialectical Behavior Therapy (DBT) (Linehan 1993), Mindfulness Based Cognitive Therapy (MBCT) (Segal et al. 2002), Mode-Deactivation Therapy (MDT) (Apsche et al. 2002); Mindful-Based Stress Reduction (Kabat-Zinn 1990, 1994); Mindful-Based Relapse Prevention (MBRP) (Bowen et al. 2010). Likewise there are programs that combine mindfulness with physical movement such as yoga or yoga nidra that emphasizes the "yoking of mind and body" (Olendzki 2005; Rhodes et al. 2016; Stoller et al. 2016, etc.). Utilizing mindfulness and/or physical action such as yoga can be empowering for clients so they can expand their ability to experience positive affect and negotiate secondary trauma triggered by the initial phase of clinical work. Northcut and Kienow (2014) provide illustrations in which the physical activity of walking meditation facilitated the formation of a therapeutic alliance with a survivor of military sexual trauma.

Vujanovic et al. (2011) have shown in their research that certain types of mindfulness training may be inadvisable during early phases of PTSD treatment if participants are unable to focus attention on current experience. For example, MBSR may not be applicable if long silences or the process of listening to tapes for extended periods cannot be tolerated. MBSR recommends PTSD survivors be ruled out of training if not in concurrent treatment for PTSD. Instructor guidance exercises of shorter duration may be more feasible, such as 5–10 min rather than the 30–45 min suggested in MBSR. Colleagues and scholars at McGill University developed a pre-MBSR interview screening sheet (Dobkin et al. 2011) that asks potential participants to describe prior group experiences, relate prior experiences of trauma, current substance use and misuse. There is also an orientation process during which the program is explained, the expectations and time commitment are clarified, and the person's intention for pursuing the program is explored. Despite orientation to the process, Pigeon et al. (2015) found a high rate of misconceptions about MBSR persisted with the 78 veterans in their research despite the extensive verbal and written instructions prior to beginning the training. These findings seem to suggest that hopes and fantasies about what may transpire during mindfulness training may be particularly unrealistic despite receiving pragmatic clarification ahead of time. Clinicians need to be aware of those potential expectations which can interfere with the helpfulness of any mindfulness training.

A more beneficial heuristic for understanding how mindfulness can enhance therapeutic work may be envisioning a "window of tolerance" that provides a framework for thinking about the emotional and physiological zone in which a client can function without disrupting functioning (Ogden 2009; Siegel 1999). Whether we have experienced trauma or not, we experience a certain level of stress daily and are still able to continue our daily lives (i.e., we can feel and function). However, if the stress level exceeds a certain point we begin to forget things, become irritable, and become symptomatic. If the level of stress is traumatic, we respond with either hyperarounsal or hypoarousal; both states prevent us from integrating our challenging emotional states. In clinical work, clinicians assist clients by trying to titrate the arousal until there is a baseline of functioning or window of tolerance. Once that level is attained then the delicate dance begins by trying to expand that tolerance level to allow for memories, repressed or dissociated emotions, and new behaviors to emerge and be integrated. This is similar to Vygotsky's (1978) Zone of Proximal Development in which another adult or more capable peer can guide someone to function beyond the level of what can be accomplished alone, but not beyond what is possible with someone else. Therapists with experience in mindfulness can scaffold a facilitating environment that is "safe but not too safe" for the client. What this means is that therapy can be disruptive when it accesses dysregulated arousal, or stirs up memories or feelings that have not been previously integrated. The challenge is negotiating the "edge" of the "regulatory boundaries of the window of tolerance" (Ogden 2009, p. 3). Certainly, we titrate when and how to push for or allow clients to access emotional content based on biopsychosocial-spiritual factors that influence the present moment, but clients need to be able to develop a tolerance for experiencing what may have not been previously integrated in a supported way. Our job is to be able to clearly assess and intervene as best as we can during the progression of that process.

Conclusion

Mindfulness has appeared to take the country by a storm in the last 15–20 years despite its long history in different religious traditions around the world. During the writing of this chapter, *Time* Magazine produced a special issue on "Mindfulness: The New Science of Health and Happiness". Empirical studies, in addition to public interest, are demonstrating support for the neurophysiological benefits of incorporating mindfulness into the daily routine of everyday life.

The components of mindfulness, attention, exposure, and acceptance of what is happening in the moment facilitate practitioners' having compassion and equanimity for themselves and about others. However, as with therapeutic processes, these are subjective experiences that have different repercussions based on individuals' psychological, sociological, and biological contexts. Social workers must continue to be mindful of introducing any trend or technique into practice without sufficient training, personal and professional experience, and qualitative and quantitative support. In our rush to embrace what appears to offer tremendous hope for our personal and professional effectiveness, we can not lose sight of the twin foci of mindfulness: private and public peace.

References

Apsche, J. A., Ward, S. R., & Evile, M. M. (2002). Mode deactivation therapy (MDT): A functionally based treatment. *Behavior Analyst Today, 3*(4), 455–459.

Bishop, S. R., Lau, M., Shapiro, S., Carlson, L., Anderson, M. D., Carmody, J., et al. (2004). Mindfulness: A proposed operational definition. *Clinical Psychology: Science and Practice, 11* (3), 230–241.

Borden, W. (2016). Taking multiplicity seriously: Therapeutic action and clinical pragmatism. *Greenstone Memorial Lecture.* April 22, 2016. Personal Communication.

Bowen, S., Chawla, N., & Marlatt, G. A. (2010). *Mindfulness-based relapse prevention for addictive behaviors.* NY: Guilford.

Brach, T. (2003). *Radical acceptance: Embracing your life with the heart of a Buddha.* NY: Bantam.

Bruce, N. G., Manber, R., Shapiro, S. L., & Constantino, M. J. (2010). Psychotherapist mindfulness and the psychotherapy process. *Psychotherapy Theory, Research, Practice, Training, 1*(1), 83–97.

Bucci, W. (1982). The vocalization of painful affect. *Journal of Communication Disorders, 15,* 415–440.

Bucci, W. (1984). Linking words and things: Basic processes and individual variation. *Cognition, 17,* 137–153.

Bucci, W. (1985). Dual coding: A cognitive model for psychoanalytic research. *Journal of the American Psychoanalytic Association*, 571–607.

Chodron, P. (1999). *Turning toward pain.* Retrieved from http://www.beliefnet.com/wellness/health/physical-health/pain-management/turning-toward-pain.aspx#YWzS66o0e07yuDe6.99

Crits-Christoph, P., Gibbons, M. B. C., & Mukherjee, D. (2013). Psychotherapy process-outcome research. In M. J. Lambert (Ed.), *Handbook of psychotherapy and behavior change,* (6th ed., pp. 298–340). Hoboken, NJ: Wiley.

Delizonna, L. L., Williams, R. P., & Langer, E. J. (2009). The effect of mindfulness on heart rate control. *Journal of Adult Development, 16,* 61–65. doi:10.1007/s10804-009-9050-6

Dobkin, P. L., Irving, J. A., & Amar, S. (2011). For whom may participation in a mindfulness-based stress reduction program be contraindicated? *Mindfulness, 3*(1), 44–50. doi:10.1007/s12671-011-0079-9

Engler, J. (1983). Vicissitudes of the self according to psychoanalysis and Buddhism: A spectrum model of object relations development. *Psychoanalysis and Contemporary Thought., 6*(1), 29–72.

Epstein, M. (1988). The deconstruction of the self: Ego and "egolessness" in Buddhist insight meditation. *Journal of Transpersonal Psychology, 20*(1), 61–69.

Epstein, M. (1995). *Thoughts without a thinker: Psychotherapy from a Buddhist perspective.* New York, NY: Basic Books.

Epstein, M. (2013). *The trauma of everyday life.* NY: Penguin Books.

Fulton, P. (2005). Mindfulness as clinical training. In C. K. Germer, R. D. Siegel, & P. R. Fulton (Eds.), *Mindfulness and psychotherapy* (pp. 55–72). NY: Guilford.
Fulton, P. (2014). Contributions and challenges to clinical practice from Buddhist psychology. *Clinical Social Work Journal, 42*(3), 208–217.
Greeson, J. (2009). Mindfulness research update: 2008. *Complimentary Health Practice Review, 14*(1), 10–18.
Hahn, T. N. (1998). *The heart of the Buddha's teaching*. NY: Broadway Books.
Hayes, S. C., Stroshal, K. D., & Wilson, K. G. (1999). *Acceptance and commitment therapy: The process and practice of mindful change*. New York, NY: Guilford Press.
Hicks, S. F. (2009). *Mindfulness and social work*. Chicago: Lyceum.
Horney, K. (1952). Free associations and the use of the couch. In A. Molino (Ed.), *The couch and the tree: Dialogues in psychoanalysis and Buddhism* (pp. 35–36). NewYork, NY: North Point Press. (Original work published 1952).
Jha, A. P., Krompinger, J., & Baime, M. J. (2007). Mindfulness training modifies subsytems of attention. *Cognitive, Affective & Behavioral Neuroscience, 7,* 109–119.
Jordan, J. V., Kaplan, A. G., Miller, J. B., Stiver, I. P., & Surrey, J. L. (1991). *Women's growth in connection: Writings from the Stone Center*. New York, NY: Guilford Press.
Kabat-Zinn, J. (1990, 2013 revised). *Full catastrophe living: Using the wisdom of your mind to face stress, pain, and illness*. New York: Dell.
Kabat-Zinn, J. (1994). *Wherever you go, there you are: Mindfulness meditation for everyday life*. New York: Hyperion.
Kabat-Zinn, J. (2003). Mindfulness-based interventions in context: Past, present, and future. *Clinical Psychology: Science and Practice, 10,* 144–156.
Klein, M., Mathieu, P. L., Gendlin, E. T., & Kiesler, D. J. (1969). *The experiencing scale: A research and training manual* (Vol. 1). Milwaukee, WI: Wisconsin Psychiatric Institute.
Kohut, H., & Wolf, E. (1978). The disorders of the self and their treatment: An outline. *International Journal of Psycho-Analysis, 59,* 413–425.
Lama, Dalai. (1997). *Healing anger: The power of patience from a Buddhist perspective*. Ithaca, NY: Snow Lion.
Lang, A. J., Strauss, J. L., Bomyea, J., Bormann, J. E., Hickman, S. D., Good, R. C., et al. (2012). The theoretical and empirical basis for meditation as an intervention for PTSD. *Behavior Modifcation, 36*(6), 759–786.
Lazar, S. W., Kerr, C. E., Wassermana, R. H., Grayc, J. R., Greve, D. N., Treadway, M. T., et al. (2005). Meditation experience is associated with increased cortical thickness. *NeuroReport, 16* (17), 1893–1897.
Linehan, M. (1993). *Cognitive behavioral treatment of borderline personality disorder*. NewYork: Guilford Press.
Loewald, H. (1978). *Psychoanalysis and the history of the individual*. New Haven, CT: Yale University Press.
Mitchell, S. A. (2003). *Relationality: From attachment to connectivity*. NY: Routledge.
Morgan, W. D., & Morgan, S. T. (2005). Cultivating attention and empathy. In C. K. Germer, R. D. Siegel, & P. R. Fulton (Eds.), *Mindfulness and psychotherapy* (pp. 73–90). NewYork: Guilford.
Nanamoli, B. (Trans.), & Bodhi, B. (Ed.). (1995). *The middle length discourses of the Buddha*. Boston: Wisdom.
Northcut, T., & Kienow, A. (2014). Trauma trifecta of military sexual trauma: A case study including mind and body in clinical social work treatment with a survivor of MST. In T. Northcut & R. Strauss (Eds.) *Special issue: Integrating mind and body in clinical social work. Clinical social work journal*. (vol. 42(3), pp. 247–259).
Ogden, P. (2009). Modulation, mindfulness, and movement in the treatment of trauma-related depression. In M. Kerman (Ed.) *Clinical pearls of wisdom: 21 leading therapists share their key insights* (pp. 1-13). NewYork: W. W. Norton.
Olendzki, A. (2005). The roots of mindfulness. In C. K. Germer, R. D. Siegel, & P. R. Fulton (Eds.) *Mindfulness and psychotherapy* (pp. 241–261). NY: Guilford.

Pigeon, W., Allen, C., Possemato, K., Bergen-Cico, D., & Treatman, S. (2015). Feasibility and acceptability of a brief mindfulness program for veterans in primary care with post-traumatic stress disorder. *Mindfulness, 6*(5), 986–995. doi:10.1007/s12671-014-0340-0

Pstein, M. (1984). On the neglect of evenly suspended attention. *Journal of Transpersonal Psychology, 16*(2), 193–205.

Rhodes, A., Spinazzola, J., & van der Kolk, B. (2016). Yoga for adult women with chronic PTSD: A long term follow-up study. *Journal of Alternative and Complementary Medicine*, 2016 Mar *22*(3):189–196. doi:10.1089/acm.2014.0407. Epub 2016 Feb 10.

Rubin, J. B. (1997). Psychoanalysis is self-centered. In C. Spezzano & G. J. Gargiulo (Eds.), *Soul on the couch: Spirituality, religion, and morality in contemporary psychoanalysis* (pp. 79–108). Hillsdale: Analytic Press.

Segal, Z. V., Williams, J. M. G., & Teasdale, J. D. (2002). *Mindfulness-based cognitive therapy for depression: A new approach to preventing relapse*. New York, NY: Guilford Press.

Shapiro, S. L., & Carlson, L. E. (2009). *The art and science of mindfulness: Integrating mindfulness into psychology and the helping professions*. Washington, D.C.: American Psychological Association.

Shapiro, F., Carlson, L. E., Astin, J., & Freedman, B. (2006). Mechanisms of mindfulness. *Journal of Clinical Psychology, 62*(3), 373–386.

Siegel, D. (1999). *The developing mind*. New York: Guilford.

Slagter, H. A., Lutz, A., Greischar, L. L., Francis, A. D., Nieuwenhuis, S., Davis, J. M., et al. (2007). Mental training affects distribution of limited brain resources. *PLoS Biology, 5*(6), e138.

Steinberg, C. A., & Eisner, D. A. (2015). Mindfulness-based interventions for veterans with posttraumatic stress disorder. *International Journal of Behavioral Consultation and Therapy, 9* (4), 11–17.

Sterba, R. F. (1934). The fate of the ego in analytic therapy. *International Journal of Psycho-Analysis., 15,* 117–126.

Stoller, C. C., Greuel, J. H., Cimini, L. S., Fowler, M. S., & Koomar, J. A. (2016). Effects of sensory-enhanced yoga on symptoms of combat stress in deployed military personnel. *American Journal of Occupational Therapy*, January/February, *66*(1), 59–68.

Storolow, R. D., & Atwood, G. E. (1992). *Context of being: The intersubjective foundations of psychological life*. New York: Routledge.

Strauss, C. A., Coeytaux, R., McDuffe, J., Williams, J. W., & Nagi, A. (2011). Efficacy of complementary and alternative medicine therapies for posttraumatic stress disorder. *Veterans Affairs Department of Research and Development, Health Services Research and Development Service's (HSR&D's) Evidence-based Synthesis Program (ESP)*. Retrieved from https://www.ncbi.nlm.nih.gov/pubmedhealth/PMH0033346/

Szczygiel, P. (2016). Maneuvering difficult emotional terrain in psychotherapy: A Buddhist-informed conceptual framework. *Clinical Social Work Journal, 44*, 241–251.

Thurnauer, E. (2016). *Cultural competence and mindfulness-based treatment with Asian Americans: A literature review*. Unpublished manuscript. New York University Silver School of Social Work DSW student.

Vujanovic, A. A., Niles, B., Pietrefesa, A., Schmertz, S. K., & Potter, C. M. (2011). Mindfulness in the treatment of posttraumatic stress disorder among military veterans. *Professional Psychology: Research and Practice., 42*(1), 24–31.

Vygotsky, L. (1978). *Mind in society*. Cambridge, MA: Harvard University Press.

Chapter 4
Beginning With the Body: The Neurobiology of Mindfulness

Natalie Beck

Mindfulness techniques are increasingly being utilized within the mental health field in conjunction with a number of therapies. Derived from Buddhist practices, mindfulness allows an individual to stay focused on the present as a way of increasing awareness into an individual's internal processes. In order to gain a more substantial understanding of mindfulness, this chapter will explore the neurobiological underpinnings of the process of mindfulness. With an understanding of the neurobiology, the therapeutic relationship will then be discussed to understand how mindfulness in the therapist and the client impacts the interpersonal therapeutic relationship in treatment.

Case Illustration

Within my current clinical work, it is not uncommon to have clients storm out of sessions, slam doors, burst into tears, or exclaim how uncomfortable treatment is. I facilitate an intensive outpatient treatment (IOT) program for substance use and many of my mandated clients are in the early stages of abstinence from alcohol and other drugs. The group meets three days a week for three hours each session and group members are required to attend the group for a total of 16 weeks. For many individuals, entering treatment through the group is a first attempt at navigating their world, internally and externally, without substances. For the newly sober, daily living can be a frustrating, exhausting, and overwhelming experience. Any additional stressors only increase the tediousness of managing another day of sobriety.

N. Beck (✉)
Institute for Clinical Social Work, Chicago, USA
e-mail: nataliemariebeck@gmail.com

T.B. Northcut (ed.), *Cultivating Mindfulness in Clinical Social Work*,
Essential Clinical Social Work Series, DOI 10.1007/978-3-319-43842-9_4

While group members are referred to the group due to substance use disorders, there is a large degree of variance between severity of addiction, length of use, and the type of substance used. Process addictions such as self-mutilation, eating disorders, and gambling are often present comorbidly in treatment. Additionally, group members vary in age, socioeconomic background, race, gender, and sexual orientation. Substance use treatment within the group is also often complicated by dual diagnosis with another mental illness. Within the group, diagnoses for major depressive disorder, generalized anxiety disorder, attention deficit hyperactivity disorder (ADHD), bipolar disorder, and posttraumatic stress disorder (PTSD) are common. One of the most prominent uniting factors for all group members within the group has been a shared experience of trauma. Individuals who have experienced trauma are twice as likely to use substances as a way of coping, with 20% of those diagnosed with PTSD also having a diagnosable substance use issue (Garland and Roberts-Lewis 2013). For some, this has included childhood physical or sexual abuse, adulthood sexual violence, domestic violence, or living in communities that have high levels of violence and conflict. These substance users who have experienced trauma are "predisposed to utilize avoidant and other maladaptive coping strategies because of an inability to withstand the distress associated with trauma exposure" (Fetzner et al. 2014, p. 475). For this reason, traumatic experiences increasingly emerge and are disclosed as the group progresses and individuals feel safer in reflecting on the events that led them to seek out substances throughout their life.

These layers to each individual add to the rich dynamic that exists within the group and leads to a shared sense that each person has their own story that has shaped their substance use history and, in turn, their sobriety. However, from a treatment perspective, it can often be difficult to facilitate a group where there are so many varying needs and presenting problems, despite the common focus. Within the group, despite varying presenting diagnoses, common complaints center around feelings of anxiety when attempting to accomplish daily tasks, intense episodes of anger, difficulty controlling and expressing emotions that had previously been avoided while using substances, and an inability to feel relaxed or alleviate stress. From the onset of the group, new coping skills were regularly introduced and discussed as a way to offer new solutions to these internal threats to emotional regulation. Mindfulness meditation that focuses on staying in the present moment allows substance users to avoid old habits that existed within addiction, where the present moment was avoided through substance use (Appel and Kim-Appel 2009). Consistent practice of mindfulness meditation helps to decrease stress, anxiety, depression but also increases emotional regulation and the capacity to refrain from substance use by reducing cravings (Brewer et al. 2009). Mindfulness practices for substance users with trauma histories also offer protective factors for positive mental health well-being that lower risk for more severe posttraumatic stress symptoms and substance cravings that can intensify these symptoms (Garland and Roberts-Lewis 2013). Due to the high prevalence of trauma histories within the group and the tendency to avoid painful affective states and traumatic memories, mindfulness practices seemed relevant to our clinical work.

After much resistance, the group agreed to try a mindfulness breathing exercise. Despite the early resistance, group members were surprised to find that they enjoyed the activity. I invited a therapist trained in mindfulness meditation to introduce and lead mindfulness techniques for an hour each week over an 8-week period. The group was provided psychoeducation on mindfulness and introduced to several ways of completing a mindfulness meditation including breathing-focused meditations and body scan meditations that allow individuals to be present and aware of their bodily states. Group members were encouraged to practice mindful meditation for at least 10 min each day. The last 15 min of each group was committed to a mindfulness meditation. Participation in mindfulness practices varied significantly outside of the group but all members continued to engage while in group.

After eight weeks, what was most noted by group members and myself was the increased ability to engage in conversations regarding the connection between mind and body that were previously much more difficult. Group members were better able to identify bodily differences in emotional experiences. This further allowed group members to identify emotional triggers that contributed to relapse by increasing self-awareness. Early recognition of emotional experiences through increased body awareness allowed individuals to implement coping strategies before emotions escalated beyond manageability and led to emotional dysregulation. Mindfulness practices also enabled the group to address symptoms stemming from several layers of different diagnoses that otherwise may have been difficult to address. As a clinician, the mindfulness practices further allowed me to better manage overwhelming affect and contain strong emotion when it presented in group. Through an increase in reflection and awareness of emotional and cognitive processes, both group members and myself were able to relate more effectively on an interpersonal level.

In order to better understand how these individual changes contributed to a more effective interpersonal experience within the group, it is necessary to explore research that outlines the changes that take place within the brain during traumatic experiences and the changes that can occur within the brain when mindfulness practices are regularly utilized. This understanding of the neurobiological changes that occur during mindfulness will ultimately lead to a more in-depth understanding of how mindfulness can not only aid in the treatment of trauma but can increase the interpersonal connection between clinician and client, both in group work and in individual treatment.

Clinical Application and Relevance: Introducing Neurobiology

While therapists may often times find themselves treating a specific diagnosis, the brain is not structured in a way that is consistent with textbook symptomology. On the contrary, individuals experience pathology in a dynamic way that encompasses their environment, history, and biology. Trauma and the proceeding diagnoses that can follow are limited examples of how the brain can have responses that fit into multiple categories or diagnoses. van der Kolk et al. (2005) note that the diagnosis of posttraumatic stress disorder (PTSD) often does not fully capture the experience of individuals who have experienced trauma, nor does the diagnosis have the capacity to explicate the experience of individuals who suffer from comorbidity with PTSD that frequently occurs for many trauma survivors. Moreover, early experiences of trauma do not necessarily result in PTSD, but can also lead to a variety of different trauma-related diagnoses such as phobias, panic reactions, dissociative identity disorder, or borderline personality disorder in response to the trauma that was experienced; the capacity to develop different diagnoses in response to a trauma is impacted by factors such as age, personality predisposition, and the severity and type of trauma (van der Kolk 1988). Given this reality, treatment must respond to the deficits that exist within a diagnostic model that does not fully account for the complex and varied responses to trauma that individuals can have.

In this light, mindfulness can be viewed as an intervention on the adapted processes of the brain, rather than on a set of symptoms experienced by an individual. As Bernstein et al. (2011) point out, mindfulness has been found to be effective in the treatment of adults who have had exposure to trauma because mindfulness has a transdiagnostic factor that addresses multiple modes of psychopathology while promoting overall mental well-being. In fact, mindfulness skills within clinical practice have been shown to alleviate symptoms of anxiety, depression, substance abuse, chronic pain, and symptoms of borderline personality disorder while also promoting resiliency for recovery from traumatic stress by increasing an individual's capacity to work through "trauma-related thoughts, memories, affective states, and related physiological cues" (Bernstein et al. 2011, p. 100). From this perspective, while mindfulness should not be considered a blanket treatment for all presenting issues, it has been found to be effective in treating trauma and other disorders at various levels because it has the ability to reach beyond the targeted symptoms. The ability of mindfulness to address a number of conditions in conjunction with therapy allows it to be a particularly useful intervention within clinical practice. The neurobiology affecting and impacted by mindfulness thus becomes important as a treatment intervention but also as a tool for allowing the clinician and client to meet on an interpersonal level, as will be discussed.

Trauma and the Brain

The traumatized brain and the changes that can occur following a traumatic incident or series of traumatic incidences have been well documented within mental health literature (Brewer et al. 2010; Davidson 2003; Cozolino 2010; Dickie et al. 2011; Doctor and Shiromoto 2010; El Khoury-Malhame et al. 2011; Fetzner et al. 2014;

Nelson and Carver 1998; van der Kolk 1988, 2002, 2006; van der Kolk et al. 1985, 2005). This section will provide a brief summary of existing research that explains the neurobiological changes in response to trauma in order to better understand how mindfulness can aid in healing the traumatized brain. The human brain has around 100 billion neurons that all interact with one another and contribute to a network that communicates between various areas of the brain (Makinson and Young 2012). When an individual encounters a traumatic event, the neurotransmitters that control attention and arousal are activated and trigger the release of the stress hormones catecholamines and cortisol (van der Kolk 2002). At the same time, the amygdala is activated while the prefrontal cortex is deactivated in the brain. The amygdala is part of the limbic system and is considered the center for all of an individual's basic emotions. The amygdala is also connected to the frontal cortex and receives visual, auditory, and sensory inputs from this area (Doctor and Shiromoto 2010). The thalamus, hypothalamus, and hippocampus send information to the amygdala. Due to this crucial role as receptor from multiple areas, the amygdala is considered to be the center of the fear system and orchestrates responses and determines emotional value based on the stimuli it receives both internally and externally. The amygdala is also responsible for the creation of emotional memory, both conscious and subconscious, and has been considered the area of the brain that stores traumatic emotional memory for this reason. Moreover, the amygdala is the main area of the brain that is responsible for responding to stimuli from the environment and creating a response in the body. In individuals who have experienced trauma, the exaggerated fear responses and over activation to emotionally arousing situations are directly linked to activity in the amygdala and can result in anxious symptomology (El Khoury-Malhame et al. 2011). When the amygdala believes there is a threat to the body, it activates the prefrontal cortex and autonomic system.

The autonomic nervous system is comprised of three separate systems: the sympathetic nervous system, which controls the sympathetic adrenal response and prepares the body to respond during high stress situations; the parasympathetic nervous system, which works on saving energy within the body during digestion; and the enteric nervous system, which controls the digestive organs. Of particular interest is the sympathetic nervous system whose sympathetic adrenal response is also referred to as "fight or flight" response where an individual responds to fear or heightened stress. Simply put, the sympathetic nervous system is responsible for preparing the body for outside threats through actions such as suppressing digestion and engaging in a survival response while the parasympathetic nervous system is responsible for disengaging from a survival response and reactivates normal patterns of digestion and body regulation when a distressing signal is no longer being sent. In this way, the sympathetic nervous system initiates the response to a threatening event while the parasympathetic nervous system acts as the counterpart that returns the brain to normal levels of functioning no longer aimed at surviving in the face of an external threat.

However, these systems function properly in response to manageable, expected threats from the environment. In instances of extreme stress, the executive control of the prefrontal cortex over the amygdala is diminished and the amygdala can generate responses that are independent from the prefrontal cortex (Makinson and Young 2012). When this occurs during trauma, the amygdala can continue to generate responses that are over exaggerated to the stimulus even after the traumatic event is over (Makinson and Young 2012). The amygdala can also be activated during states of disgust, sadness, and anger, in addition to fear, showing that it has a crucial role in generating surprise and excitement during high arousal states (Suvak and Barrett 2011). These findings highlight that the amygdala is not dependent on fear-based experiences but can be activated in a more general hypervigilant state of arousal that responds to various stimuli in the environment (Suvak and Barrett 2011). For example, the hypervigilance and sensitivity that survivors of trauma experience can lead the individual to be triggered by sights, sounds, smells, or other sensations associated with the original trauma. In protecting the individual from further trauma, the amygdala remains active to ensure continued survival. For this reason, mindfulness practices, which allow for increased relaxation and body awareness, can aid in helping the brain switch from sympathetic nervous system responses driven by the amygdala to parasympathetic nervous system responses that recognize more participation from the body without overemphasis on what is occurring externally.

During a traumatic event, while heavy activation is occurring in the limbic system and the autonomic nervous system, activity in other areas of the brain decrease. Most significantly, neuroimaging studies indicate that the medial prefrontal cortex has decreased activity during trauma (Dickie et al. 2011). The prefrontal cortex functions within the brain as the executive control over judgment and inhibition while regulating emotions and controlling working memory, impulsivity, attention, and decision making. In addition, it is the prefrontal cortex that curbs the response of the limbic system and initiates the body's stress response systems during normal periods of stress (Makinson and Young 2012). However, during traumatic experiences, the regulatory top-down control of the prefrontal cortex on the amygdala is weakened, which results in a difficulty to disengage from the threat in the environment (El Khoury-Malhame et al. 2011). This means that an individual experiencing trauma no longer has the ability to use the prefrontal cortex and practice regular judgment or regulate their emotions or impulses. During these states, the amygdala and larger limbic system are in charge of creating emotional interpretations of the event through the smells, sounds, and sensations at the current moment as a way of remembering the experience and protecting against such threats in the future (van der Kolk 2002). Without significant input from the prefrontal cortex, these memories of stimuli serve as triggers to protect the individual; the amygdala's main priority is ensuring survival rather than increasing understanding. The lack of involvement from the prefrontal cortex and any executive response also makes it difficult for these memories to be formulated in an appropriate response to these stimuli when experienced again in the future. Thus, the top-down processing of the brain that utilizes cognition to manage emotional and sensorimotor processing does not occur during traumatic events (van der Kolk 2006). This means that for individuals who are triggered by a sensation that is not currently a threat but is associated with a traumatic memory, the processing of the brain does not allow the individual to recognize the difference in sensation or stimulation. A traumatic response is initiated, despite no real threat to survival. For example, an individual who has experienced trauma due to gun violence may hear a loud noise from a car starting that the survival brain associates with gunfire and therefore a threat. In a survival response, the individual may lower to the ground or duck to avoid the external threat of gunfire because the prefrontal cortex is not able to override the amygdala and gather further information and judgment that the loud noise is from a nonthreatening car.

Further, during trauma, the Broca's area of the brain, the region that enables individuals to formulate feelings into verbal expression, is not activated either. This further leads to a nonverbal experience of an event because the brain is both in a reactive, survival mode rather than in a mode to create language for experience. Thus, traumatic experiences that are largely experienced outside of the prefrontal cortex create nondeclarative (i.e., implicit and not requiring conscious thought) memories that are reexperienced nonverbally (Nelson and Carver 1998). What this means is that when individuals remember traumatic experiences, due to the construction of memory and the mental state at the time of the trauma, they are frequently unable to put the experience into words because no verbal memories have been stored that would allow them to reexperience or process the event in a verbal narrative. This not only makes talk therapy exceptionally difficult, but can also contribute to an individual's tendency to avoid stimulation as a way to avoid becoming aroused by a traumatic stimulus for which they have "no words" for what they are feeling. For this reason, the tendency of traditional therapies to ignore the bodily responses to traumatic events and reexperiencings only further complicates clinical work (van der Kolk 2002). In studying the coping of an incident that occurred at a preverbal level through techniques like mindfulness, a bridge is formed in the previously separated somatic and the cognitive in experiences of trauma (Anderson and Gold 2003). Clinicians can create physical safety through mindfulness practices that ease into bodily sensations that may be uncomfortable when memories of trauma get triggered. This safety thus increases the ability of the clinician to help the survivor generate language for what she feels and what she remembers. Clarifying how mindfulness impacts the brain helps us understand how it can be used within the treatment of trauma to alleviate symptoms and disturbances, and as a way to explore further implications for treatment of other mental health issues.

Mindfulness and the Brain

Mindfulness as a technique may offer individuals a way to separate themselves from the sensory experiences of the trauma, which may then allow them to process what they have experienced in a new, more manageable way. Mindfulness is understood as involving both an awareness of the present moment and an acceptance of emotional experiences without any self-judgment (Vujanovic et al. 2011). Within mindfulness, awareness of the present, through recognition of what can be seen, heard, tasted, smelled, and felt throughout the entire body without preoccupation with the past or future, is utilized as a tool for tuning the individual into the here and now, rather than remaining focused in thoughts and judgments. Being nonjudgmental, a main tenant of mindfulness derived from the Eastern practices that influence mindfulness, allows the practicing individual to experience her body and the world around her without the need to categorize anything as "good" or "bad." What an individual experiences is simply the experience and the need to label it is unnecessary.

During the practice of mindfulness meditation, multiple areas of the brain are activated simultaneously and function in a synergistic manner to impart change across the brain (Hölzel et al. 2011). In a process termed neural integration, prefrontal neurons are activated during mindfulness practice and extend to various areas of the brain and body, which inevitably contributes to an increased sense of well-being as well as increased insight. In neural integration, when both the cognitive and emotional areas of the brain are activated, the brain restructures and creates neuroadaptations through neuroplasticity (Makinson and Young 2012). Specifically, when both the amygdala and the prefrontal cortex are engaged in mindfulness meditation, not only the negative effects are able to be regulated through integration of the cognitive and the emotional, but also the cortisol levels, a hormone released during stress, are lowered (Bergen-Cico et al. 2014). Over time, when an individual utilizes the prefrontal cortex in regulating experiences rather than relying on the amygdala that is active during trauma and survival responses, the hippocampus is also affected in the brain. The hippocampus is the area of the brain that regulates cortisol and other hormones that contribute to stress-related symptoms and diseases (Bergen-Cico et al. 2014). By controlling the release of stress hormones, the brain is able to adjust back into a mode of functioning that is not based on responding to potential threats. Instead, the brain can use the prefrontal cortex to judge and perceive the environment realistically rather than through the lens of past trauma and the amygdala's need to preserve survival. Mindfulness practices that activate areas of the brain that previously had limited activity due to trauma responses create neuronal pathways to other areas of the brain. These new "neuronal networks" are integrated into the regular top-down processing of the prefrontal cortex that occurs. Over time and with repeated connection, these networks become the new default networks for processing information instead of the previous networks that were created in response to trauma (Hinton et al. 2013). Going further, mindfulness practices also incorporate the body in a way that allows for sensory experiences to be integrated with cognitive regulation. Mindfulness practices utilize selective attention and working memory to process sensory experiences of the body in a top-down modulation of alpha rhythms in the sensory neocortex that allows for a cognitive processing of what is initially felt so that experiences can be felt and then understood in a regulated manner (Kerr et al. 2013). In other words, mindfulness allows the practicing individual to experience physical sensations in the body while cognitive areas in the brain are active, making it easier for individuals to cognitively understand what they are feeling. This directly contrasts with the experience individuals have during trauma when cognitive areas of the brain are shut down or limited and experiences are not recognized on a verbal level. The cognitive processing of bodily experiences aids in clinical work by increasing the ability of the client to express what she feels and experiences with the clinician, thereby increasing the client's ability to process the experience and also allowing the clinician to have better insight into the client's experiences.

A Conceptual Framework for Understanding the Neurobiology of Mindfulness

In order to better understand how the complex systems of the brain interact during mindfulness practices, the conceptual framework constructed by Hölzel et al. (2011) can offer clarity. In their framework, after conducting a meta-analysis of recent neurological studies, Hölzel et al. (2011) outline how regular practitioners of mindful meditation produced long-term changes in multiple areas of the brain and contributed to increased (1) attention regulation, (2) body awareness, (3) emotional regulation, and (4) changes to an individuals' perspective on the self. These four areas of improvement are brought about by different areas of the brain and have implications for a number of clinical presenting issues. Using this framework, changes in the brain will be discussed along with clinical research that exemplifies the claims provided within the framework.

Attention regulation. The anterior cingulated cortex (ACC) is the area of the brain that is responsible for interpreting the conflicts between separate streams of incoming data that are incompatible by using executive attention. Attention can be maintained during mindfulness meditation in spite of distractions in the environment when the ACC works in conjunction with the fronto-insular cortex to switch between different brain networks as a way of maintaining cognitive control (Hölzel et al. 2011). This top-down approach is possible through rapid firing neurons in these areas of the brain that control signals and responses during cognitively demanding tasks. When an individual utilizes mindfulness practices, these areas of the brain are activated and become skillful in quickly filtering out distractions that do not contribute to the identified focus. Over time, and with consistent practice of mindfulness techniques, cortical thickness of gray matter has shown to be increased in the ACC, which further reinforces an individual's ability to maintain attention on a task (Hölzel et al. 2011). Individuals also report increases in executive attention, orienting, and alerting to stimulus. For example, an individual may find that while attempting to meditate, they are distracted by the noises of others around them, the smell of food coming from another room, and curiosity about what movies are playing in theaters. Through continued mindfulness practice, the brain becomes trained in recognizing the stimulus but also allowing the stimulus to be recognized, so that the thoughts pass through rather than distract and pull the individual from the meditation they were originally focusing on.

Within clinical studies, attention regulation through mindfulness has been posited to be a possible intervention to aid individuals with PTSD in decreasing emotional numbing and hypervigilance by placing nonjudgmental attention on difficult emotional states (Kearney et al. 2012). Smith et al. (2011) reported in a study on urban firefighters with PTSD that those who utilized mindfulness-based interventions experienced greater cognitive flexibility that allows an individual to think about multiple ideas at once or to easily switch attention between ideas and an increased ability to pay attention to what is presently occurring. These abilities to be more cognitively flexible and more present-minded also facilitated the ability to be more regulated emotionally and led to a decrease in posttraumatic stress triggers. In a study on mindfulness practice with veterans diagnosed with PTSD, Bormann et al. (2014) found that an increase in mindful attention resulted in decreased stress, rumination, and anxiety while also improving self-compassion. Attention regulation was also shown to contribute to a reduction in PTSD symptomology in women who utilized yoga practice that included mindfulness meditation (Dick et al. 2014). Focusing attention allowed these participants to tolerate the urge to avoid aversive internal experiences, which contributes to PTSD symptom severity and a prolonging of symptoms over time. Increases in attention also facilitated an easier process of regulating emotions and increasing sensory experiences, demonstrating the synergistic effect mindfulness has on the brain.

Body awareness. At this point in research, there has not been enough empirical evidence to validate claims made by practitioners of mindfulness meditation that there is an increase in body awareness. However, recent studies have found activation in areas of the brain that is typically activated during body awareness that is also activated during mindfulness practices. The insula, located in the fissure that separates the temporal lobe from the parietal and frontal lobes, and its gray matter is the portion of the brain that contributes to visceral awareness and interoceptive accuracy (Hölzel et al. 2011). During mindfulness practices that focus on staying in the present moment, this area of the brain is activated along with the thalamus and the secondary somatosensory cortex, the area of the brain that interprets exteroceptive sensory events, which are bodily perceptions through the five senses of sight, taste, touch, sound, and feeling (Hölzel et al. 2011). Activation in all these areas contributes to a bottom-up processing of external stimuli that allow the sensory experiences of an individual to be fully processed within the body before being processed on a cognitive level, thus leading to the interpretation that this activity in the brain contributes to an increased sense of body awareness. For individuals who complete an 8-week mindfulness meditation program, gray matter concentration has increased in the temporo-parietal junction, which is the structure within the brain that is responsible for the feeling of embodiment or awareness of bodily states, only furthering the claim that mindfulness practices alter the brain to allow individuals to become more aware of their bodily sensory experiences (Kabat-Zinn 1994).

Clinical studies have also validated these reports, especially with the practice of mindfulness techniques that utilize bodily movements, such as yoga. Yoga and other techniques that utilize physical sensations are believed to be more effective than seated meditation because such techniques draw the body into the mindfulness practice and further teach the participant new skills within the context of the body (Dick et al. 2014). For individuals with PTSD, yoga could be exceptionally helpful by increasing the tolerance for recognizing internal sensations and perceptions (van der Kolk 2006). More specifically, for survivors of sexual or physical trauma, the body may itself be a connection to the trauma. In working with survivors of military sexual trauma, a case level study by Northcut and Kienow (2014) notes how military personnel who are survivors of sexual violence have layers of difficulty surrounding their body and the violence that occurred. As members of the military, the body as a trained and skilled entity is a physical representation of the job assigned to each soldier. However, following an act of sexual violence, the body also becomes the location of the trauma, thus transforming the body from an asset of labor into an object of pain. In providing guided meditations, mindfulness body scans that bring awareness to the body's present status, and walking meditations, the study highlighted how the participant was able to detach from thoughts and experience bodily sensations (Northcut and Kienow 2014). This process of detaching from thoughts so as to ground the individual back within the body parallels the bottom-up processing that occurs in the brain when individuals report feeling more sensory awareness after mindfulness practice. While top-down processing may be beneficial for regulating emotions and maintaining attention, the sensory experiences that connect an individual to the body are effective in allowing the person to reexperience the body while also encouraging a return to typical, routine actions such as hygiene maintenance that are often lost when intrusive thoughts, feelings, and memories are unmanageable.

Emotional regulation. As discussed within the section on the neurobiology of trauma, individuals who have difficulty regulating their emotions have an excess of activity within the amygdala, the area of the brain that is designed to detect affective stimuli and a decrease in the prefrontal activity that would typically monitor and maintain the amygdala's responses through judgment, reason, and impulse control. However, through the practice of mindfulness, the brain is returned to a top-down processing of events where the prefrontal cortex is activated and the amygdala shows a decrease in activation. During mindfulness, the ACC, which helps to regulate attention, also works to monitor control processes while the prefrontal cortex monitors affective states, thereby becoming involved in responding to inhibitions. The activations within the brain that help to regulate emotions are also speculated to be the factors that contribute to findings in improved mental health for practitioners of mindfulness practice and lead to stress reduction, as well as a reduction in depressive symptoms (Hölzel et al. 2011).

Clinical research validates the claims that emotional regulation stemming from mindfulness practices contributes to a better sense of mental health as well. In mantram (concentrative) practice, frequency of practice was correlated with a reduction in intrusive thoughts, anxiety, and depression, thus leading to a reported higher quality of life (Bormann et al. 2014). Within expressive writing, mindfulness was shown to be a trait that negated alexithymia and contributed to participants having a much more emotionally regulating experience when writing about traumatic experiences than individuals who were found to have low scores of mindfulness. The ability to be more emotionally regulated when discussing trauma allowed the individuals to experience a more therapeutic exchange due to the individual being able to better tolerate and stay engaged with the topic (Poon and Danoff-Burg 2011). Therapeutic transformation also took place in the form of improved emotional regulation within a mindfulness program for veterans. Participants presented with issues including anger, hypervigilence, guilt, shame, intrusive memories and thoughts, the tendency to avoid, and emotional numbing; when any of these issues arose, participants were encouraged to experience them in the present and to address them as they arose, thus allowing participants the opportunity to learn the skills necessary to regulate themselves (Kearney et al. 2013). In these examples, mindfulness practices allow for the creation of a "space" that aids the brain in forming new ways of interpreting and processing emotional information in a controlled, cognitive way.

Changes to a sense of self. Much like body awareness, it is difficult to empirically prove a change to a sense of self, despite the long-held statements made by practitioners of mindfulness that have experienced a shift in identity that allows them to be less "static" in their conception of their sense of self. However, Hölzel et al. (2011) still attempt to explain the brain changes that take place when an individual experiences a change in the perspective on the self by noting that when this shift occurs, there is increased gray matter concentration in the posterior cingulated cortex, the temporo-parietal junction, and the hippocampus. Gray matter is dense in neuronal cells and leads to an increase in functioning in the areas where it is concentrated. These areas of the brain, in combination with the medial prefrontal cortex, form the brain network that is referred to as a theory of the mind due to this network's ability to draw from the past, conceive the future, speculate alternative perspectives of the self, and think about how others may interpret and view a situation (Hölzel et al. 2011). The theory of the mind is understood to allow individuals to understand the subjective experiences of others outside themselves and to allow this recognition to inform their own subjective experience. Following mindfulness practice, it is conceivable that this brain network is associated with "the perceptual shift in the internal representation of the self" (Hölzel et al. 2011, p. 549). A change in the ability to relate to the self in new ways and with alternative perspectives to the self through the recognition of others allows the mindfulness practitioner to widen the internal world that understands the self.

Within trauma treatment, the idea of being aware and present within an identity of the self is particularly useful, especially for clients who experience depersonalization, which is "characterized by subjective experiences of unreality and detachment in one's sense of self" (Michal et al. 2007, p. 693). During the practice of mindfulness, individuals are encouraged to not only feel embodied within the experience, but to become aware of themselves in relation to their body. Moore et al. (2009) highlight their finding that mindfulness exercises allow individuals to experience a sense of self by using awareness and insight to construct narratives that accurately describe who they view themselves to be in the current moment. This ability to stay present and connected with the self can allow clients to experience and express their internal awareness and more effectively encode new information and experiences associated with improved mental health.

Interpersonal Neurobiology: Bringing the Clinician into the Room

The neurobiology of the individual who is utilizing mindfulness techniques can experience a shift in the dynamic that occurs within the therapeutic relationship between clinician and client. From an interpersonal perspective, the internal world of the client is not completely separate from the clinician. The human brain is a complex and complicated organ that exists and functions within one singular body. However, from the moment a human is born, that human is in relation to others. Within the text *The Neurobehavioral and Social-Emotional Development of Infants and Children*, Tronick (2007) discusses a mutual regulation model that ultimately contributes to dyadically expanded states of consciousness between two individuals. While Tronick (2007) describes the model through a parent–infant interaction, the model can also be useful in discussing the relationship that a clinician and client create. When mindfulness is an entity within the therapeutic relationship, the ability to relate and participate within the mutual regulation model is increased, as will be discussed.

The mutual regulation model of parent–infant interaction is a model that suggests that between the parent and infant, the interactive goal is to "achieve a state of mutual regulation, or reciprocity" that is created and maintained through interactive behaviors that are "primarily affective displays" (Tronick 2007, p. 178). A common example of this is when an infant mirrors the affective display of a smiling parent by smiling back. If the parent stops smiling, the child will respond accordingly, only to resume smiling if the parent resumes smiling. This sense of reciprocity that is strived for is created through the actual *process* of attempting to establish intimacy and connectedness. Unlike other goals, which may be achieved as a result of the successful attempts to connect with one another, the mutual goal of both individuals to meet one another, successful and unsuccessful, creates a reciprocal relationship where both individuals are in a consistent state of finding one another. The mutual regulation model is created by two people who want to meet and understand each other. What this means is that the ongoing interaction between the parent and child to reach one another and to understand one another's affective states is what contributes to this model. In addition, this ability to understand and express to one another is an interaction that is honed over time as the infant develops a broadened "range and use of facial expressions and vocalizations" while also deepening "the infant's capacity to interpret the parent's expressions… and master subtleties of affective displays and social cues as well as nuances in the communicative meanings of changes in tempo and rhythm" (Tronick 2007, p. 190). These developments are usually stabilized between 3 and 9 months of the infant's life and allow for predictability between the dyad's interactive patterns with one another. This allows both individuals to communicate more effectively within a positive interaction in the relationship and repair mismatches, which facilitates a secure attachment.

In order for this model to exist, it is understood that both the infant and the parent are fully differentiated entities from the moment that the infant enters the world. The infant is able to evaluate its environment and is able to experience impinging events that disrupt the infant's affective system. The infant's evaluation or appraisal of an interaction is thus communicated to the parent and to the outside world through the infant's ability to create an affective display. When the infant creates an affective display in order to express such evaluations, the infant is afforded "significant communicative power, particularly with a sensitive and responsive partner, enabling him to initiate, modify, and maintain the exchange" (Tronick 2007, p. 179). What this means, in other words, is that within positive interactions, an infant experiences an impingement on their world and this discomfort and change is expressed by the infant to another as a way of scaffolding or processing the experience. A "good enough" parent is be able to recognize what the infant is affectively communicating and by recognizing and responding to the infant's affective communication, is able to create a mutually regulated state. This is considered to be a positive, healthy interaction between the two, but within the relationship, this interaction has expected moments of imperfection that are marked by mismatched exchanges even when the infant has a "partner who is willing to modify her own behavior to match her reading of his communication" (Tronick 2007, p. 180). When there is a mismatch, the infant is forced to change his affective expressions as a way of self-regulating his emotional state and attempting to reconnect with the parent. The process of mismatched affect is not only common, but according to Tronick (2007), is also necessary in the development of the child's ability to self-soothe and eventually allows these self-regulatory skills to be translated into skills that can help the infant with coping. At this point, however, it should be noted that coping, as distinguished by Tronick (2007), is considered a response to exaggerated and extended stress that goes beyond the normal strain of mismatched states within the dyad. Coping enters the realm of negative interactions, while simply having mismatched affective expressions lies within the realm of expected positive interactions between the parent and child.

A dyadic consciousness results from this interaction between the parent and child which assumes each person is a self-organizing system that can form states of consciousness. These states of consciousness, also referred to as states of brain organization, can work with another individual's system to construct more coherent and complex states (Tronick 2007). Infants are reliant on others to regulate their physiological homeostatic state. This regulation process includes managing the infants' emotional states, behaviors, and the caregiver's regulatory contributions which include expressions and touches. As a result the infant's regulating experience is comprised of both internal and external pieces that all contribute to the intersubjective system that exists between parent and child (Tronick 2007). Within this system, the child is not simply mimicking the parent but is creating her own responses that communicate implicit meaning and emotion within the dyadic display as the infant experiences it. However, within the system, when the two individuals contribute to creating a dyadic state of organization, the state itself is greater and has more complexity and coherence than the states that are experienced solely by the parent or by the infant individually (i.e., the whole is greater than the sum of its parts). In order for this to happen, both individuals must take on pieces of the other's state of consciousness which expands the singular state of consciousness they experience on their own. During these "moments of meeting," change can occur within the relationship. For the infant, there is an opportunity to develop through the process of taking on pieces of the parent through the dyadic state. As a result he or she is able to develop individual skills within the relationship providing the interaction is healthy. During therapy, when mindfulness practice increases the ability of both individuals to have more awareness of their bodily sensations and cognitive and affective states, the ability to meet one another in states of consciousness is increased. This ability to form a new state of consciousness allows for greater affect regulation and attachment within the therapeutic relationship, as experienced in the parent–infant dyad.

However, the mutual regulation model developed by Tronick (2007) is not the only evidentiary support of interpersonal neurobiology for mindfulness practice. In addition to the developments that occur within the brain in response to an "other," the structure of the brain is organized in such a way that it allows for knowledge and memory to be transmitted in ways beyond the exchange of words. Developed within the infant and maintained throughout adulthood are two distinct types of memory and knowledge: explicit and implicit. The explicit, or declarative, knowledge and memory that exist within an individual can be described as the conscious, aware memories stemming from the left hemisphere of the brain that can be described and understood through language by the person. On the other hand, implicit, also called procedural, knowledge and memory are the memories and knowledge that are outside of conscious awareness and exist beyond the capacity for language so that it may inform feeling and experiences but cannot be formulated on the conscious level in the way that explicit knowledge and memories can. According to Schore (2011), the "early developing right brain generates the implicit self, the structural system of the human unconscious" (p. 75). This means that the implicit portion of memory and knowledge is experienced unconsciously and therefore contributes to the "motivational and emotional processes that are essential to adaptive functioning" (p. 77) as the right hemisphere of the brain develops. For Tronick (2007), implicit relational knowing "operates largely outside the realm of verbal consciousness and the dynamic consciousness" (p. 414) and is defined as "the procedural knowledge of how to do things with others… that encompasses normal and pathological knowings and integrates affect, fantasy, behavioral, and cognitive dimensions" (p. 413). This information and way of knowing is always evolving and updating during daily interactions with others and contributes to more advanced understandings of interactions and knowing.

The right hemisphere of the brain not only contributes to daily and momentary experiences, but actually plays a larger contributing role than the left hemisphere of the brain that generates explicit knowledge and memory, despite the dominance that this type of knowledge and memory has on conscious awareness. Rather than merely existing in implicit cognition, the right brain also controls implicit affect, implicit communication, and implicit self-regulation which ultimately contribute to a "relational unconscious" that has the ability to communicate with self and others on nonverbal, unconscious levels outside the awareness of the conscious mind (Schore 2011, p. 78). This unconscious experience permeates all relationships, including the therapeutic relationship. In referring back to the understanding of the client who may not have verbal memories of trauma, this relational unconscious participates in treatment that can expand beyond what is said, much in the same way that mindfulness is able to reach beyond the capacities of language and verbal narrative.

For Wallin (2007), the unconscious, implicit experience of the therapist is not only present, but is so potentially powerful that the ignoring of one's subjective experience as a therapist can be detrimental to the therapeutic relationship by unconsciously causing the therapist to influence the client's experiences and perceptions without even realizing. In addition, Tronick (2007) discusses "moments of meeting," where two individuals within a relationship are able to have a shared moment of mutually constructed regulation on an implicit level that is productive rather than destructive. In the parent–infant dyad, implicit procedural knowledge within relationships is something that is developed in a dyadic state and informs the way in which the infant will relate to and interact with others throughout the remainder of their life (Tronick 2007). The interchanges that take place between the infant and parent are not necessarily able to be verbalized and the infant may go through life reenacting these patterns of relating without ever having explicit knowledge of all the ways in which relationships are impacted. Given this idea, it is clear that implicit/procedural knowledge is not only necessary to the therapeutic relationship as it plays out in countertransference and transference interactions, but it carries more weight in the way that it impacts individuals' lives while existing beyond the individual's full awareness. The treatment of traumatic memories that cannot be fully expressed thus also becomes an area where the clinician can either help or hinder, based on the recognition of their own implicit knowledge and communication to the client. Due to this importance, understanding how mindfulness can facilitate the "meeting of minds" is crucial to clinical work.

Introducing Mindfulness into the Therapeutic Relationship

In thinking about mindfulness, the complexity of the dyadic therapeutic relationship becomes a fertile territory for offering self-regulating skills. Much like the infant–parent dyad, where the parent is scaffolding the infant in its affective experiences while also being impacted by the child, the therapist, and client that practice mindfulness together or separately are introducing their newfound skills into the relationship without ever having to explicitly state that they are utilizing such skills. With an implicit, dynamic exchange always taking place, the benefits of mindfulness techniques can be shared each time a clinician attempts to scaffold an emotional experience of a client while utilizing emotional regulation or attention regulation.

Further, patients that "habitually evoke responses from the therapist that seem to recreate the problematic past can also be expected to pull implicitly for responses that fulfill unmet developmental needs" (Wallin 2007, p. 182). In entering the enactment but beginning to make changes, it is as Wallin (2007) suggests that opportunities for new relationships reveal themselves and allow for a change within the client. So while a client enacts repeated relationships, she is also pulling for needed relationships and is thus opening the door for therapeutic change to occur within the session. Introducing mindful awareness and regulation thus allows the client to experience the enactment while also giving them the skills to manage their own emotions and feelings without creating a cycle of dysregulation and distress that is known and familiar to them. Moreover, enactments create stressful moments within the therapeutic context that offer the opportunity for the therapist to offer a corrective emotional experience that "can lead to the emergence of more complex psychic structure by increasing the connectivity of right brain limbic-autonomic circuits" (Schore 2011, p. 84). For the clinician, being mindfully aware not only offers a new skill, but also allows the clinician to be more fully present to the occurrence of enactments and to respond in the present moment in a regulated way, as mindfulness so strongly advocates for. This response not only creates a mutually regulated experience, but also allows for lasting changes within the brain that offer the client a chance at more successful future interactions outside of the therapy office. As the client continues to practice mindfulness and engage positively in the relationship with the clinician, the ability to form mutually regulated experiences with others will also increase, as an infant with a positive relationship with a parent will throughout the lifespan.

Conclusion

The field of neuroscience is still a relatively new field with many questions about the human brain left to be answered. Within the realm of mindfulness practices, such unanswered questions are abundant, but what has been discovered is that mindfulness techniques are correlated with positive changes in the brain that lead to emotional regulation, attention regulation, psychological flexibility, increased integration of the mind and body, and increased overall mental health. By understanding the complex changes that may occur for a client during mindfulness practices, clinicians can better tailor their clinical work to address the needs of each individual client. In this chapter, a focus has been placed on addressing the needs of clients experiencing trauma. However, the neurological changes that take place during mindfulness practice are shown to impact individuals regardless of presenting problems and diagnoses. For this reason, it is encouraged to focus beyond symptomology when thinking about mindfulness interventions and stay present in the body: what is happening in the brain and in the therapy room all contribute to a complex experience that can have long-term effects on both client and clinician. By adapting an interpersonal neurobiological understanding of mindfulness, clinicians can join clients in a collaborative creation of new modes of thinking and consequently experiencing.

References

Anderson, F. S., & Gold, J. (2003). Trauma, dissociation, and conflict: The space where neuroscience, cognitive science, and psychoanalysis overlap. *Psychoanalytic Psychology., 20*, 536–541.

Appel, J., & Kim-Appel, D. (2009). Mindfulness: Implications for substance abuse and addiction. *International Journal of Mental Health and Addiction, 7*(4), 506–512.

Bergen-Cico, D., Possemato, K., & Pigeon, W. (2014). Reductions in cortisol associated with primary care brief mindfulness program for veterans with PTSD. *Medical Care, 52*, 25–31.

Bernstein, A., Tanay, G., & Vujanovic, A. A. (2011). Concurrent relations between mindful attention and awareness and psychopathology among trauma-exposed adults: Preliminary evidence of transdiagnostic resilience. *Journal of Cognitive Psychotherapy, 25*(2), 99–113.

Bormann, J. E., Oman, D., Walter, K. H., & Johnson, B. D. (2014). Mindful attention increases and mediates psychological outcomes following mantram repetition practice in veterans with posttraumatic stress disorder. *Medical Care, 52*, 13–18.

Brewer, J., Sinha, R., Chen, J., Michalsen, R., Babuscio, T., Nich, C., et al. (2009). Mindfulness training and stress reactivity in substance abuse: Results from a randomized, controlled stage I pilot study. *Substance Abuse, 30*(4), 306–317.

Brewer, J. A., Bowen, S., Smith, J. T., Marlatt, G. A., & Potenza, M. N. (2010). Mindfulness-based treatments for co-occurring depression and substance use disorders: What can we learn from the brain? *Addiction, 105*(10), 1698–1706.

Cozolino, L. (2010). *The neuroscience of psychotherapy: Building and rebuilding the human brain* (2nd ed.). New York: Norton.

Davidson, R. J. (2003). Affective neuroscience and psychophysiology: Toward a synthesis. *Psychophysiology, 40*(5), 655–665.

Dick, A. M., Niles, B. L., Street, A. E., DiMartino, D. M., & Mitchell, K. S. (2014). Examining mechanisms of change in a yoga intervention for women: The influence of mindfulness, psychological flexibility, and emotion regulation on PTSD symptoms. *Journal of Clinical Psychology, 70*(12), 1170–1182.

Dickie, E. W., Brunet, A., Akerib, V., & Armony, J. L. (2011). Neural correlates of recovery from post-traumatic stress disorder: A longitudinal fMRI investigation of memory encoding. *Neuropsychologia, 49*(7), 1771–1778.

Doctor, R. M., & Shiromoto, F. N. (2010). *The encyclopedia of trauma and traumatic stress disorders*. New York, NY: Facts on File.

El Khoury-Malhame, M. M., Reynaud, E., Soriano, A., Michael, K., Salgado-Pineda, P., Zendjidjian, X., et al. (2011). Amygdala activity correlates with attentional bias in PTSD. *Neuropsychologia, 49*(7), 1969–1973.

Fetzner, M. G., Peluso, D. L., & Asmundson, G. J. G. (2014). Tolerating distress after trauma: Differential associations between distress tolerance and posttraumatic stress symptoms. *Journal of Psychopathology and Behavioral Assessment, 36*(3), 475–484.

Garland, E. L., & Roberts-Lewis, A. (2013). Differential roles of thought suppression and dispositional mindfulness in posttraumatic stress symptoms and craving. *Addictive Behaviors, 38*(2), 1555–1562.

Hinton, D. E., Ojserkis, R. A., Jalal, B., Peou, S., & Hofmann, S. G. (2013). Loving-kindness in the treatment of traumatized refugees and minority groups: A typology of mindfulness and the nodal network model of affect and affect regulation. *Journal of Clinical Psychology, 69*(8), 817–828.

Hölzel, B., Lazar, S., Gard, T., Schuman-Olivier, Z., Vago, D., & Ott, U. (2011). How does mindfulness meditation work? Proposing mechanisms of action from a conceptual and neural perspective. *Perspectives on Psychological Science, 6*(6), 537–559.

Kabat-Zinn, J. (1994). *Wherever you go, there you are: Mindfulness meditation in everyday life* (1st ed.). New York: Hyperion.

Kearney, D. J., McDermott, K., Malte, C., Martinez, M., & Simpson, T. L. (2012). Association of participation in a mindfulness program with measures of PTSD, depression and quality of life in a veteran sample. *Journal of Clinical Psychology, 68*(1), 101–116.

Kearney, D. J., McDermott, K., Malte, C., Martinez, M., & Simpson, T. L. (2013). Effects of participation in a mindfulness program for veterans with posttraumatic stress disorder: A randomized controlled pilot study. *Journal of Clinical Psychology, 69*(1), 14–27.

Kerr, C. E., Sacchet, M. D., Lazar, S. W., Moore, C. I., & Jones, S. R. (2013). Mindfulness starts with the body: Somatosensory attention and top-down modulation of cortical alpha rhythms in mindfulness meditation. *Frontiers in Human Neuroscience, 7,* 1–15.

Makinson, R. A., & Young, J. S. (2012). Cognitive behavioral therapy and the treatment of posttraumatic stress disorder: Where counseling and neuroscience meet. *Journal of Counseling & Development, 90*(2), 131–140.

Michal, M., Beutel, M. E., Jordan, J., Zimmermann, M., Wolters, S., & Heidenreich, T. (2007). Depersonalization, mindfulness, and childhood trauma. *The Journal of Nervous and Mental Disease, 195*(8), 693–696.

Moore, S. D., Brody, L. R., & Dierberger, A. E. (2009). Mindfulness and experiential avoidance as predictors and outcomes of the narrative emotional disclosure task. *Journal of Clinical Psychology, 65*(9), 971–988.

Nelson, C. A., & Carver, L. J. (1998). The effects of stress and trauma on brain and memory: A view from developmental cognitive neuroscience. *Development and Psychopathology, 10*(4), 793–809.

Northcut, T. B., & Kienow, A. (2014). The trauma trifecta of military sexual trauma: A case study illustrating the integration of mind and body in clinical work with survivors of MST. *Clinical Social Work Journal, 42*(3), 247–259.

Poon, A., & Danoff-Burg, S. (2011). Mindfulness as a moderator in expressive writing. *Journal of Clinical Psychology, 67*(9), 881–895.

Schore, A. N. (2011). The right brain implicit self lies at the core of psychoanalysis. *Psychoanalytic Dialogues, 21*(75–100), 2011.

Smith, B. W., Ortiz, J. A., Steffen, L. E., Tooley, E. M., Wiggins, K. T., Yeater, E. A., et al. (2011). Mindfulness is associated with fewer PTSD symptoms, depressive symptoms, physical symptoms, and alcohol problems in urban firefighters. *Journal of Consulting and Clinical Psychology, 79*(5), 613–617.

Suvak, M., & Barrett, L. (2011). Considering PTSD from the perspective of brain processes: A psychological construction approach. *Journal of Traumatic Stress, 24*(1), 3–24.

Tronick, E. (2007). *The neurobehavioral and social-emotional development of infants and children*. New York: W.W. Norton & Company.

van der Kolk, B. A. (1988). The trauma spectrum: The interaction of biological and social events in the genesis of the trauma response. *Journal of Traumatic Stress, 1*(3), 273–290.

van der Kolk, B. A. (2002). Posttraumatic therapy in the age of neuroscience. *Psychoanalytic Dialogues, 12,* 3.

van der Kolk, B. A. (2006). Clinical implications of neuroscience research in PTSD. *Annals of the New York Academy of Sciences, 1071,* 277–293.

van der Kolk, B., Greenberg, M., Boyd, H., & Krystal, J. (1985). Inescapable shock, neurotransmitters, and addiction to trauma: Toward a psychobiology of post traumatic stress. *Biological Psychiatry, 20*(3), 314–325.

van der Kolk, B. A., Roth, S., Pelcovitz, D., Sunday, S., Spinazzola, J., van, K. B. A., & Courtois, C. A. (2005). Disorders of extreme stress: The empirical foundation of a complex adaptation to trauma. *Journal of Traumatic Stress, 18*(5), 389–399.

Vujanovic, A., Niles, B., Pietrefesa, A., Schmertz, S., Potter, C., Roberts, M. C., et al. (2011). Mindfulness in the treatment of posttraumatic stress disorder among military veterans. *Professional Psychology: Research and Practice, 42*(1), 24–31.

Wallin, D. J. (2007). *Attachment in psychotherapy*. New York: Guildford Press.

Chapter 5
Beginning with the Social Worker: Yoga Nidra Meditation as a Means for Self-inquiry, Growth, Effectiveness and Resiliency

Corinne Peterson, Amy Zajakowski Uhll and Susan Grossman

> *As you welcome your wholeness, you become a light for those who follow in your footsteps. We are all brothers and sisters on our healing journey together.*
>
> —*Richard Miller*

Introduction

Social workers are unique in that they work in a myriad of settings, in a variety of roles. Throughout a career, the individual social worker may work as a caseworker, therapist, administrator, teacher, researcher, advocate, activist—even wearing many hats at the same time. She might be employed by a large, bureaucratic organization, or self-employed. The work is often very difficult, with long hours, and challenging (even dangerous) situations. Sometimes the rewards are readily apparent, and sometimes so subtle they are barely perceivable. No matter what hat she wears, the social worker has chosen to dedicate her life to service on a broad scale, working at the micro and macro levels to alleviate problems for those suffering from sociological, psychological, and economic difficulties. This fundamental dedication serves as a foundation throughout her career.

Yet the path is not an easy one and often not as straightforward and romantic (or idealistic) as it seemed at its inception. Burnout and secondary trauma are also part of the likely path of the social worker, at some point in her career. In addition, each social worker comes with her own past history and life experiences. There is always

C. Peterson (✉)
iRest® Yoga Nidra Meditation, Therapeutic Yoga and Massage, Chicago, IL, USA
e-mail: corinne.peterson@gmail.com

A.Z. Uhll
Chicago Center for Integration and Healing, Chicago, IL, USA
e-mail: jazajuhll@yahoo.com

S. Grossman
Loyola University Chicago, School of Social Work, Chicago, IL, USA
e-mail: sgrossm@luc.edu

T.B. Northcut (ed.), *Cultivating Mindfulness in Clinical Social Work*,
Essential Clinical Social Work Series, DOI 10.1007/978-3-319-43842-9_5

personal healing to be attended to, and that inner work has reverberation into the work in the world. As the renowned Buddhist nun Pema Chodron states, "*We work on ourselves in order to help others, but also we help others in order to work on ourselves*" (Chodron 2008, p. 78).

As evidenced by this book, there is more and more information coming out about mindfulness and its effectiveness with various populations. Social workers, and many of those involved in caregiving professions are often looking for techniques that can help clients and communities. What is often overlooked is the profound benefit of these same practices for the caregiver. As practitioners, we (the authors) have been exploring the impact of iRest® Yoga Nidra Meditation in our various roles. Our understanding of the profound implications of this practice continues to deepen as we bring it into therapy, supervision, mentoring, teaching, advocacy, and administration. It is through our collective experience that it has become abundantly clear that these practices are not just for the populations we serve but essential for us as well. In this chapter, we focus on the ways in which these practices enable us to be more responsive practitioners, whether working directly with individuals in the therapeutic context, or teaching future social workers. We also discuss the ways in which they enrich our lives and by connection, the lives of those with whom we work.

In the following sections, there are three voices with different yet overlapping narratives. We begin with a description of the iRest protocol to provide a foundation for understanding the practice. This first voice is a yoga instructor with a social service background who specializes in working with trauma. The second voice is that of a psychotherapist, who is also an administrator and mentor. A social work college administrator is the third voice. She is also a seasoned researcher, professor, and advocate. Through our three voices we speak to the impact of iRest in our personal and professional lives.

What Is iRest Yoga Nidra Meditation?

by Corinne Peterson, M.P.H.

Like many yoga teachers, I began practicing yoga and meditation because of physical pain, and internal emotional suffering. From this personal suffering came a deep desire to help others relieve their suffering as well. Prior to becoming a yoga instructor, I worked and volunteered in several social service settings in Chicago's Latino communities. For over 15 years I was both a direct service provider and an administrator in settings including foster care, domestic violence, and homeless shelters. As I developed as a yoga teacher, I was able to bring the teachings into the workplace with clients and staff. For the past 18 years I have had a private practice. At this time, I primarily work with people with trauma histories, and the therapists who serve them.

Throughout the years my journey to help others has gone hand-in-hand with my own personal growth. I have seen my own path reflected in the many social workers I have known throughout the years. Both yoga and social work seek to end suffering, and that desire is usually both personal and professional. Over this time I have also explored many mindfulness approaches, and finally came to appreciate iRest as an extremely effective practice. I have seen many clients and practitioners benefit profoundly from this approach to meditation.

Yoga Nidra is an ancient meditative practice that has recently been gaining popularity in a variety of forms. Similar to the practice of yoga postures, various systems have been developed over the years. One such system, the practice of iRest, evolved from the studies and teachings of Richard Miller, Ph.D. Miller is a clinical psychologist who has been integrating yoga and other wisdom teachings with western psychology for over 45 years. He has gained particular recognition for using yoga nidra to help military veterans with posttraumatic stress disorder (PTSD). During initial research at Walter Reed Army Medical Center, he was asked to come up with a different name for his approach to yoga nidra, concerned that the words "yoga nidra" might be rejected by the very veterans they were hoping to serve. Careful consideration evolved the name "Integrative Restoration" or "iRest" for short (Miller 2015, p. 2). Miller's organization, the Integrative Restoration Institute, continues to expand to serve the broader population, including hospitals, clinics, hospice, homeless shelters, sex trafficking, community programs, and schools.

The words "yoga" and "nidra" come from the Indian Sanskrit language and have many translations. The following definition offers a glimpse into the practice of yoga nidra:

> Yoga: the view, path, and means by which you experience your interconnection with yourself and all of life.
>
> Nidra: changing states of consciousness, such as waking, sleeping, and dreaming, which include sensations, emotions, thoughts, and images (Miller 2015, p. 18).

As previously mentioned, iRest takes as its premise that we are already whole and complete. Through this wholeness, we are able to directly experience our interconnectedness with life. Within this deep interconnected wholeness, we also attend to the present moment as experienced in the body. The practice is rooted in direct somatic experience. This includes various emotions and beliefs as they arise. iRest teaches us to welcome our experiences, even the most challenging.

The iRest Framework

> The body is always present, the mind is a time traveler. When you can bring your attention to the sensation here, in the body – you are the very presence you seek.
>
> —Amy Weintraub (personal communication, April 21, 2015)

As with most yoga nidra practices, iRest is based on the Panchamaya model (aka Panchamaya Koshas). This is an ancient model that can help us understand our human experiences. This model traditionally describes five layers of our physical experience. These "layers" are often called "dimensions" or "sheaths." As humans, we experience these layers somatically, as felt-sense in the body. The first layer is the physical *Body*. It is physical and tangible. We can feel the solidity of our muscles and bones. The second layer is the *Breath*. It is subtler, yet we can feel how it moves in and out; how our body expands with each inhalation and releases with each exhalation. The third layer includes *Feelings and Emotions*. We can feel sensations like temperature or tension. Emotions like anger or fear or happiness can also be felt as sensation in the body. The fourth layer is that of *Thoughts and Beliefs*. Through quiet listening, we realize that they are also felt somatically, though we often think they are only in the mind. The fifth layer is that of *Joy*. This joy has a subtler felt-sense, and may be experienced through gratitude, kindness, or compassion. In iRest an additional layer is added that invites specific inquiry into the separate sense of "I." This is felt as the perception that we are separate from the world around us, rather that part of the wholeness of life. The practice of iRest helps us cultivate the ability to feel these layers as physical sensations. This ability improves over time through consistent practice.

Inherent in this Panchamaya model, and yoga philosophy in general, there is an understanding that the tangible world of form is always changing, coming, and going. The layers previously described are constantly changing and moving through us. Our bodies, breath, feelings, emotions, beliefs, and joy are impermanent. For example, our bodies will age, and our emotions can change from one day to the next (or even one minute to the next). Within this ancient perspective, there is also an underlying sense of a deeper permanence, an Awareness that is unchanging. Sometimes this is felt as "Presence" or "Being" or "Witnessing Awareness" or "Wholeness." However translated, it speaks to a deeper experience beyond words that is often hard to describe but can be felt. This Awareness is often likened to the clear blue sky and the layers are weather patterns moving through. Sometimes there is sunshine, other times storms swoop in. Sometimes we just have a cloudy day. But the sky is the continuous backdrop through which the weather moves.

In iRest, mindful attention is brought to each layer, these metaphorical weather patterns, with a sense of welcoming and curiosity. Through this attention, the layers gradually quiet, the mind calms and this unchanging Awareness is felt and witnessed within the practitioner. The sense of welcoming and curiosity is fundamental to the iRest practice, as we demonstrate in the narratives to follow. Through following the protocol as it unfolds, we intentionally cultivate openness instead of trying to ignore or push away uncomfortable sensations. Physical discomforts, uncomfortable emotions, or challenging beliefs are considered messengers or allies that may bring insight or information. Ultimately, we are developing the ability to deeply listen and befriend ourselves. It is through this ability to "be with" ourselves, rather than deny ourselves, that we can recognize our deeper wholeness that is peaceful and calm amidst even the most challenging circumstances.

The Panchamaya model provides the basic outline for the 10-step iRest protocol. This protocol is often delivered as a guided practice in group settings, and can be done through the use of recorded practices. The protocol also provides a framework for dyads (one-to-one meditation) and shorter micropractices that can be used throughout the day.

The 10-Step Protocol as a Guided Practice

Setting the Stage—Unlike other forms of mindful meditation which are often done seated, iRest can be practiced in any position. Most commonly it is practiced lying down, with support under the head and knees. The practitioner[1] is asked to get as comfortable as possible to feel completely supported. When coming to the practice from a place of comfort, the body can more deeply rest, and attention can be directed inward toward each aspect of the protocol.

Moving through the Protocol—The iRest protocol consists of 10 stages. First, we set the stage for the practice with Heartfelt Desire, Intention, and Inner Resource. Then we bring attention to each layer: Body, Breath, Feelings/Emotions, Beliefs/Thoughts, and Joy. After attending to each dimension, there is a "stepping back" or a defocusing into Awareness. At the end of the practice, while resting in a sense of Wholeness, participants are asked to recall their Heartfelt Desire and Intention, as they move back into their daily life.

Here are salient aspects of each stage of the protocol:

1. **Heartfelt Desire**—We begin the practice by identifying what we most want in life, a deeper longing that is connected to that which is most important to us. Some may word this as a "heartfelt mission," "heartfelt path" or even a prayer. It helps clarify our deeper motivations and connects us to the flow of Life. The Heartfelt Desire is the simple felt-sense of the life force that is animating every cell in our body. By simply feeling this life force, we experience a deep felt-sense of value, meaning and purpose, just as we are—that is prior to anything we do in the world. Just our basic beingness has value, meaning and purpose (Miller, personal communication, July 2015). Connecting with one's reason for practicing brings deep personal meaning to the practice and support in daily life. It is expressed in present tense, and we experience it as if it were already true in this moment. Examples might include:

[1]Please note that I use the word "practitioner" as a personal preference. In yoga the term "student" is often used, but this indicates that there is a learning involved, rather than an internal experiencing that is being facilitated. A psychotherapist who uses iRest in their practice would likely say "client", and a doctor would use "patient".

- *I am whole, healed, and healthy.*
- *My thoughts, words, and actions agree and align with one another.*
- *I am deeply connected to myself, to others, and to life.*
- *I am at peace with myself and the world.*
- *I accept and appreciate myself.*
- *I am a compassionate, loving, and kind person.*

2. **Intention**—We then come to a short-term intention for the specific practice. Intentions are the vows that support our realizing of Heartfelt Desire. They can help define and support behavior change, including shifting attitudes. They are also expressed in present tense, and experienced as if it were true in this moment. Examples might include:

   - *I exercise and eat healthy foods to strengthen and nourish my body and mind.*
   - *I show up on time, respecting my relationships with others.*
   - *I pay attention and notice when I am getting reactive. I take time to mindfully respond.*

3. **Inner Resource**—Our Inner Resource is that within us which is already healthy and whole. It has never been harmed or damaged. It is already a place of contentment, peace, security, safety, strength, ground, ease, and well-being. Inner Resource is ultimately the feeling of being, and of the life force that is living us. Sometimes it is referred to as "inner sanctuary,", "inner refuge," or "safe place." Each practitioner finds their own pathway to eliciting the felt-sense of their own inner resource. These may include:

   - *A place in nature (real or imagined).*
   - *A special room which is comfortable, filled with favorite things.*
   - *Being in the company of a special person, wisdom figure or spiritual guide.*
   - *A word or phrase (calm, peaceful, ease, safety...).*

   Images can be useful to help orient the practitioner to this felt-sense of ease in the body. However, Inner Resource is not the image itself, but is the felt-sense of the image that links us with that felt-sense of connection to that which is unchanging. Everyone can feel this. Some come to it innately, others find that a skilled instructor can help identify a connection that is personally resonant.

   The ultimate Inner Resource is the innate, simple feeling of being that has always been with us. It is always pure, spacious, beyond time, beyond need or lack, complete and always whole. It is the ground of security, ease and well-being that can never be harmed, does not need healing and is always whole. It just needs to be remembered. By connecting with our Inner Resource at the beginning of the practice, we have a safe place to return to whenever we would like to reconnect with our inner safety. This can be particularly useful during the practice (or in everyday life) when we experience sensations that are overwhelming.

4. **Bodysensing**—The body is the first layer we attend to, noticing sensations in different parts of the body. By feeling into the body we begin to befriend it and listen to the messages it sends us. Through consistent practice, we increase our capacity to feel various sensations in the body. By learning to feel these more tangible sensations (arm, toes, etc.), it helps to foster the skill of feeling sensations as they arise in more subtle form (anger, excitement).
5. **Breathsensing**—The breath layer is more subtle than the body, yet it can still be felt. We can sense the expansion and release of the inhalation and exhalation as it moves in and out of the body and continue to increase our capacity to experience sensation. As several authors point out (Miller 2015; Van der Kolk 2014), by breathing mindfully, we are helping the regulation of the central nervous system. Over time the system becomes more responsive, the sympathetic nervous system (fight/flight/freeze) begins to calm and parasympathetic nervous system (rest/renew/heal) becomes more prominent. With regular practice they come more into right relationship with each other. The balance between the sympathetic nervous system and the parasympathetic nervous system is measured by heart rate variability (HRV), an indicator of overall well-being and resilience to stress (Miller 2015, pp. 81–82; Van der Kolk 2014, pp. 266–267).
6. **Feelings and Emotions**—In this layer, the word "Feelings" refers to particular sensations in the body, such as warmth, coolness, heaviness, lightness, comfort, and discomfort. The internal experiences of "Emotions" can include angry, sad, excited, bored, guilt, satisfaction, shy, etc. The variety and richness of human emotion is endless, yet few of us are fully aware of the rainbow of our internal emotional landscape. Richard Miller likens *Emotions* to a pot that holds ingredients, and *Feelings* as ingredients in the pot (Miller 2015, pp. 94–95). As with all layers, Feelings and Emotions are welcomed as messengers, with the understanding that anything that is refused becomes more ingrained, and processing is delayed. It is common to want to push down or ignore emotions that are uncomfortable. For example, anger is an unacceptable emotion for many people, but with iRest we have the opportunity to engage it in meditative inquiry. We can ask ourselves, "What does it feel like in the body?" Then we can explore, "What is it doing here? Does it have a message for me? Is there an action this anger is asking me to take?" Instead of pushing away challenging emotions, we can experience them as bringing helpful information.

   iRest also offers other ways of inquiring into feelings and emotions. Sometimes we explore the opposite of a feeling or emotion. We can feel the present sensations (e.g., anger or tension), and then we can explore what its opposite might feel like (e.g., calm or relaxed). We go back and forth, experiencing the felt-sense of each. Then we experience them both at the same time, which often dissipates the challenging emotion and reveals the restful experience of wholeness. This process can also help to build our resiliency when challenging emotions arise. Through the practice we become familiar with tolerating uncomfortable sensations and can navigate them more easily when they arise in everyday life.

7. **Beliefs and Thoughts**—As humans, we all carry thoughts and beliefs that guide our movement and interactions in the world. Sometimes we are cognizant of those beliefs, sometimes they are subconscious, and sometimes we carry conflicting beliefs. Beliefs and thoughts are all temporary, some are short lived, and others more engrained with a longer life cycle. Quite often we take our beliefs to be completely true and don't question them. We might not even be aware of some of our guiding beliefs. Or we might try to talk ourselves out of a belief, thinking, "I really shouldn't think that way because ________." In either case, these unprocessed beliefs can become even more engrained. Many common beliefs are a variant of "Something is wrong with me." This might be as concrete as "If I were thinner, I would be happier." During iRest meditation we have a chance to explore beliefs and welcome them in as messengers bringing us information and guidance. We can notice what a belief feels like in the body. We can engage with it, feeling what an opposite belief might feel like. For example, "I am perfect just as I am," or "I appreciate my body for all that it does for me." Exploring opposite beliefs helps us to understand our deeper motivations, and we begin to understand that we are not our beliefs, but that they are also something that changes over time, like clouds moving through the sky. We come to a deeper knowing that all experience is part of our wholeness.
8. **Joy**—This is the subtlest layer, referring to a felt-sense of Joy that is already part of our experience. This is a joy that is deeper and more permanent. It is different than the temporary joy we derive from pleasurable experiences, like eating something tasty, enjoying a good movie, or the addict's temporary relief giving into the object of their addiction. The more permanent joy may also be experienced as an inner smile, gratitude, kindness, and compassion. It is already in us, and as the more accessible sensations quiet down (body, breath, emotions, etc.), we are able to directly experience this truth. There is a saying in neuroscience that, "neurons that fire together wire together" (Hanson 2013, p. 10). By lingering in our felt-sense of joy, we are actually rewiring our brains.
9. **Witnessing Awareness**—After sensing into each layer of being, we "step back" into simply witnessing our experience. This witnessing opens up into a broader perspective of Awareness that is often experienced as open, spacious, expansive, grounded, stable and/or a deep equanimity. Awareness is like the unchanging, clear blue sky in which the other layers are temporary, moving through like clouds (or sometimes thunderstorms). Here we take a broader view and are not caught up in experience. Our True Nature emerges as an inner knowing felt deeply in our being.
10. **Integration/Experiencing Wholeness**—This is the integrative stage of the iRest protocol. Here we rest in the experience of our own wholeness and interconnectedness with Life. We often feel a deep sense that everything is ok, just as it is. There is nothing we need to do. Changing sensations may come and go, yet there is a feeling of deep trust. We completely rest in Wholeness.

Completing the Practice—At the end of this formal practice, we make a slow transition back into our daily lives. First, we allow our Heartfelt Desire and Intention to return. We notice any accompanying insight that we may want to make note of. Then we slowly begin to sense our surroundings, the body and breath, and begin to slowly stretch and move. As we transition back into the day we can feel the practice linger with us like a perfume that permeates our lives.

"Off the Mat": iRest Dyads and Micropractices

As with the guided practice, both micro-practices and dyads help cultivate the ability to be with all that arises in the present moment with a sense of welcoming and curiosity, even the most difficult and the most joyous of life's experiences.

Micropractices—Another way of exploring iRest is with mini-practices throughout the day. The 10-step protocol can be considered as ten separate practices combined sequentially. Each can be practiced at a moment's notice at any time throughout the day. Through neuroscience advances, we know that these short mindfulness practices can have a huge impact on the structure of our ever-changing brains (Hanson 2009, p. 17). For example, when confronted with a difficult situation, we can sense into our Inner Resource, or when making a decision we can feel whether it feels in alignment with our Heartfelt Desire. When fusing with an uncomfortable emotion we can explore its opposite. Or we might simply be walking outside on a beautiful day and feel our connection with all of life.

Dyads—iRest can also be experienced one-to-one with a teacher. In this process, the individual and the teacher are both present in meditative awareness. As in a guided practice, the individual welcomes whatever is arising as sensation in the body with a sense of curiosity. But instead of moving through the sequential protocol, the body becomes the guide. Feelings, emotions, beliefs, and thoughts arise in their own time and the teacher helps the individual stay present to the experience. Dyadic regulation and the activation of mirror neurons can explain how this process occurs, as the teacher's calm presence serves as a model in the midst of disturbing sensations (Graham 2013, pp. 24, 199).

Now that we have briefly described the philosophy and practice of iRest, the remainder of this chapter looks at how the practice of iRest can be instrumental for social workers in both micro- and macro-level work. This next section focuses on work with clients in a therapeutic setting and details how the practice facilitates a deeper therapeutic bond while supporting both therapist and client. Following this discussion, we focus on the experience of a practitioner and application of iRest to social work practice in macro settings.

iRest Yoga Nidra as a Tool for Therapists

by Amy Zajakowski Uhll, L.C.P.C.

As therapists, we, ourselves, are the tools of our craft. Our personal history and present experience enter the therapy room with us and influence the clinical relationship. I became interested in becoming a psychotherapist when I served as a full-time volunteer in a domestic violence shelter 25 years ago. I have specialized in working with individuals with a history of trauma throughout my career including working in community mental health and with refugees seeking political asylum. I initially trained in psychodynamic theory, but through my work in trauma and growing awareness of neurobiology, I became interested in integrating my psychodynamic, relational work with a body-centered focus. Ten years ago I also engaged in advanced training in Sensorimotor Psychotherapy. For the last 4 years I have been the Director of a group practice that specializes in trauma, and specifically in the integration of relational and body-centered thought in psychotherapy. My role includes providing administrative leadership, supervision, and direct practice with clients.

Research has demonstrated that, regardless of clinical theory or technique, the therapeutic relationship is an extremely powerful factor in positive therapeutic outcome (Norcross, Beutler and Levant 2005 in Siegel 2010). A critical component of that relationship is the empathic communication that occurs between client and clinician. Neuroscience and attachment research have demonstrated that much of that very important communication occurs in the nonverbal realm (Ogden and Minton 2006; Schore 1994; Siegel 2001). Our very sense of self, a sense of integration and basic safety, is developed in our early preverbal experiences with a primary caretaker (Wallin 2007). At each moment in the process of therapy we are engaging with our clients at many different levels both verbally and nonverbally. When we devote our attention exclusively to our cognitive processes we are limiting our scope to a narrow range. "We risk allowing the words we exchange in therapy to monopolize our attention when we don't remind ourselves that beneath the words there is a flow of crucially important experience" (Wallin 2007, p. 115). These experiences cannot be accessed in therapy through our traditional "talk therapy" methods. They must be accessed through the nonverbal realms that include tone, posture, sensation, movement and the dance of nonverbal information.

We, as practitioners, are taught that we must be careful that our own issues don't contaminate the treatment in some way or harm our clients. We may feel that in order to address this concern we must keep ourselves completely out of the room—become a blank slate. However, in order to work in the present moment and connect to the experience of the client, the therapist must be aware of his or her own experience. A mindfulness practice is necessary so that we can cultivate an awareness of ourselves in the present moment, and move more fluidly within the multilayers of conversation that occur in thought, feeling, and sensation.

Our clients often come to us with stories of horrible events and difficult circumstances that cause them pain. However, their ongoing suffering is often caused by avoidance of their own internal experience. Anxiety, shame and depression can be the result of avoiding deep feelings such as grief, loss, anger, and longing. Many clients fear this inner experience because it feels chaotic and overwhelming. This is particularly true for those who have a history of trauma. Many of the behaviors we would describe as self-destructive—drug usage, compulsive behaviors, suicidal ideation, or self-harm can be viewed as attempts to manage this overwhelming experience. "Traumatized people are often afraid of feeling. It is not so much the perpetrators (who, hopefully, are no longer around to hurt them) but their own physical sensations that are now the enemy" (Van der Kolk 2014, p. 208). Individuals often enter a practice of meditation or mindfulness hoping for some kind of relaxation or ease. However, as individuals begin a mindfulness practice they often touch into experiences that are terrifying and painful. We, as therapists, know the deep value of sitting in the present moment at these times. Neuroscience has taught us that through the social engagement system our calibrated and attuned response to this terror can help soothe the client's central nervous system (Ogden and Minton 2006, p. 170).

We have discussed the importance of a mindfulness practice for the practitioner. iRest is a mindfulness practice that can be particularly helpful for social work practice. iRest is anchored both in ancient practice and current psychology. As noted throughout this chapter, it holds the belief that we have an Inner Resource, something that has remained whole, integrated and undamaged by any of the things that have happened in our lives. As therapists, we are often challenged to sit with incredible pain. Our capacity to remain present and aware of both our own Inner Resource and that of our clients in the face of this pain is itself healing. Our practice of iRest helps us to embody it ourselves. Supported by our own experience of wholeness we can sit with another's pain confident in the capacity of all individuals to heal.

iRest's teaching on Heartfelt Desire can also be transformative in the clinical relationship. Often when individuals come into therapy they are acutely attuned to their suffering and not able to wish or hope for anything. At the same time, they may have longings and desires of which they are unaware or these longing and desires may be difficult for them to access. As practitioners, we may also often become oriented toward their suffering, yet instead of working toward simply a decrease of symptoms we can practice orienting toward a fuller, richer, more peaceful life for both our clients and ourselves. Practicing with an embodied, full sense of our own Heartfelt Desire develops our capacity to orient toward the Heartfelt Desire in our clients.

Recent research in the trauma world has demonstrated that it is essential to work in the present moment in order to help our clients settle their highly dysregulated central nervous systems and live a more peaceful day-to-day life (Ogden and Minton 2006; Siegal 2001). As therapists we often collude with our clients in avoidance of their pain because it is difficult for us to sit with and can touch our own wounded places. However, touching the cast-off experience in a regulated way is often what's needed for healing. The practice of iRest can assist the therapist in developing the capacity to regulate his or her own self in the face of a client's deep pain. Because it is a body-centered mindfulness practice, it accesses the resources of the body to anchor in the present moment. Through the iRest work with emotions and beliefs, the therapist can then strengthen the capacity to touch the painful places and return to safety. This is regulating for both client and therapist. It can help protect the therapist from vicarious trauma. The practice of iRest strengthens our capacity to connect to difficult stories by allowing them to enter our experience and then move through us. We experience vicarious trauma and burnout when the painful things we sit with daily enter our experience and become stuck. A mindfulness practice helps to increase the capacity to tolerate both pain and joy.

Recently I had a session with a woman that I had seen in therapy for 5 years. Ellen was planning to move out of state with her partner because of a job change. She experienced the belief that her mother hadn't wanted her and we had often worked with her deeply felt-sense that she did not deserve to feel, to think or to exist. Her therapy was often difficult, intense and moving. About six weeks before she was leaving, I asked her in session how she was feeling about ending our therapy. She began reporting that she was feeling nervous about leaving but had gained some really good skills. She described these skills and the achievements she felt she had made. She planned to seek out a therapist in her new city but wasn't sure if she would do it right away. While she was talking I felt vaguely distracted and I observed a clenching sensation in the pit of my stomach. I know from my own practice of mindfulness that my body sensations can give me important information about my emotions. I realized that I was bracing in my core. On some level the material that my client was presenting was hopeful and optimistic. I became curious about my own present experience and practiced relaxing my stomach muscles, deepening my breath, and began to become aware of my own sense of sadness and loss at the coming separation in our relationship. I focused my attention for a moment on releasing my muscles and letting myself feel the sadness. As I did that her reporting also started to shift. She began to identify that she was going to miss me—not only her therapy but also me as a person. She explored how proud she was of the work that we together had done and she identified her sense of connection in the room. She described that when our work began she experienced me as "just a therapist" and now she felt that I was an actual person and in our relationship she knew that she existed. We both became tearful as we shared both our sadness at the parting and our joy over the changes she was able to make in her life. In this circumstance I hadn't reported my own inner experience. However, as I brought it into mindful awareness something shifted in her experience as well which enabled us both more flexibility to experience a wider ranges of experience.

In another example, Sarah has a history of sexual abuse by her father and has worked long and hard both in therapy and in her own iRest practice to help stabilize her posttraumatic symptoms. She has a long history of job difficulty, drug abuse and engaging in destructive, often violent, relationships. She had worked hard in her therapy to achieve a sense of stability in her daily life. She had gone to graduate school and had a job in social services in which she was very successful. One day in therapy she was describing a conflict that she was having with her male supervisor. She was discussing her feelings that her job requirements were too demanding and decided that she was going to ask for some changes in her job description. This all sounded very reasonable. However, as she was talking I began to notice that I was feeling a sense of urgency and noticed a desire to help her "solve" her work issue by giving her advice. I paused a moment to mindfully observe my own internal experience and noticed a sense of agitation in my brow and my arms. I also noticed a sense that I wanted to move toward her and convince her to advocate for herself with her boss, to protect herself. I took a moment to acknowledge this sense of activation and grounded myself by observing my feet in contact with the floor. I commented to her that I had noticed that I was feeling agitated and wondered if we should pause in our efforts to solve her work problem. In that moment she became aware of a growing sense of fear. She recognized that she felt if she asked for a change in her job responsibilities she would be saying "no" to her boss and the very thought of telling him "no" was activating a sense of terror within her. She immediately commented, "I don't think this is about my supervisor—this is about my dad." Because of her own iRest practice we were able to sit together with both the sensation of terror and her feelings of fear until they eased in the present moment. Without my own practice of mindfulness in the session I would have worked with her to develop a course of action and she would have gone off to talk to her boss unaware of her sense of terror. My effort to "fix" her problem was an attempt to avoid my own fear. It may have communicated to her that I was also afraid of the intensity of her terror and that it wasn't safe to experience it with me in the session. Simply bringing the experience into mindfulness together helped us both to widen our capacity to experience her fear together and to recognize the difference between the present and the past.

It is clear that the practice of iRest can be an invaluable tool for those working with clients in a therapeutic setting. In this next section, we hear how the practice can be helpful for social workers practicing in macro settings through the author's role as a Social Work administrator and teacher.

iRest in Other Social Work Contexts

by Susan Grossman, M.A., Ph.D.

Meditation isn't what you do, it's who you are.

—*Richard Miller*

My path as a social worker has been long and varied. My first job, as a recent college graduate, entailed working with youth in a wealthy community on the North Shore of Chicago. I soon discovered that direct practice with individuals was not my true calling however, and returned to get my Master's degree in social work with an emphasis on community development and social welfare policy. A child of the late 60s and early 70s, my intention was to change the world and right all social injustices. Over the years, that intention has remained, but I have learned that all change—personal and/or social—takes time and is not a solitary effort. As I reflect below, iRest has helped me in accepting this reality. I worked for several years with policy makers, researchers and service providers on issues related to homelessness and domestic violence. I loved those aspects of my work involving evaluation and program development and saw that data derived from these activities could facilitate advocacy for change. Subsequently, I returned to school to obtain my doctorate, going on to engage in research and teaching at a social work program in Chicago. In my research and writing, I have focused on issues related to poverty, violence and social inequality, particularly as they affect women, and teach classes on social welfare policy and research methods. I also transitioned into an administrative position more recently because of a desire for change and new challenges. Ironically, this work has brought me back full circle to direct practice in a way I never expected as I am called upon to address difficulties and concerns among students, staff, and faculty.

I came to iRest having established a meditation practice built on Jonathon Kabat-Zinn's work on Mindfulness Based Stress Reduction (Kabat-Zinn 1994, 2013) and Vipassana or Insight meditation (Rosenberg 1998; Salzberg and Goldstein 2002). I began practicing to relieve stress and increase calm in what felt like a very busy and hectic life at the time. As my practice deepened, however, I came to see that meditation was not about the absence of thoughts or feelings. If anything, meditation practice helped to clarify exactly what I was thinking and feeling and sometimes I did not welcome this awareness.

Like other meditative practices, iRest allows me to hold a space so that I can observe my thoughts and feelings. Yet connecting with my inner life seems easier for me because so much of the practice is grounded in the body and in a felt-sense of things in congruence with observation. Much of my work day involves the use of my intellect to understand and approach things, so operating from my feelings and senses is challenging; I cannot neatly explain all that is happening in a conceptual way, disrupting my usual orientation. Changing my usual perspective is also quite delightful as through the practice, I continue to learn that everything I think is not necessarily correct or "true" and that my felt-sense of things—what is happening in my body and in my feelings—can be a sign post to truth as well. Indeed, learning to trust this felt-sense and the feelings that arise, even when they are the difficult feelings of sadness, loneliness and anger, has led to a shift in how I teach, work with students and think about effecting change in the world.

As an administrator, the ongoing demands from students, faculty, and other administrators for attention and time frequently pull me away from the present. I am sometimes left feeling disjointed and disconnected from others and myself. Here is where my ability to apply what I have "learned on the mat" to the real world is put to the test. A student may end up in my office because he or she has clearly not "followed the rules." He or she may have taken courses out of sequence or failed to meet the graduation application deadline. While it is not usually possible to go through a full practice at such times, frequently I use these situations as opportunities for engaging in the micro-practices mentioned at the start of this chapter. For example, I use Bodysensing to feel what is happening in my body, and tune into my feelings and emotions, as well as beliefs and thoughts. Sometimes I am aware of anger and the heat rising to my face or I sense the tension in my body. At other times I am aware of my belief that I need to "fix" the situation for the student and sense tightness in my chest or queasiness in my stomach, sensations I associate with anxiety. Pausing to acknowledge these beliefs and feelings, I consider my Heartfelt Desire, which may reflect a desire for others ("All beings are happy and safe") or something I desire for myself ("I am a compassionate and kind person"). I may also connect with my Intention (which in this instance, is often to be fair in my response). These micro practices help me to avoid acting out my own issues and allow me to have a more mindful connection with the student even when the outcome may be one the student does not like.

I have become increasingly aware as I have practiced longer, of a growing ability to wait and sit with the unfolding of an interaction whether it is between me and a student who is worried about his or her ability to remain in school, or me and a faculty member who is angry about a teaching assignment. Pausing to feel the sensation in my body grounds me in the present place and time. From this place, I then move on to consider the different feelings that are also arising at the moment in that encounter and use that information to guide my responses. Remaining mindful of my intention is key in shaping my response to each interaction as well. I also try to tune into any sensation of something not feeling "right" or "easy" as a way to help me recalibrate my reaction. Perhaps most difficult to sit with are the feelings that arise when a student or faculty member becomes angry or tearful in an encounter. As my co-authors have noted, here is where my practice of iRest is particularly helpful. I have seen how sitting with these difficult feelings, inviting them in so to speak, paradoxically lessens their power to control my response and allows me to react with more awareness and less often on "autopilot."

I believe that my ability to sit with what is occurring has also been strengthened by my ongoing understanding and experience of the belief, inherent to the practice of iRest, that individuals are already whole and healthy and that our natural movement is toward health and healing. I resonate with this philosophy as well because I see it as complimentary to the strengths based perspective of social work. From this viewpoint, our role as therapists, teachers, change agents, and administrators is really one of facilitator to the extent that we support the movement toward wholeness. Yet this understanding of the individual as whole and healed at each moment all too often results in concern that such acceptance will lead to stagnation. Indeed in our iRest class, many of us, who have been involved in social change efforts for much of our lives, have grappled with the question of exactly what acceptance means. We have worried that acceptance means that we will no longer be motivated to change either the world or ourselves; that acceptance means passivity.

Over time, I have come to see that this is not what is meant by acceptance within the iRest framework. Rather, to the extent that the practice of iRest engenders a deeper embodiment and mindfulness of what is at any point in time, it has allowed me to both accept the truth of a situation and consider change at the same time. I understand in a deep sense what is "really" happening, and I also have clarity about what needs to change and why. Acceptance in this framework does not mean throwing up my hands and saying that nothing can change. Instead, it means acknowledging what is and moving forward from there. To bring this back to a social work lens, until a woman who is being abused by her partner fully understands that abuse is occurring and the nature of that abuse, it may be difficult for her to move toward changing her relationship to her abuser or to leave the abusive situation. Similarly, a caseworker dealing with a neglected child cannot develop an effective service plan until she acknowledges the myriad of problems, many of which will not be easily fixed, facing a single parent who is poor. Indeed, if we are to be effective change agents, the more we understand our own intentions, beliefs and feelings about an action in which we are engaged, including the overwhelming sense of futility and sadness we may sometimes feel when we recognize the number of systems that add to the problems of our clients, the greater our chances of promoting a change that reflects the desires of those for whom we are advocating and not our own agendas.

For me, there is also an element of this understanding of ourselves as whole and healthy that allows me to understand that in the end, things cannot go wrong. This is facilitated by the larger sense described in the previous section, arising from the process of iRest, that everything is part of a common whole through which we are all connected. What each of us does affects another in some way and what may sometimes seem like a negative experience may in another context be positive. In essence, one outcome is not worse than another, but part of the unfolding that is occurring at that point in time. At another time, another outcome may occur and that is the unfolding that works at that point in time. In essence, there is an equanimity that arises as a result of doing this work. This equanimity is not a blind acceptance. Rather, it sustains me as I work toward a goal. It also protects me from becoming burned out when things do not unfold in the way that I had hoped. It helps me to continue moving forward toward my goal. Feelings arise as I work toward one outcome and they guide me to the next right thing given the situation as it is at that moment. This is particularly helpful when so much of my work involves working toward social change and addressing social problems that are quite entrenched. Rather than getting discouraged, although this does happen too, I can consider each outcome as one step in a larger unfolding.

There is also an awareness embedded in this same framework, that we alone are not responsible for any given outcome. That is, I acknowledge that other people, both those involved in working for change and those who oppose our efforts also have heartfelt desires and intentions that will shape what happens. This is particularly salient when I am teaching. I may have a specific direction or goal in terms of what students learn in a class each class session, and yet I have come to realize that my goal is not the only thing shaping student learning. Indeed, the checking in and recalibrating process facilitated by my practice is a critical tool when in the classroom. For example, students often struggle with the concept of probability sampling. The logic is sometimes hard for some of them to understand and some students only grasp the concepts intuitively. Here again, I find the micropractices helpful for tuning into my own feelings and emotions, as well as the felt-sense of the classroom when confusion arises. Where is there tension? What feels easy and/or “smooth” in terms of my explanation or their understanding? What is too “logical”? What direction seems to make the most sense to follow in terms of where the students are heading with their understanding? How can I support their approach to understanding certain concepts and still make the logic clear? What am I sensing each time I make a change? And where does that lead me? When I hold true to this process, I believe it deepens the learning experience for students and enriches my skill as a teacher.

This practice is not always easy. Sometimes I cannot get past the words or concepts I want the students to understand. I can only convey an idea one way and it is difficult to relax and work with the class, moment by moment tuning in so that I can access other explanations or ways of understanding. Similarly, throughout the day, as I move from one role to another, in the frenzy of activities I can easily ignore what is currently happening in my interactions with students and faculty members because I feel pressured to get something done and to move ahead to the next item on the list. If I remember my practice and pause, breathe, and sense back into my body to ground myself again in the present, I am deeply rewarded by my greater ability to respond from a place of clarity and connection.

Conclusion

Social workers must often address both individual and societal pain and trauma in their work. It is clear that the capacity to remain present in the face of this pain is healing to individual clients and whole communities. Mindfulness, at its most fundamental, helps us to experience our own wholeness and to recognize it in others. Quite often mindfulness practices are presented as tools solely for clients, but they are a tremendous resource for social workers as well. In this chapter, we have shared our experience with iRest Yoga Nidra Meditation as an effective mindfulness practice. Through examples of personal experience, we have demonstrated the usefulness of this practice in a myriad of settings.

iRest is a particularly body-centered practice that is anchored both in ancient practice and current psychology. It begins from the belief that we have within us something that has remained whole, integrated and untouched by any of the things that have happened in our lives. When we practice this belief with iRest it helps us to fully embody it ourselves. Supported by our own experience of wholeness, we can be truly present to others’ experience, confident in the innate capacity to heal. This has profound implications for how we approach ourselves and our work. It is our deepest desire that students enter the field of social work with tools that can help them mitigate the stressors inherent in the work, whether they work as therapists, casemanagers, administrators, or academics. iRest as a powerful tool of transformation that will serve the practitioner throughout their career and beyond.

References

Chodron, P. (2008). *The pocket Pema Chodron*. Boston, MA: Shambhala Publications.

Graham, L. (2013). *Bouncing back: Rewiring your brain for maximum resilience and well-being*. Novato, CA: New World Library.

Hanson, R. (2009). *Buddha's brain: The practical neuroscience of happiness, love and wisdom*. Oakland, CA: New Harbinger Publications.

Hanson, R. (2013). *Hardwiring happiness: The new brain science of contentment, calm, and confidence*. New York, NY: Harmony Books.

Kabat Zinn, J. (1994). *Wherever you go, there you are: Mindfulness meditation in everyday life*. New York, NY: Hyperion.

Kabat Zinn, J. (2013). *Full catastrophe living (revised edition): Using the wisdom of your body and mind to face stress, pain and illness*. New York, NY: Bantam.

Miller, R. (2015). *The iRest program for healing PTSD: A proven-effective approach to using Yoga Nidra meditation and deep relaxation techniques to overcome trauma*. Oakland, CA: New Harbinger Publications.

Ogden, P., & Minton, K. (2006). *Trauma and the body: A sensorimotor approach to psychotherapy*. New York, NY: WW Norton and Company.

Rosenberg, L. (1998). *Breath by breath*. Boston, MA: Shambhala Publications.

Salzberg, S., & Goldstein, J. (2002). *Insight meditation: A step-by-step course in how to meditate*. Louisville, CO: Sounds True.

Schore, A. N. (1994). *Affect regulation and the origin of the self: The neurobiology of emotional development*. Hillside, NJ: Lawrence Erlbaum Associates.

Siegel, D. (2001). *The developing mind: How relationships and the brain interact to shape who we are* (1st ed.). New York, NY: Guilford Press.

Siegel, D. (2010). *The mindful therapist: A clinician's guide to mindsight and neural integration*. New York, NY: W.W. Norton & Company.

Van der Kolk, B. (2014). *The body keeps the score: Brain, mind, and body in the healing of trauma*. New York, NY: Viking.

Wallin, D. J. (2007). *Attachment in psychotherapy*. New York, NY: Guilford Press.

Chapter 6
Beginning with the Training: Training Clinicians in Essential Methods for Integrating Mindfulness into Clinical Practice

Michael Rogan

Mindfulness has entered the mainstream of mental health treatment, and has been supported by clinical and neuroscience research findings, though meta-analyses of research about the efficacy of mindfulness yield both positive (Gotink et al. 2015) and negative (Goyal et al. 2014) results. These different findings suggest that utilizing mindfulness as an intervention can be challenging and exacting: clinical efficacy has been found to be sensitive to client and treatment protocol characteristics (e.g., Williams and Crane 2014). As a psychotherapist and research neuroscientist I am familiar with the clinical research about current treatment modalities that use elements of mindfulness (e.g., Kabat-Zinn 2003; Segal et al. 2012), and with the growing body of neuroscience research about mindfulness as a neurobiological phenomenon (see Paulson et al. 2013). However, my most important qualification in this endeavor is over 30 years of dedicated practice and study of the meditation practices from which clinical mindfulness techniques were derived, within the living Buddhist traditions taught by lineage masters.

My clinical practice has involved the flexible use of mindfulness techniques and processes, sometimes in quite small doses, within the constraints of a standard therapeutic session, and often in support of other clinical priorities and treatment modalities. This approach has been developed out of need to work with a diverse population of clients, at both high and lower levels of function, many of whom live with great distress and intense and persistent environmental stressors. This treatment has taken place in a variety of settings including community mental health clinics and community college walk-in counseling centers, where more formal utilization of manualized mindfulness-based treatment models may be neither feasible nor suitable for the client and setting. I present here a different, non-manualized approach, where one investigates with the client what aspects of her life are workable with the essential elements of mindfulness, and shape an ability to

M. Rogan (✉)
LCSW, Psychotherapist and Neuroscientist, New York, USA
e-mail: Michael@MichaelRoganPhD.com

T.B. Northcut (ed.), *Cultivating Mindfulness in Clinical Social Work*,
Essential Clinical Social Work Series, DOI 10.1007/978-3-319-43842-9_6

mutually communicate details of experience so that mindfulness can be cultivated and evaluated. In this way, existing beneficial coping and soothing functions and behaviors may be developed into a precise and effective mindfulness practice.

Training for Clinicians: Modeling a "Small Dose" Intervention

This chapter is based on an experiential training course for clinicians that I developed to teach core competencies for a flexible use of mindfulness in mental health treatment. Though the approach I present here has not been tested in clinical trials, it is wholly consistent with time-tested traditional mindfulness practices and pedagogy, as well contemporary therapeutic models that are supported by clinical research. It is specifically tailored to be workable in the scenario that does not lend itself well to empirical study—the broad and sometimes chaotic array of activity, circumstances, and client characteristics that are a part of every-day mental health practice.

At the outset, I emphasize that for a clinician to make use of mindfulness as an intervention, all competency ultimately derives from the clinician's own thorough experiential grounding in mindfulness and mindfulness training. A mastery of didactic information is insufficient. As others have suggested (Segal et al. 2012), a year of consistent, daily formal mindfulness practice may be considered a minimum qualification for using mindfulness effectively with clients. Further, it is essential that one's personal mindfulness practice be supervised by an experienced practitioner so that it is precise and fruitful—it is very easy for these simple practices to lose their fidelity and become just another vague soothing and coping mechanism. With this depth of experience, clinicians can learn to design and deliver a mindfulness intervention for each client, often delivered in quite small "doses," as circumstances permit, over multiple sessions.

To teach these clinical skills, I engage with clinicians in group sessions over several weeks, working directly with each group member with this "small dose" intervention—up to 10 min per clinician per session. This involves a progressive development, across sessions, of support, assessment, didactic information, instruction, inquiry, development of precision in self-report, correction of technique and concepts. The goal of this progressive approach is to gently bring about an ability to engage in mindful experience that is self-sustaining in everyday life. The group format maximizes learning, as clinicians witness others receiving their interventions, become aware of others' use of language to describe experiences, ways in which difficulties are experienced and expressed as well as individual differences in sensitivity and reaction to correction.

While the clinical course models client treatment, it is more rigorous and programmatic: to drive experiential learning, clinicians agree to try to take on specific mindfulness practices (up to 10 min a day) and participate in detailed exploration of their practice acquisition and technique precision over the course of training in group sessions. More broad didactic information and case material is also presented to explore the impact of special client characteristics on this process. For clinicians who have significant experience with their own mindfulness practice, this group course provides experience with how to design and deliver a customized, progressive mindfulness intervention. For clinicians with little background in mindfulness practice, the course is intended to jump-start a personal practice and provide cautionary perspective on the need for personal practice prior to implementing mindfulness as an intervention.

Becoming Familiar

The topic of meditation is very broad, and has had diverse expressions across cultures and history. A description that I find particularly useful as a general guide to this endeavor is a Tibetan word for meditation, *gom*, which may be translated as "to become familiar with" (Mingyur and Swanson 2010, p. 15)—that is, to become familiar with your mind and mental events. For those entering mental health treatment, the mind is often experienced as confused and conflicted—a place of struggle. Meditation practices provide a way to develop non-adversarial familiarity with mental events, cutting through habitual patterns of thought.

The present volume concerns a subset of foundational meditative practices broadly termed *mindfulness*, and it is important for the reader to know that neither in the West, the East, the clinic, the laboratory nor within the various traditional practices is there a single understanding of this term. Mindfulness-like experiences and practices have been described and explored in many religious, spiritual, cultural traditions. In the West, mental health interventions have for the most part been based on the Hindu and Buddhist traditional methods, which are themselves quite diverse across history and regions as they developed over thousands of years across Asia. It is beyond the scope of the present work to address this diversity, and so I will define terms as they are used in this chapter.

In common usage, mindfulness is a term that identifies an *experience*, as well as a set of *techniques* that may be used to bring about that experience. As this is a discussion within a clinical context, we may well start with the definition used to frame the early clinical trials of mindfulness as a mental health intervention: According to Kabat-Zinn (1994), mindfulness is "paying attention in a particular way: on purpose, in the present moment, and non-judgmentally" (p. 4). This definition captures essential elements of mindfulness: attention, being in the present moment, and nonconceptual experience. In practical terms, mindfulness techniques typically involve conscious attention to sensations, such as those that occur during breathing. It is the feeling of sensation that provides the orientation to the present moment: sensations can only be felt in the present—as they occur.

Mindfulness: Deliberate and Spontaneous

In the clinic I have found it important to recognize the distinction between explicit mindfulness training which brings about an experience of mindfulness through a *deliberate act of attention* and the experience of mindfulness itself, which is independent of deliberate effort and can be naturally occurring. That is, one can be present in experience, with attention and without judgment, without there being first a deliberate and purposeful direction of attention. From some traditional perspectives, nondeliberate experiences of this nature are the subject of much exploration and often involves different nomenclature. For example, a distinction can be made between effortful and non-effortful practices: "The deliberate effort to meditate is called mindfulness. Mindfulness is attentive, in that there is a sense of being alert, conscientious and careful" (Urgyen et al. 1994, p. 187). Mindfulness can also evolve into "awakeness," an effortless experience, which "is free of an observer and something observed" (Urgyen et al. 1994, p. 187). These and many more distinctions have been a matter of lively discussion and debate over millennia. In clinical practice, rather than lay stress on the nuances of experiential terminology, I describe *spontaneous mindfulness* as follows: *moments of direct experience of life that have a simple satisfying quality, uncomplicated by preoccupations with the past and the future, and free from burdensome attitudes about self and other.* I find this description useful because most people recognize having had at least flashes of such experiences and are able to endorse them as genuine and valuable (for example: "It was when I was in a new place, and turned and saw a beautiful view, so unexpected").

Soothing Behaviors: Elements of Mindfulness

People also may have mindfulness-like experiences more routinely, in the absence of any special training or instruction, or novel events. In particular, it has been quite helpful to observe that many of the effective soothing behaviors reported by clients include essential elements of mindfulness. While mindfulness is not in itself *necessarily* soothing or calming, most people who appear for treatment have prior experience of finding some relief of mental distress using elements of mindfulness such as, for example, an open attention to certain sensations (such as the sensations of exercise, or those arising from fresh, clean clothing—see *Client Case: J takes a ride*).

Client Case: J takes a ride

A client in outpatient psychiatric treatment had some cognitive impairment and paranoid ideation. Her journey to the clinic would typically be dominated by distressing thoughts about how the other passengers on the bus don't like her, look down on her, and so forth. Her primary therapist described J in the course of a 5 week mindfulness training I conducted for hospital psychiatric staff. Asked about how J may benefit from some mindfulness intervention, I asked more about this client and what was notable about her—signs of good function. It turns out she always carefully dressed herself, in clean clothes, before heading out. I suggested the clinician ask her about her clothes and what she likes about them. She was able to report a surprisingly detailed description of the sensory experience of her clothing—texture, smell, "stiffness," and how she was aware of it moving against her skin. I suggested this be used as a way to make the client aware of how a sensory awareness gave her "a break" from her negative thoughts, and how she could notice other sensations if she wanted to—cultivating a more generally useful mindful experience. At our last training session the clinician reported that J described her trip on the bus as "like a ride," where she was aware of the movement and how she and the others on the bus were swaying together through bumps and turns—a trip also notable for the absence of report about negative thoughts. This is an example of how one can work with a spontaneous mindful experience and cultivate it to a more generally effective experience. It also points to the emergence of a spontaneous sense of kinship with others—a quality that often develops with mindfulness practice.

These soothing behaviors may be engaged in deliberately or habitually without much awareness. That mindfulness can be spontaneously discovered and valued is not surprising, as it neither is an exotic state nor a complex achievement—it is a natural baseline awareness of mind, alert and at rest. The identification of *spontaneous mindful experience* in clients' lives opens up a route to cultivation of mindfulness that does not require tasking the client with novel explicit training, and I have found this route to be an essential part of using mindfulness as an effective intervention. Illustration of this can be seen in most of the cases presented in this chapter.

Cultivation Versus Training

The traditional path for mindfulness involves explicit training—a time set aside from other activities when specified techniques are practiced for a certain length of time. This is also the path taken by prominent clinical models that use mindfulness techniques. While this is a time-tested and effective method for those who engage in it, it is a simple fact of mental health treatment that many of those seeking treatment are not up to taking on "one more thing to do," let alone sign-on for the 45 min per day of mindfulness practice prescribed, for example, by MBCT (Segal et al. 2012). Many clients experience a degree of distress and environmental stressors that don't leave much energy or interest in new skill learning. Others can be puzzled, feeling that their problems are being trivialized by the suggestion that simple mindfulness techniques can bring them any benefit. Still others are fully occupied with pressing concrete issues or emotional crises that require the use of other interventions, and there is no time for sessions dedicated to exploration of mindfulness.

What is indicated most often is a gradual approach in which some time in each session is spent assessing and fostering a conscious orientation to mental events in the present moment, either through the deliberate use of mindfulness techniques or through identification of already-occurring mindful experiences. For many clients, this path of cultivation is very productive, and for some it can develop eventually into a more conventional daily practice.

In the following, I will first describe the basic mindfulness techniques which are used in my clinical training course, and which also may be used at some point with clients, depending on their receptivity. These techniques also point to the nature of mindful experience, and thus illustrate what steps may be taken to cultivate that experience outside of a formal training.

Mindfulness Is Simple and Precise: Assessment, Verification, Correction

The challenge is that mindfulness is wholly experiential, nonverbal, nonconceptual and nonjudgmental, but paradoxically it is cultivated and supported through didactic explanation, verbal exploration of experience, and correction of imprecise effort.

The implementation of mindfulness I have found useful in my clinical practice involves a selection of technically simple variations consistent with established treatment models, but drawn more directly from my own training and familiarity with foundational techniques found in the living Theravadin (e.g., Amaro 2015) traditions, and Tibetan *mahamudra* (e.g., Thrangu 2003) and *dzogchen* (Urgyen et al. 1994) traditions. The basic instruction has two elements: the first is to place attention on a sensory *object of mindfulness* such as the sensations that occur during the act of breathing, or the sensation of hearing ambient sound. For example, in the words of Thrangu (2003), "You simply direct your attention… to what you hear. You may or may not be hearing something in particular, but by directing your attention to what you hear, you become aware of sound in general, and you rest your mind on that" (p. 40). The second element of the instruction involves a metacognitive awareness of mental events: when you notice that thoughts have captured your attention, so that you are no longer attending to the object of mindfulness, you simply direct your attention to what you hear. This points out the two essential elements of this technique: placing attention on sensations and a metacognitive awareness of mental events. In terms of brain functionality, this variety of mindfulness technique may be considered a kind of attentional training (Malinowski 2013).

Though the technique is simple, it clearly involves several competencies, including, at least, the availability of sensation to conscious experience, the ability to place attention and be aware of where it is placed, and an ability to communicate experience with sufficient precision that the correct use of technique can be assessed. In adapting these traditional approaches to the clinic I have broken them down to several processes, which may be brought to the client in small doses across sessions, in response to material raised in session and according to the client's receptivity.

1. ***Preliminary assessment***
2. ***Didactic explanation: attention, sensation, thinking, agency***
3. ***Preparation for practice: experience and communication***
4. ***Providing instruction and practicing with the client in session***
5. ***Inquiring about experience: shaping precision of technique***
6. ***Discussing how to anchor practice in daily life***
7. ***Recognizing emergent qualities.***

Preliminary Assessment

I think it is uncontroversial that everyone would benefit from a conscious orientation to the present moment, relief from preoccupations with the past and the future, some time spent in relative freedom from burdensome attitudes about self and others, and a greater familiarity and flexibility with how mental events arise and pass away. A mindfulness intervention is one way of bringing all this about, but which (if any) mindfulness approaches may be workable for a given client is a separate question that requires assessment. The first thing to ascertain is whether the client can appreciate a framing of her clinical issues such that mindfulness "makes sense" as a treatment approach. This involves finding out the client's view of what the problem is, what makes it better and worse, and what are the special client characteristics that need to be considered.

What is the problem?

If, as has been stated above, mindfulness is a natural baseline of the awake mind, how is it that it can seem so elusive? This can be framed as follows: A lifetime of mental and emotional habits and reactivity tend to obscure natural mindful experience, covering it up with an uncomfortable but familiar neurotic tangle of worries, regrets, strategies, and expectations. This tangled state obstructs satisfying connection with others, clear purposeful action, and simple direct experience of everyday life. For those who appear for mental health treatment, these obstructions can be quite acute—they may be in response to powerful adversities (acute loss, trauma, abuse, problems with health and security), but often the causes are not so clear-cut.

The client's reasons for seeking treatment generally provide sufficient rationale for introducing mindfulness as a worthwhile approach. Most mental health problems involve specific issues that can directly be impacted by mindfulness, and some of these issues may be elicited from the client during assessment:

- Too much time spent thinking/worrying/engaging in internal dialogue
- Thoughts and feelings that are sometimes disruptive, stressful, and repetitive—not helpful

- Habitual responses that are both maladaptive and stable—seemingly out of reach of change
- Little agency with regard to mental events—one is swept along by what comes into mind
- Poor ability to report experience and activities: evidence of automaticity
- Perceived conflicts and problems may be real and entirely valid, but the intensity of the reaction to them is counter-productive.

Participation in assessment at this level requires that the client develop an ability to distinguish between the *information content* of thoughts about problems and conflicts, which may in fact be accurate and valid as matters of concern, and *mental activity itself*, which may be obsessive or ruminative and therefore not be a helpful response to these problems.

It is vitally important to recognize, with the client, that it is valuable and adaptive to engage in thinking, planning, assessment, and reassessment of one's life and experience, problem solving and anticipation of troubles that might be ahead. Mindfulness can be presented as a way to take a break from this activity when it proves to be excessive and exhausting. Most clients are receptive to being able to take this kind of "vacation" and intrigued by the proposition that they may be able to do this by choice. However, not all clients consider their mental activity to be problematic in itself—some fully endorse every minute of their problem solving, analysis, and review of to-do lists as being essential activities. I have found this attitude in clients, and also in clinician trainees (see *Clinical Training Case C*).

Clinical Training Case C: My thoughts are too important.

C was a successful psychiatrist, wanting to learn about mindfulness for use with clients. In assessment and preparation for practice, C was unable to come up with any time of day during which he felt it was worthwhile to "interrupt" his thoughts, which he believed were at all times effective and valuable. He did not consider his thought processes to be problematic, and felt that any time spent not thinking would be time he would have to make up later, because his thinking was effective and efficient.

After the first in-session mindfulness practice (3 min., feel the breath) he reported his mental activity candidly, but in the midst of the report appeared to be surprised and embarrassed at what he was revealing: that his thoughts were racing, fragmentary, and had an unexpected lack of orderliness. Despite the fact that others in the group made similar reports, and this was discussed as a very common discovery when first using mindfulness techniques, C subsequently became guarded in his self-report, and withdrew from training after the third session.

To assess and bring a client "on board" with mindfulness as a valuable tool, good questions to ask are:

- How much of the time that you spend thinking is really useful (e.g., not simply repetitive)?
- Do you think it would be better (more efficient, effective) if you didn't respond so intensely when you thought about these real problems?

When is it better/worse?

Next, it is useful to explore with the client "when is it better?"—when are these distressing symptoms absent or less intense and when is the client more free to experience pleasure and connectedness in daily life. Highlighting the fact that distressing mental activity waxes and wanes is an important step in appreciating that these issues are changeable and subject to influence by events and also by purposeful action. Soothing behaviors may be identified that involve elements of mindfulness such as sensory awareness, as with the case of J mentioned earlier. Other soothing/coping behaviors may be revealed that are not compatible with mindfulness techniques, and it is important not to devalue these soothing behaviors, but instead to offer mindfulness as an additional alternative. For example, clinical trainee E found soothing visualizations more important than mindfulness.

Clinical Training Case E: Soothing visualizations

In my clinical training course, E, a clinical social worker, declared previous experience with meditation, which, upon inquiry, seemed to consist entirely of generating soothing and "uplifting" imagery and scenarios. In inquiry after our first in-session mindfulness practice (feel the breath), E expressed surprise at being told he was not following the instructions, apparently not having understood that engaging in visualization of beautiful images was not part of the technique. E was encouraged to not abandon his practice of visualizations, but to also reserve a different time for mindfulness practice. However, the ability to soothe himself with pleasant visualization was for him so valuable that he was reluctant to consider a technique that did not deliberately cultivate this kind of experience. When he was able to spend some time using the mindfulness technique (feeling the breath) with some precision, he reported that the experience was "harsh" and "felt deprivational"—suggesting that broader underlying psychological issues were being revealed by the disruption of soothing behaviors. In the context of relatively brief clinical training, E found mindfulness to be of limited benefit for him, and preferred his visualization practice. As a result he realized, and declared, that he would not be able to use mindfulness as a clinical intervention.

The cases described thus far point to an important consideration when introducing mindfulness to people in a clinical setting, and why clinical competence in mindfulness is essential. Mindfulness training must be used carefully in a clinical context: it is not a tranquilizer. In its traditional form, mindfulness practice is *intended* to be disruptive and destabilizing of the status quo—the status quo being, generally, the domination of experience by a tangle of thoughts about past and future. There are two main classes of problems that can occur as people take on a mindfulness practice: those that occur when the instructions *are not* used accurately, and those that occur when instructions *are* used accurately:

When the instructions are not used accurately

It is typical for people to hear the simple instructions for mindfulness, and rather than follow them, engage instead in their own particular variety of neurotic exertion, which may include excessive strain, self-criticism, performance anxiety, feeling incompetent, or overwhelmed. At the beginning, this tendency should be expected and addressed in careful communication and assessment, so that people can be protected from "mindfulness practice" that is really a session of intensified and sometimes painful neuroticism. When this tendency is pronounced, a variety of methods may be used as a remedy. For example, short practice periods during therapy sessions are recommended, giving opportunity for communication and reinforcement of the precision of technique, before sending people off to practice alone at home.

When the instructions are used accurately

It is important to remember that mindfulness has the intended effect of disrupting habitual patterns of mind, and this may include patterns of coping and self-soothing. Most people who appear for clinical treatment have a hard-won repertoire of coping and soothing strategies, which may operate with or without awareness. These may not be well designed, but they generally do contribute to stability and a sense of control. I have found it remarkable that many people, even those who experience great distress in their daily lives, have naturally discovered elements of mindfulness practice and make use of them in their coping and self-regulation. However, most people have other coping and soothing methods based on the mental routines that are quite vulnerable to disruption by mindfulness training. It is important to monitor people in session while they begin to practice, particularly those suffering from severe anxiety, obsessiveness, or trauma. When mindfulness instructions are followed with precision, unexpected troubles may come to awareness as layer upon layer of distraction dissolve.

Special Client Characteristics

When obtaining clinical and medical history, several issues are of importance in deciding if or how to proceed with a mindfulness practice. In my experience, the most common are:

Medical illness/physical pain

For those with medical illness or injury involving chronic physical pain, neurological symptoms, or recurrent episodes of illness, attention to somatic sensation may be aversive or anxiogenic. People with these issues can be averse to reporting negative somatic experiences, as they may be avoidant of the matter. With these clients it is important to gently explore somatic sensation and medical symptoms prior to beginning mindfulness practice. Mindfulness practice or any attention to somatic sensation at home should not be encouraged until in-session experience can be explored and found to be safe. It should be noted that many clients can tolerate quite unhelpful levels of distress, and it is not advisable to simply rely on their spontaneous verbal report. In-session practice should be done under close observation for signs of distress—these include changes in posture and respiration, movements and muscular tension, and expression in face and eyes (see *Client Case L*).

Client Case: L at checkout—serious illness, somatic avoidance

L appeared for treatment after a second bout of cancer, now again in remission. Though he had no current physical symptoms or pain and emphasized that he "felt fine" his illness had put considerable strain on his relationships and financial stability, and these were the presenting issues he wished to address in his sessions.

In our first sessions he was able to talk about a need for "a break from all the noise in his head," and this indicated a mindfulness intervention might be useful. In the first session that addressed mindfulness, he was not able to report sensations with readiness or detail, but was able to notice the sensations of air entering his nostrils as he breathed. We decided to try this as an object of mindfulness in our first attempt at practice. However, after a minute of practicing together, he showed signs of distress in his face, hunched over slightly and bowed his head. We immediately stopped the practice and upon inquiry it turned out that the breath, with it's diaphragmatic movement, was too close to his abdominal "danger area," where he had experienced pain and nausea during illness, and this suddenly turned the practice into a very aversive experience. He revealed a morbid preoccupation with his somatic sensations—being always on the alert for signs of illness—which he had not reported before.

Sound as an object of mindfulness did not work well for L as he was particularly, characteristically, irritable, and if asked to notice the ambient sounds in the room prior to practice he would complain about "all the noise" that was intruding into the session room. In exploration about when, in the day or during the week, things were better for him, he reported that walking to and from his appointments during the day were peaceful "breaks" for him. We therefore explored using the sensations of walking as an object of mindfulness. However, in subsequent report about this experience, it turned out that it was the visual sensations during walking outdoors that were his object of mindfulness. This developed into a useful practice for him, including an ability to practice in session using visual sensation as the object of mindfulness. After several weeks of regular practice, a particular report was notable: At the grocery checkout counter, he was annoyed that the person ahead of him was causing some kind of delay. L found that he spontaneously became attentive to his groceries on the runway, the colors and shapes, and was aware that he was markedly less agitated than he would normally be in such a situation. Still in the midst of delay, he looked up and saw the cause of the delay—the woman ahead of him was having trouble getting her food stamps to work and was clearly embarrassed at the attention she was attracting. In a notable departure from his usual irritability, L reported feeling "sorry for her" and politely looking away as the situation was resolved, noticing an unusual amount of patience with the delay.

Traumatic memories/dissociative symptoms

People who are subject to re-experiencing traumatic memories or dissociative symptoms should first be established in good therapeutic alliance with the clinician (by any number of conventional means) before engaging in mindfulness practice. Careful didactic explanation of the value of orienting to the present moment, to the clinician, and to the room, can be followed by gradual guided orientation to sensations present in the therapeutic setting. This preparation is valuable in re-orienting to the present particularly if someone has dissociated or is re-experiencing a past trauma. Beginning in-session mindfulness practice should be reserved for times when the client is most stable, and done with verbal guidance, a minute at a time, under close observation for signs of distress or dissociation. In my experience, the amount of verbal guidance of mindfulness—"I feel the breath, I feel my body in the chair," etc., can be modulated by the clinician to help maintain contact with the client.

Anxiety, Panic, Obsessional Thinking

Individuals with these symptoms may experience heightened anxiety when attempting to use mindfulness techniques (see *Client Case Q*). In all such cases, it is important to recognize that mindfulness techniques are potentially destabilizing and can lead to increased distress even when used accurately.

Client case Q: Frightening results

Q appeared for treatment with severe social anxiety. After a few sessions she was open to trying mindfulness practice as a way to deal with her anxiety, which recently had caused her to "get dizzy and need to sit down on the curb" on the way to a job interview. Because of her high level of anxiety, (shortness of breath was one of her frequently reported anxiety symptoms), we used ambient sound as the object of mindfulness, which seemed to interest her, as she said the ticking of the clock in the room was "nice." At the end of our first 3 min of in-session practice, however, she shifted into a visibly stiffened posture, with more rapid respiration and a hard frightened gaze. Upon inquiry she reported that it was "nice" at the start, but after "settling down" she noticed the flow of thoughts going through her mind, which she experienced as chaotic and frightening. It is likely that her habitual self-distraction and avoidant attitude about the contents of her thoughts protected her from noticing their profusion until she started to "settle down" by using the mindfulness techniques. We discontinued mindfulness for several weeks to focus on more psychodynamic treatment, exploring what was being so energetically avoided. After her anxiety was reduced by this means, she was able to again try mindfulness in session, without being afraid of her mental events, and with greater feelings of agency. Mindfulness practice then became a useful part of her daily routine, credited by her for disrupting the habit of thinking of elaborate anxious scenarios in advance of social interactions.

Depression

When a client is in the midst of a depressive episode, mindfulness in stillness can be too dulled by depressive symptoms to be useful as an intervention. Instead, it can be effective to combine mindfulness with general principles of Behavioral Activation (Kanter et al. 2009). In short, have the client engage in simple mindful physical activity, with emphasis on the sensations of the activity. For example, wash a dish and feel the sensations - the weight, water, temperature, textures, sounds. This attentional placement can bypass cognitive and mood obstacles and foster increased physical activity and sense of agency.

Didactic Explanation

Once the preliminary assessment is done, the clinician can proceed to deliver some didactic information to the client, and move toward defining and cultivating mindfulness. Didactic descriptions about mental events and mindfulness are only useful to the extent that they motivate and bring about accurate practice and mindful experience. As is evidenced by the vast literature that has accumulated about mindfulness over the millennia, there is a great deal that one can say about this experience. Indeed there are times when it is important to explain things in order to remove obstacles to practice. However too much didactic information can quickly become an obstacle in itself, leading the client to spend time pondering and attempting to master an understanding of the didactic material, even during practice time, rather than putting it to use and gathering the fruit.

It is also true that there are many ways of motivating practice and dealing with obstacles – these different ways may each point accurately to mindful experience, but may seem contradictory on a didactic level. This is not a problem in itself, but clients may become confused with a superfluity of explanatory discourse, or get side-tracked into a dissection of paradoxical issues and nuances. There is not sufficient room here to express all the different points that can be raised to motivate and support a precise mindfulness experience. Many points will be apparent to clinicians who have sufficient personal mindful experience and training, and these should be used judiciously to directly address specific issues as they arise with clients. I present here a few key points that I have found to be particularly useful and easy to communicate to a broad client base.

What mindfulness is not:

- Visualization or an act of imagination
- Exploration of the content of thoughts, feelings, or habitual patterns
- Stopping or improving thoughts, feelings, or habitual patterns
- Exertion toward attaining a special state, including being relaxed, calm, or comfortable.

What mindfulness is:

While some degree of relaxation or calm may occur in the course of mindfulness, it is important to understand that by using mindfulness techniques we are not attempting to achieve a goal, we are *enacting a process* and *noticing* what happens. The process is simple, and it involves the placement of attention on sensory experience: "I feel the sensations of the breath. When I notice that I'm not feeling the breath, I feel the breath, right away." This process brings about an experience of the present moment—that is because sensations only occur in the present, and that's when we can feel them. (One can also remember past sensations, or imagine sensations, but most people find it easy to distinguish these from present sensation). Feeling sensation is essentially non-conceptual, non-fabricated and direct, and involves some openness to experience. This openness may be quite constrained in some clients, and it is helpful to emphasize that it is not to be expected that one will "feel the breath" clearly and directly for an extended period of time—even a second may be a long time. It is important to orient the client to the fact that very brief experiences of sensation, fractions of a second, are valid mindfulness experiences: "It only comes in little bits." Emphasis on this quality of experience can be particularly helpful for those with attentional disorders, who may find onerous any call to direct their attention. In fact, one need only place attention on the breath—it is not necessary to somehow *grip* the breath with one's attention. It is understood that attention will shift after placement—that is not a failure.

In the course of practice, thoughts and emotions arise, and this is not a problem. It is hard for most people to understand that mindfulness does not involve shutting down or managing thoughts—that one does nothing to thoughts, one just feels the breath. The clinician needs to be on guard for this "thought management" impulse, which arises again and again, often in the guise of judging the goodness or badness of practice as it is taking place.

Attention and Agency

It is important to introduce to clients the voluntary and involuntary nature of attention, and how events come to conscious awareness. Though these may sound like somewhat demanding abstract concepts, they are in fact easily pointed out and experienced, and most clients profit from this exploration.

We can attend to specific things if we wish to, but our system is also built so that our attention is captured by important things that happen around us. An unexpected loud sound, for example, captures our attention because we need to know what's going on and deal with it if necessary. Our attention can also be captured by thoughts when they carry a strong emotional charge. Indeed, one may say that one of the adaptive values of emotion processing as an evolved function of the brain is the identification and assessment of "what is important" to oneself. So, news of an impending court date that represents a risk to our livelihood carries an emotional charge and commands our attention. Subsequent recall of the court date also can capture our attention in a way that is helpful to get things done in preparation. However recall of the court date can also lead to ruminative and stressful thinking that is not helpful. In particular, it does no good to have one's attention captured in this way at 4:00 AM when sleep is needed. Thus, actually important thoughts can drive attention in a way that is maladaptive and exhausting.

It is also a common problem that certain thoughts have an emotional importance that they do not deserve—for example, memories of events or personal interactions that are long over, beyond any reach of purposeful action, but which for some reason have acquired an exaggerated importance and recur in the mind with an urgency that compels attention and drives a sequence of habitual thought. Clients are often quite able to recognize that the urgency associated with some thoughts is unwarranted and unwanted, but that awareness does not prevent these thoughts from capturing attention and dominating experience.

Mindfulness techniques build up a strength of mind that allows us to place our attention where we want to, rather than have it be helplessly driven by any thoughts that may happen to occur. If, during practice, our attention is captured by other things, we are able to place our attention once again according to our choice, in a simple gentle way. Some clients respond well to this as an assertion of agency—an ability to have impact on one's own state. Sometimes it is useful to explain this with some care, as some clients, particularly those exhausted by years of ruminative, obsessive thought patterns, may not be aware that this is actually a potential of their minds—that a non-combative agency regarding attention to mental events is a possibility.

Preparation for in-Session Practice

Sensation, Attention and Communication About Experience

The mindfulness techniques presented here are simple but require precision: attention is placed on sensation, and sensations are felt in "real time". Though this may seem simple enough, in fact it cannot be taken for granted that this instruction will be followed. This is a critical point, as "thinking" about the breath, or engaging in imagery about what the air and the lungs and "energy" may be doing during breathing will not cultivate mindfulness.

For most people, sensation is not reliably available to conscious experience, despite best efforts and clear intellectual understanding of the matter at hand. Though this situation can be greatly exacerbated in certain conditions (trauma, for example) this is not in itself an issue of mental illness—it is part of the human condition: "We have some relationship with body, but it is very uncertain and erratic. We flicker back and forth between body and something else—fantasies, ideas. That seems to be our basic situation." (Trungpa 2010, pp. 23, 24).

Verifying that sensation is being felt during mindfulness practice is complicated by the general uncertainties that always surround communication about experience. The client's use of language may not coincide with the clinicians expectations, but this does not necessarily mean that the underlying experience or use of technique is imprecise. In an attempt to point clients toward sensory experience, and to verify that sensation is being felt during mindfulness practice, I prepare for the first in-session practice with a discussion of sensation vocabulary (e.g., cool, warm, smooth, rough, pressure), and with a discussion about how somatic sensation works: it is the result of activity of peripheral sensory neurons that signal an occurrence at a specific location in the body. For example, one may feel the sensations of the breath in various parts of the nose, mouth, throat, the movement of the chest and abdomen, the shifting of one's clothing against the skin as the chest and abdomen move—all these are locations where the breath can be felt, and any or all are quite workable objects of mindfulness.

Operationally, in order to clarify communication, I inquire about their sensory experience (what was felt, and where in the body was it felt) and then reflect client's statements back to them, with a modification which reflects a small difference in the kind of precision of expression that I am after—this becomes an inducement for the client to consider other possibilities of language and restate their experience in a way that points more directly to physical sensation by including sensory and location words. This reflection technique (which for shorthand purposes I will refer to as "reflect with precision") is inspired by the "agreeing with a twist" method of Motivational Interviewing (Miller and Rollnick 2012), a set of techniques that I have found to be very useful in psychotherapy practice: "Agreeing with a twist contains the benefits of reflection and of inviting the person to consider things in a different light" (p. 202).

Here is an example of exploring sensation and communication about the breath in preparation for practice. After every few exchanges, the client is invited to take a little time and feel the breath once again.

Clinician: "Take a little time now and notice the sensation of the breath. What did you notice?"
Client: "I'm thinking about the flow."
(This may be an imprecise description of sensation, or it may be an indication of engaging in imagery about the breath.)
Clinician: "You were feeling the flow of the air."
Client: "Yes, coming in and out."
Clinician: "You're feeling the air as it comes in and out of your body as you breathe.
Client: "Yes."
Clinician: "Where in your body do you feel it? Let's take another couple of breathe."
Client: "In my nose."
Clinician: "You feel the air coming in and out of your nose as you breathe. Do you notice anything about temperature as you breathe? Let's take another couple of breaths."
Client: "It's cool when I breath in."
Clinician: "Where do you feel the coolness when you breathe in?"
Client: "In my nose. At the tip."

The clinician can be reasonably assured at this point that the client has been able to place attention on the sensations of the breath. It is not clear to what extent this process of exploration involved a refinement of communication, or a redirection of attention toward sensation—probably some aspects of both.

Objects of Mindfulness

The techniques described here involve placing attention on a particular sensation, which can be referred to as the object of mindfulness. If someone reports that running or knitting or using the elliptical machine at the gym provides a natural mindfulness-like experience, then that should be encouraged and specifically cultivated into a true mindfulness practice, using the sensations of those activities as the object of mindfulness. In the absence of such an obvious choice, there are several considerations that should guide the choice of an object of mindfulness for practice, including the person's reactions and sensitivity to the possible object. Client Case L, described above, illustrates some of these issues.

The object of mindfulness should be neutral, or at least not carry aversive associations. For example, the breath can be problematic for those with asthma, and also for those with severe anxiety or panic attacks, as the breath can become a morbid center of focus during crisis and therefore be a "worrisome" thing to pay attention to at any time. The breath can also be a problematic choice for people who have had voice training, or exposure (but not good training) in yogic breathing techniques: in these cases the clinician should explore whether the client's breathing may be too heavily managed and associated with performance anxieties. If the experience of the breath is encumbered in any of these ways, the sensation of hearing ambient sound is a good alternative as an object of mindfulness. However, there are some exceptions: some people have particular irritability around sounds, and random sound is not neutral for them ("all this noise!"). Others have living situations full of unwanted noise, so that specific attention to sound outside of session may be anxiogenic. Sensations of the body in contact with the chair, hands on the lap, the visual scene, may also be explored as useful objects of mindfulness.

Provide Instruction and Practice with the Client in Session

When providing instruction in session, I explain that I am going to do the practice, and I invite the client to join me as I narrate the process that I am engaging in. Thus I give the instruction in first person. The accumulation of experience of being mindful together in the therapeutic setting becomes an invaluable resource when difficult material arises in treatment, and in recovery from dissociative symptoms.

I ask that eyes be kept open, lowered with soft gaze: this helps with alertness, allows the practice to be usable in more situations, and also allows the clinician and the client to be aware of each other's presence during practice. This allows the clinician to be able to observe any signs of distress or tension in the client: for the clinician, during practice in session, the client is also an object of mindfulness. The client benefits from being exposed to the nonverbal as well as the verbal manifestations of practice in the clinician. Contemporary meditation masters have spoken of the potential beneficial impact of this exposure in therapeutic situations. In a discourse about PTSD and trauma, Tsyokni Rinpoche (2013) refers to the affect of a clinician, who is a meditator, on a patient as a therapeutically important kind of *darshan*—"if you have a good stable compassionate cognitive calmness, of course it influences the other."

The Language of Instruction

The clinician's use of language in describing the technique and leading mindfulness practice in session is important, as it is becomes internalized and used by the client. I have learned to simplify the language I use in providing instruction. Many common word choices can easily become problematic in a clinical situation. My comments here do not represent my opinion about what is "correct" but rather what I have found to be useful. This very simplified view of instruction language has been inspired by teachings of Dzogchen, which is truly virtuosic in its nonconceptuality (Urgyen et al. 1994). In particular, I have found it extremely helpful to keep to language that minimizes any call to exertion, imagery, or abstract conceptualization, as it is easy for these to become "hooks" for obsessiveness and anxiety.

For example, a commonly heard instruction is "return (or come back) to the breath". This gives the impression of the client having gone somewhere and traveling back—an image that I believe tends to unhelpfully and inaccurately solidify the "realness" of thoughts. This may seem a fine point, but in my view it is an entirely unnecessary complication that may interact negatively with clinical vulnerabilities, and is very easily avoided. Words like "concentrate on" or "focus on the breath" are evocative of special effort (and thus opportunities for failure), and are best avoided: I find that clients are all too ready to turn mindfulness practice into a strenuous and exhausting activity. Even talk about "placing attention", which is useful in didactic explanation, is too abstract and conceptual for use at the point of instruction, and is best avoided when leading practice. Another unnecessary piece of imagery is "let go of the thought"—why introduce this idea of physicality? In fact one need not engage in an operation of letting go of anything—one need only feel the breath. Instead of all these possibilities, I recommend simply and consistently saying, "feel the breath".

Essential elements of mindfulness practice:

Whether the practice involves sitting still, or engaging in activities of daily life, the recommended sequence of instruction is as follows, with sample language in quotes:

- **Set intention**: I remind myself what I am doing and why—endorsing the process, not an outcome.
  - "For this practice time I will be awake and alert, I will gently apply the technique, and I will be curious about what happens."
- **I feel the object of mindfulness**
  - "I feel the physical sensations of the breath."
- **I allow thoughts to come and go**
  - "Thoughts and emotions come and go as I feel the breath."

- **Metacognitive awareness**
  - "If I become involved in thinking – worries, plans, talking to myself—and as soon as I notice this…."
- **I feel the object of mindfulness**
  - "I feel the physical sensations of the breath"

It is not necessary that mindfulness practice take place in the standard formal way—sitting still for a defined period of time. Rather it is necessary to find out how the client may most easily and readily engage in the essential elements of mindfulness. As mentioned, this may be discovered in client's report of soothing behaviors, or may be chosen as having some already existing motivation behind it. In my experience, this has manifested in quite a large range of activities, and the challenge for the clinician and the client is to see that these activities are transformed into mindfulness practice by including the essential elements described above. When doing activities mindfully, it is easiest if the sensory object of mindfulness derives as directly as possible from the activity itself. Some of the activities that I have worked with effectively are:

- Exercise (Feel the movement of the body, changes in posture, etc.)
- Knitting (The feeling of movement, texture, colors, sounds)
- Doing the dishes (The feeling of the water, temperature, weight, texture)
- Clearing mountains of clutter (the weight of each magazine as it goes in the trash)
- Walking the dog (The feeling of movement, sight of dog)
- Riding the subway (Movement of the body, sights and sounds).

There are other variations that may be used to make practice more possible for a person experiencing agitation and restlessness of mind or body, and those with ADHD or similar difficulties. For such clients, one can choose a technique that involves more mental activity. One useful example is what I call "cycling"—in which the instruction is to have several different objects of mindfulness (breath, sound, sight), and during practice engage in moving attention from one object of mindfulness to another in a set pattern, staying on each for a particular duration of time. This kind of more "busy" techniques can satisfy the urge for change and nevertheless allow mindfulness to develop and practice to continue.

Inquiry and Correction

After practice in session, or when talking about practice done outside of session, it's important to check in on the essential points, to be sure that the use of technique is precise. This generally amounts to identifying deviations from the simplicity of technique—there is usually considerable deviation in early exposure to mindfulness—and gently suggesting the correct technique as being easier (which it invariably is). It is also useful to use reflection methods, such as the *reflection with precision* method mentioned above, to develop an understanding of the client's experience through exploration, rather than jump to conclusions based on their initial word choices.

First, be clear about what sensations were being felt during the client's practice, and redirect the client toward actual sensation if necessary. Next, as the client describes what happened during the practice time, be aware of language that indicates effort/failure ("It was hard" or "not so good," "focus," "concentrate"), imagery or thought management ("I pictured a blank white screen to stop the thoughts," "I tried to stop thinking"). It is important to normalize these diversions, and point out that they are not unusual and are likely to continue to some degree, but they are not part of the technique. Finally, refresh the original simplicity of the practice by giving the simple instruction.

Anchoring Practice in Daily Life

Whether the client's practice is a formal sitting practice, or takes place during activities, daily practice should be encouraged as it is most helpful. It is better to shape the practice so that daily practice is doable, than to have an ambitious plan that the client does not execute on a daily basis. Having practice take place at specific, planned times of day, before or after other regular activities (right after morning coffee or tea, for example), is a good way to anchor the practice in the daily routine.

Recognizing Emergent Qualities

As already described, the attempt to be mindful and engage in practice can have destabilizing and potentially distressing effects. The clinician should also be on the look-out for signs of improved function or mood that are typical results of precise mindfulness practice. Among these are evidence of more choice points, where the client has a new ability to choose among courses of action rather than reflexively engage in habitual patterns: "Usually I would have just left when it started to get difficult, but instead I was able to pause and express myself more clearly." There is also, typically, evidence of more sympathetic awareness of others, and a sense of kinship. Traditionally this can be viewed as an emergence of compassion as the noise and confusion of the mind settles down with ongoing practice. In my experience, this is a quite common result of mindfulness interventions, and can be noted in some of the cases already described, as well as the following:

Client Case W: Compassion in flood

W had been participating in a client group about mindfulness in daily life, and had been practicing mindfulness for 10–20 min a day for about 6 months. He generally had positive reports about his practice, attributing to it a reduction in anxiety, greater stability of mood, a greater range of activities and "having more fun." In one session he reported waking to find water coming through the ceiling of his apartment from a pipe leak in the apartment above. As this had happened with some regularity over the decades that he lived in this apartment, W was instantly very angry at the landlord for "not keeping things in shape." He made an angry call, and awaited the repairman, rehearsing the angry speech he would give him. When he answered the doorbell and opened the door, he looked at the repairman's face and saw that "he was frightened" and this caused W's anger to dissipate and allowed him to have a more calm and business-like discussion about the work that needed to be done. "For the first time in my life I didn't have a shouting match." W reported that this was one of several times he noticed feeling more "warmly" toward others—something that had increased his social exploration and feelings of being more comfortable in daily life.

Conclusion

Mindfulness, like most other effective mental health interventions, is not a one-size-fits-all solution. Traditional Buddhist training takes this very much into practice: in the traditional view there are *84,000 teachings* because that's what it takes to meet the needs, capacities, and circumstances of each individual. The clinician's own mindful experience, accumulated through diligent daily practice, can provide the best guide for insight into how best to cultivate mindful experience with clients. It is important to recognize, however, that each clinician's experience with mindfulness training is shaped by the clinician's own characteristics and circumstances: a clinician who does not have ADHD or severe anxiety may be surprised by the obstacles faced by clients with these challenges, and not have direct experience with how these obstacles can be overcome. Thus it is hoped that a growing literature about the use of mindfulness in clinical practice will provide insights into the many conditions, concerns, obstacles, characteristics, and alternatives that need be accommodated in the clinic. While clinical trials addressing broadly defined conditions such as depression and substance abuse have been conducted with some success, it is to be hoped that systematic approaches to addressing more particular issues related to symptomatology, medical health, as well as environmental and relational conditions will be developed so that clinicians can successfully customize mindfulness interventions for their clients.

References

Amaro, A. (2015). A holistic mindfulness. *Mindfulness, 6*(1), 63–73. http://doi.org/10.1007/s12671-014-0382-3

Gotink, R. A., Chu, P., Busschbach, J. J. V, Benson, H., Fricchione, G. L., & Hunink, M. G. M. (2015). Standardised mindfulness-based interventions in healthcare: An overview of systematic reviews and meta-analyses of RCTs. *PloS One, 10*(4), e0124344. http://doi.org/10.1371/journal.pone.0124344

Goyal, M., Singh, S., Sibinga, E. M. S., Gould, N. F., Rowland-Seymour, A., Sharma, R., … Haythornthwaite, J. A. (2014). Meditation programs for psychological stress and well-being: a systematic review and meta-analysis. *JAMA Internal Medicine, 174*(3), 357–68. http://doi.org/10.1001/jamainternmed.2013.13018

Kabat-Zinn, J. (1994). *Wherever you go, there you are: Mindfulness meditation in everyday life*. Hachette Books. Retrieved from https://books.google.com/books?id=QnYBXlX2bPwC&pgis=1

Kabat-Zinn, J. (2003). Mindfulness-based interventions in context: Past, present, and future. *Clinical Psychology: Science and Practice*. http://doi.org/10.1093/clipsy/bpg016

Kanter, J. W., Busch, A. M., & Rusch, L. C. (2009). *Behavioral activation: Distinctive features*. Routledge. Retrieved from https://books.google.com/books?hl=en&lr=&id=L699AgAAQBAJ&pgis=1

Malinowski, P. (2013). Neural mechanisms of attentional control in mindfulness meditation. *Frontiers in Neuroscience, 7*, 8. http://doi.org/10.3389/fnins.2013.00008

Miller, W. R., & Rollnick, S. (2012). *Motivational interviewing: Helping people change*. Guilford Press. Retrieved from https://books.google.com/books?hl=en&lr=&id=o1-ZpM7QqVQC&pgis=1

Mingyur, Y., & Swanson, E. (2010). *Joyful wisdom: Embracing change and finding freedom*. Three Rivers Press. Retrieved from https://books.google.com/books?hl=en&lr=&id=5btipqRM8nAC&pgis=1

Paulson, S., Davidson, R., Jha, A., & Kabat-Zinn, J. (2013). Becoming conscious: The science of mindfulness. *Annals of the New York Academy of Sciences, 1303*(1), 87–104. http://doi.org/10.1111/nyas.12203

Segal, Z. V., Williams, J. M. G., & Teasdale, J. D. (2012). *Mindfulness-based cognitive therapy for depression, second edition*. Guilford Press. Retrieved from https://books.google.com/books?hl=en&lr=&id=1_NcsDZ17icC&pgis=1

Thrangu, K. (2003). *Pointing out the dharmakaya* (vol. 25). Snow Lion Publications. Retrieved from https://books.google.com/books?id=Fi5w-wNj0D8C&pgis=1

Trungpa, C. (2010). *The heart of the Buddha*. Shambhala Publications. Retrieved from https://books.google.com/books?hl=en&lr=&id=BdCjGgmMJcoC&pgis=1

Tsoknyi, R. (2013). Wisdom in Aging: Waking Up the Mind and Revitalizing the Subtle Body September 20–26, 2013, Garrison, New York, in 2013. https://www.youtube.com/watch?v=rj7rvvX6JJA&feature=youtu.be

Urgyen, T., Kunsang, E. P., & Schmidt, M. B. (1994). *As it is, volume 2*. Rangjung Yeshe Publications. Retrieved from https://books.google.com/books?id=23OQ9ozpYgsC&pgis=1

Williams, J., & Crane, C. (2014). Mindfulness-based cognitive therapy for preventing relapse in recurrent depression: A randomized dismantling trial. *Journal of Consulting and Clinical Psychology*, 82(2), 275–286. Retrieved from http://psycnet.apa.org/journals/ccp/82/2/275/

Chapter 7
Beginning with the Clients: Mindfully Reconciling Opposites with Survivors of Trauma/Complex Traumatic Stress Disorders

Robin Carnes and Terry B. Northcut

The world is full of suffering. It is also full of overcoming.
Helen Keller

Introduction

When I was 18 years old I found myself at a weekend yoga retreat held at an old farm in rural Virginia.[1] This was long before yoga enjoyed the modern day mainstream popularity it does now. I still remember the kinesthetic state I was in after the first class. I felt something down-shift inside me. I noticed a calm alertness I hadn't felt in…maybe ever. At the time, I couldn't articulate what I experienced; I just knew I needed more of it. Though it took me about 15 more years before I got serious about yoga as a regular part of self-care and health maintenance, this weekend planted the seed for a journey I never could have foreseen. In this chapter, I discuss that journey, the development of the "Warriors at Ease" Program, the challenges of mindfulness including reconciling opposites, and establishing a supportive environment for trauma survivors in mindful yoga.

Since 1995, when I quit my unfulfilling job as a management consultant, I have been avidly teaching and practicing mindful yoga and meditation. After several years of experience as a group facilitator, curriculum developer, and professional trainer in the corporate world, I began bringing yoga and meditation to groups of people who, due to a variety of economic and social factors, would be very unlikely to step inside a yoga studio. I worked with "at-risk" teen girls in a lock-down public

[1]Note: When the personal pronoun is used throughout the paper, it refers to the first author Robin Carnes.

R. Carnes (✉)
Warriors at Ease, Silver Spring, MD, USA
e-mail: rdcarnes@gmail.com

T.B. Northcut
Loyola University of Chicago School of Social Work, Chicago, IL, USA
e-mail: tnorthc@luc.edu

T.B. Northcut (ed.), *Cultivating Mindfulness in Clinical Social Work*,
Essential Clinical Social Work Series, DOI 10.1007/978-3-319-43842-9_7

high school and ran a volunteer yoga program at a homeless shelter and halfway house in downtown Washington DC for 10 years. After a deadly subway accident, Washington Metro management asked me to teach "meditation and breathing" to their employees traumatized by witnessing the wreckage. In all these situations and more, I had to find a way to bridge the gap between the upper middle class, primarily White, Sanskrit chanting, Hindu-tinged culture of U.S. yoga studios I currently taught and practiced in, and the practical suffering of the folks who thought yoga was for…well, somebody else. I found out that to be effective I not only had to change **how** I was teaching, but I had to change **what** I was teaching as well. Many people don't realize, even many yoga practitioners themselves, that every yoga and meditation practice is designed to have an impact on the practitioner that includes the physical, emotional, cognitive, and nervous systems. I needed to understand the neurophysiological impact of these practices and learn to administer them skillfully, because each one has the potential to address the underlying cause of trauma symptoms as well as provide relief from the symptoms themselves.

In 2005, my life took an unexpected turn as I began working on the Department of Defense's (DoD) first study of meditation. The pilot study was designed to find out if active duty service members with high scores on the PTSD Symptom Checklist (PCL) at Walter Reed Army Medical Center would participate in a 9-week study, attend class regularly, practice independently, and if their PCL scores would change as a result of this participation.[2]

It was at this time that I met clinical psychologist and yogic scholar, Dr. Richard Miller. Dr. Miller had been adapting an ancient, at that time little known, guided meditation practice called Yoga Nidra into his clinical psychology practice for over 20 years with outstanding results with a wide variety of trauma patients (Miller 2005). I asked Dr. Miller to consult on the Walter Reed study because of his uniquely suited expertise. Rachel Greene, the woman who had the original idea for the study, invited me to participate. Dr. Miller, Ms. Greene, and I worked with the staff of the Deployment Health Clinical Center and the Samueli Institute for over a year to design and recruit for the study.

While the number of participants in the study was small, study participants did come to class, did practice with their home practice CDs, and their PCL scores dropped precipitously. Just as the study ended, the DoD's Deployment Health Clinical Center, sponsor of the study, asked me to join the clinical team of their pioneering integrative Acute PTSD, Traumatic Brain Injury, and Medically Unexplained Physical Symptoms (MUPS) treatment program, the Specialized Care

[2]COL Charles Engel, Jr., MD, MPH (2) (3); Christine Goertz Choate, DC, Ph.D. (3) (4); Damara Cockfield, MPA (1); David W. Armstrong, Ph.D., FACSM (3); Wayne Jonas, MD (1) (3); Joan A.G. Walter, JD, P-AC (1); Matt Fritts, MPH (1); Rachel Greene (5), Robin Carnes, MBA (6); Kristie Gore, Ph.D. (2); Richard Miller, Ph.D. (7). 2006. Yoga Nidra as an Adjunctive Therapy for Post-Traumatic Stress Disorder: A Feasibility Study. Alexandria, VA: Samueli Institute and Department of Defense Deployment Health Clinicial Center and Walter Reed Army Medical Center. Uniformed University of the Health Sciences: MILCAM 2003: Contract MDA905-03-C-0003.

Program (SCP) as the yoga and meditation instructor. Active Duty Service Members stationed around the world and from all branches of the military were eligible for treatment at the SCP. An intensive 3-week outpatient program, the SCP saw eight patients at a time. These veterans suffered from the visible and invisible wounds of war. Further, many also came into the military with complex trauma. They presented with a myriad of diagnoses that the best military healthcare had failed to fully address. SCP patients were usually individuals, ages 20–55, 85% male, who had been treated for years in multiple military medical facilities and still had poor outcomes. The SCP was a last resort for most.

The SCP clinical team included an internist, a psychologist, a social worker, a physical therapist, myself as the yoga and meditation instructor, and at times an additional acupuncturist or massage therapist as needed. The patients were offered expert lectures on topics like PTSD and the brain, sleep hygiene, and post-deployment relationships and effective communication from various expert military health care providers. While a part of the SCP clinical team, I received regular supervision from Dr. Miller via phone and email. I saw the cohort of patients every day for 1–2 h, as the last activity of their structured curriculum. They came through the doors to see me exhausted after hours of grueling psychological and physical exertion.

From the start, the transformations I witnessed inside the small windowless room where we practiced yoga and meditation were astonishing. After a great deal of reluctance and resistanceto the experience, the vast majority of our patients reported some improvement in their sleep, their pain level, their mood, their ability to relate to their children and spouse, and their sense of meaning and purpose within a few classes. At first, I was almost as surprised as they were at how effective these simple practices, stripped down to bare bones, were. After hearing one after another tell me of their mindful experiences, I often thought to myself “I'll have what they are having!”

The patients and the skilled professionals on the clinical team taught me a great deal. I was also privileged to teach Deployment Health Clinical Center staff members in a weekly class as a way of addressing the ills of compassion fatigue. In addition, I worked with patients' spouses in a week-long adjunctive program. Those programs impressed upon me the price that military families pay for their loved ones' service. I was also given the opportunity to teach people hurt by a wide variety of traumas, e.g., childhood abuse, sexual abuse, sexual harassment and assault, medical trauma, and natural disasters. As a result, I witnessed the many ways that trauma shows up in people's bodies, hearts, minds, and spirits. Despite hearing extremely difficult and horrible traumas participants had gone through, I mostly felt extremely fortunate to be spending time with strong, courageous individuals to whom life had dealt such hard blows. Almost every person engaged in the process continued to show up because they didn't want this trauma to beat them, to take their life, and to win. Most were willing to try something new, something that at first blush seemed very weird to them. They were willing to admit that they had the wrong idea about yoga when they started to feel better.

A pattern emerged within the first few programs in which yoga and meditation was offered. The men and women would start the first week of the program angry that they had to do yoga and meditation and vocal about their disdain for the very idea. By week 3, they were often angry that they had had to suffer for so long without this kind of support, and that there wouldn't be yoga and meditation classes for them to continue their practice once they left in just a few days.

Warriors at Ease

It only took a few months of seeing these life-changing shifts in SCP patients to put a fire in my belly. Inspired by the courageous and authentic men and women I worked with, it became my mission to bring culturally informed, trauma-sensitive, and evidence-based, mindful yoga and meditation to military communities around the world. It was becoming increasingly clear, unfortunately, that the wars in Iraq and Afghanistan were not going to be brief endeavors. Simultaneously, I began to hear from yoga and meditation teachers all over the world asking about my work and wanting to help service members and veterans coming back from the wars, and as they cycled through multiple deployments, with mindful yoga and meditation. I got hundreds of emails and phone calls asking advice on how to do what I was doing. Many yoga and meditation teachers wanted to be of service to those service members who were serving our country, and they wanted help to do that well. I knew that the yoga training I had had before getting to Walter Reed was adequate for working with primarily, mentally, and physically healthy folks in a yoga studio. However, it was not adequate to address the needs of a population with a very distinct culture (a culture negatively inclined toward yoga), nor a population with a high incidence of trauma. We needed a specialized, advanced teacher training for those working in military communities.

I joined forces with several like-minded pioneering colleagues to prepare yoga and meditation professionals to teach safely and effectively in military communities. Karen Soltes, LICSW, Molly Birkholm and Colonel Pat Lillis, MD were all either teaching mindful practice to veterans or to active duty military personnel in places like the Washington DC-VA, the Miami VA or working inside the military for its adoption. We formed Warriors at Ease in 2009.

The mission of Warriors at Ease (WAE) is to bring the healing power of yoga and meditation to militarycommunities around the world, especially those affected by combat-stress, PTSD, and trauma. WAE accomplishes this by training and deploying certified mind-body professionals to settings where they can enhance the health and well being of service members, veterans, families, and health care staff at a reduced cost. To date, WAE has trained more than 700 teachers, many of whom are now actively teaching in VA Hospitals, Veteran Centers, militarybases, and military hospitals. Warriors at Easeteachers have proudly served with well over 100,000 veterans since our inception.

A plethora of research studies focused on yoga and meditation in specialized VA and DoD PTSD treatment programs continues to try to determine how best to provide cohesive, consistent programs. Results of studies have indicated that yoga for military service personnel with PTSD is effective (Johnston et al. 2015). Unfortunately, too often there is variability in the context and nature of how yoga programs are delivered (Libby et al. 2012). However, Mindfulness-Based Stress Reduction (MBSR) has shown effectiveness with veterans in alleviating symptoms of PTSD, depression and improving quality of life (Kearney et al. 2012; Kluepfel et al. 2013). iRest® Yoga Nidra has also been found to be effective with combat-related Post-Traumatic Stress Disorder (Stanovic 2011). In addition, breathing-based meditation has helped to reduce post-traumatic stress symptoms (i.e., respiration rate, startle responses, and self-report symptoms) in U.S. military veterans over a 1 note time period.

The need for new, effective, and affordable approaches to stress-related conditions including pain, insomnia, PTSD and anxiety, has given WAE the opportunity to integrate yoga and meditation into an ever-increasing number of VA and DoD facilities. The programs complement and strengthen the standard therapies for combat and other stress-related conditions. We also promote self-care and health maintenance for the military and veteran communities at large. WAE's evidence-based programing allows veterans and Active Duty Service Members (ADSM) to participate in an efficacious and empowering self-care modality that is beneficial to both their bodies and their minds.

Warriors at Ease teachers are trained to offer military and veteran students specific physical movements, breath, and meditation practices that science shows help to regulate the nervous system and activate the parasympathetic (relaxation) response, thus improving their ability to cope with pain. Just as with pharmaceuticals, there is no one-size-fits-all yoga approach, so our teachers are equipped with a wide variety of tools within their practice, including adaptive yoga techniques that allow the teacher to adapt the practice for conditions such as TBI, spinal injuries and amputations; breathing exercises; and trauma-sensitive meditation protocols, such as iRest® Yoga Nidra (described in chapter by Petersen, Zajakowski-Uhll, and Grossman this text). WAE teachers know how to work collaboratively with students to find a combination of practices for the most beneficial outcomes for each student. Utilizing programs through WAE and working with trauma survivors of noncombat related experiences has resulted in observing common themes that face every participant in a mindful yoga practice, the most striking of which is learning how to reconcile seemingly opposite and contradictory states to achieve the helpful benefits.

Reconciling Opposites

> There is a brokenness out of which comes the unbroken, a shatteredness out of which blooms the unshatterable.
>
> Rashani

There are now many texts that explain the neuro-physiology of trauma including its effects on the brain and body, as well as its common behavioral and physical symptoms (Anderson and Gold 2003; Cozolino 2010; Davidson and Begley 2012; Dickie et al. 2011; Doctor and Shiromoto 2010; Levine 2015; Miller 2003; Nelson and Carver 1998; Siegel and Solomon 2003; van der Kolk 1988, 2002, 2004, 2006, etc.). Rather than attempt to reiterate what astute scientists and clinicians have documented, a more simple thematic approach to understand how the mind and body process trauma will be utilized looking at the experiences of opposites. This approach is based both on what we know about neurophysiology and my experience as a mindful yoga and meditation instructor primarily working with trauma for over 20 years.

The philosophy and practice of yoga focuses strongly on opposites—the premise that everything in life arrives paired with its opposite (Miller 2003). It is in the conscious and purposeful holding of those opposites that said opposites are transcended and an underlying wholeness is revealed. Mindful Yoga, meditation, and trauma comprise an "alchemy" of opposites.

Stuck in the There and then Versus Present in the Here and Now

van der Kolk and van der Kolk & Najavits (2003, 2013, respectively), have described trauma as a condition of being "stuck in the there and then". That is, a person suffering from trauma relives the mental, emotional, and physical experience of the traumatizing event(s) (though it may not be consciously remembered) and is unable to decouple their present moment from the experience of the event that caused the trauma. Mindfulness is by definition a "here and now" phenomenon. So by learning to bring attention to his/her moment to moment somatic experience, mindfulness practitioners discover a portal to their own lives which is always happening only right now. Harris (2014) describes in his humorous account of learning meditation, that being in the here and now is the opposite of daily life thinking where we always expect a result. Being mindful is just "sitting with whatever is there". In so doing, the constant feeling of being in a waterfall of thoughts that include past experiences, future anxieties and obsessive ruminations, take a back seat. Harris describes it as "choiceless awareness" that allows him to move "behind the waterfall" of thoughts (2014, p. 138).

Chaotic Versus Structured

The after-effects of trauma are often described as chaotic. Alarming neurophysiological impulses arise unexpectedly, whether it is cold sweats, a flashback, or a migraine headache. The mind's attention chases after each physiological symptom as if it is trying to return a constant barrage of unruly serves in an exhausting and chaotic tennis match. All the while, the individual fights desperately to keep all of this inner mayhem under control so as to appear collected to the outside world. No surprise that people with trauma report feelings of unpredictability, instability, and disorder (Herman 1992, 1997; Northcut and Kienow 2014).

Mindfulness practices, specifically those that are trauma-sensitive, offer a sense of structure to the client. Here is a place to put your attention. Here is a way to bring it back when it wanders. Here is a way to orient your experience … a ground to put your feet on rather than floating in space bumping sharply into walls. Consistency can be the best panacea for such unpredictability. However, there are certain qualities needed in that kind of consistency. There needs to be "engaged consistency" or "consistent flexibility" as will be discussed in the next section.

Rigid Versus Flexible

One simplified way of describing a traumatic experience is when something happens that is truly overwhelming to the person to whom it is happening, he/she cannot thoroughly process what is occurring, but instead "steps away" from the physical/emotional/mental reality. As van der Kolk (2014a, b) states, "the body keeps the score," or the body remembers and stores the experience. The hugeness of the event(s) leaves the person feeling helpless and out of control. In order to mitigate the terror and vulnerability of helplessness, the trauma survivor may become quite rigid in their thinking and in their behavior. Perhaps this rigidity shows up in avoiding any and all situations that might re-trigger the traumatic response, thus narrowing one's life into specific predictable venues with specific predictable people. Another manifestation of the rigidity may be certain routines that have to be followed compulsively, or certain thought processes and beliefs that are rigid. Underlying it all is a desire to control life, to prevent the tsunami that swept over the individual unexpectedly in the past, from ever happening again (Segal et al. 2012; Thomas 2011).

Mindful yoga and meditation on the other hand, are about flexibility. In fact, that is how I used to define yoga for my beginning students at Walter Reed. Yoga is a practice that helps us be more flexible human beings. We may not have legs, or arms, or even all of our brain, but if we have breath, a body in any condition, and attention, we can do yoga. We can learn to feel comfortable in a wider variety of "poses," in a broader and deeper continuum of life situations. The seemingly paradoxical "consistent flexibility" manages and counters the relentless rigidity that has developed as a means to cope with the helpless experience of the trauma (Weintraub 2012).

The Body Is Dangerous Versus at Home in the Body

One of the most consistent reactions to trauma is the "disinhabiting" or dissociating from one's body. It is not hard to imagine why this is a very functional defense against overwhelming emotional and sometimes physically painful experiences. The individual perceives a threat so intense that staying present, actually feeling and sensing all that is occurring, becomes impossible. One's body becomes dangerous terrain, not safe for human habitation. The only way to survive is to escape via the only route possible—leaving the body, or parts of the body. Conscious somatic awareness shuts down (Herman 1992; O'Brien et al. 2008; Ogden and Fisher 2015; van der Kolk 2014a, b).

With mindful yoga and meditation, we invite people back, slowly but surely, to a life inside their body. This means feeling and sensing parts of themselves that they may not have been able to for years. The "reentry" occurs at a different pace for each person; no script or vision of the "typical" or "perfect" yoga or mindfulness exists. By its nature, being in the postures, working with the breath, and learning to abide in somatic experience is the route back home to one's body. What was once enemy territory is slowly brought back into a compassionately aware relationship and befriended. In a similar way in recent years we've seen the increase of sensory psychotherapies, designed to process and understand the "language of the body" that has been silenced through traumatic experiences (Levine 2010; Ogden and Fisher 2015). Likewise, yoga has been shown to reduce PTSD symptomatology by helping survivors tolerate physical and sensory experiences often associated with the fear and helplessness that accompanies trauma (Jindani et al. 2015; van der Kolk et al. 2014). Yoga and meditation are beginning, gradual steps that can facilitate this necessary reconnection and reorientation of mind and body.

Fixing Versus Welcoming

The human tendency toward self-improvement is a double-edged sword. We naturally have a yearning toward growth and fulfillment, and yoga and meditation can play a beautiful role in that journey. On the other hand, all of us wish to be something other than we are which often results in damaging self-criticism. This self-criticism is never more apparent than when learning to be mindful. Self-criticism amplifies or escalates to the point of criticizing a perceived inability to meditate "successfully."

People who have suffered trauma tend to have especially acute self-judgement and little tolerance for themselves. A self-image of brokenness, being tainted, or damaged can pervade their self-perception. There is no curiosity about the thoughts, feelings, and sensations that arise within, but instead many quick judgments and rejections are made about the body and the self. There is no friendliness, but instead a reflexive dislike of oneself and one's inner experience (Epstein 2013; Lang et al. 2012; van der Kolk 2014a, b; Vujanovic et al. 2011).

Thus, students may come to yoga and meditation, with a conscious or unconscious wish to fix themselves so they can be okay—to stop the bad stuff from happening. As a yoga instructor, I have to be mindful that if I convey that a certain style or experience level is a "best practice," I am conveying that students are not acceptable as they are. However, in yoga philosophy we learn that each human being is whole and complete as is, no matter how intensely she/he is suffering (Miller 2005; Weintraub 2012). This informs my perspective of myself, and my students in every aspect of interaction with them. For example, the way I assist students in their practices is by intervening very seldom once I give instructions. I intervene in their yoga posture, or breath work as little, as lightly, and as uncritically as possible. It is not about getting it right, or being super precise (which infers there's a wrong) but about being as curious and friendly toward one's experience, whatever it is, as possible. Linehan (2003) in her work with Dialectical Behavior Therapy offers a much more structured use of "radical acceptance" to reinforce and validate the present experience of clients who have great difficulty with affect regulation. The dialectic or tension between opposites is balancing acceptance of the present condition and circumstances with change. Mindful yoga, in contrast to the Linehan approach, is less structured and adaptable to each individual and what his or her body and mind can do at the present.

There is one word that best describes this most important quality of a mindful teacher and mindful student: it is the backbone of the practice of yoga. The word is "Welcoming" according to Miller (2003; and personal communications). Welcoming is a conscious, active receptivity to your own thoughts, feelings, and sensations, as well as to those of your students. Welcoming is also a curious, friendly, accepting attitude toward whatever unfolds, with no exceptions (Miller 2003).

Welcoming our own reactions as teachers or therapists is the first step in this process. As we welcome our own experience, even the feeling of being uncomfortable or fearful in the face of our students' reactions, it creates the space that has the potential to allow the students' own experiences to emerge and be worked with in a way that will ultimately provide integration between mind and body. In order to welcome our own experiences and those of our students we are assuming a basic trust in the inherent strength and resilience of ourselves and others. We develop a deep trust that the human psyche has the resources needed to process any challenges that arise in the class. It is different from the belief that we are all machines that operate based on the laws of physics or animals governed by drives and impulses. Instead we are born with inherent abilities, capabilities, and strengths that allow us to know, at some level, what we need if we are given a safe, secure yet flexible environment that can adapt to our needs (Weintraub 2012). We emphasize that our bodies know how to process experiences, including trauma, and that if we can learn to listen to the body, we will be able to move into challenging places as fast or slow as necessary.

It is important to recognize what welcoming is not. Welcoming does not mean that one never takes action to change the course of what is happening, just that whatever action is taken doesn't come from a place of fear or suppression. Welcoming does not have expectations of a certain level of accomplishment or a certain agenda for each class. Paradoxically, by trusting the client's process, and letting go of any need to speed things up or move toward an instructor's goal, the client can experience full acceptance which allows for a shift in perspective and experiences. Harris (2014) reports the Sufi Muslim quote "Praise Allah, but also tie your camel to the post" (p. 201). Figuring out what action is warranted and sufficient is one of the most difficult tasks. The only action necessary for the client is showing up for the class or appointment. The action for the teacher or clinician is to welcome the "person in the situation" at that moment. Integration happens as a result of resisting the urge to "over-act" in the moment and cannot happen if burdened with unnecessary expectations.

Fragmented and Separate Versus Attached and Connected

I've heard trauma survivors, whether combat vets or those that have suffered a sexual assault, say that they feel broken, shattered, and fragmented—separated from themselves, from others and from life itself. The defenses constructed to protect and sustain people in threatening situations, while functional, have a huge downside. The defenses put walls around certain memories, certain feelings, and certain parts of the body. They may require us to hide from ourselves and others. The vulnerability of seeing oneself and being seen as we truly are seems unbearable. Not surprisingly, traumatized people may feel very lonely and isolated, even from those they love the most because they instinctually withdraw to stay safe—just as a wounded animal may hide itself in protection (Ogden and Fisher 2015; van der Kolk 2014a, b).

The translation of the Sanskrit word *yoga* means "to yoke or bring together in union." And that is exactly what practicing mindful yoga does. In a myriad of ways the practices connect body, mind, emotions, and spirit. Experiences of strength and resilience are reconnected within a visceral way. As one veteran said of his meditation experience, "Most therapies focus on what is wrong with us. In meditation we feel what is right with us." Likewise, as the practitioner's system becomes more regulated, the fragmented bits and pieces of hurt, injury, and trauma come back to the surface and are integrated into the whole person. Individuals have a somatic experience of having the pain, but also being more than the pain. Siegel (1999), van der Kolk (2014a, b), Schore (2003), and others have described the process of "perceiving the interior" as interoception. When we have greater interoception, we are more empathic, which physiologically equals greater activity of the right insula and greater self-awareness of emotions (see chapter by Beck in this volume). For trauma survivors, regaining a relationship between the mind and body can be greatly facilitated via the process of mindful yoga (van der Kolk 2014a, b). Once the empathic capabilities are enhanced for the self, clients can be more empathic with others which also feeds back to enhance acceptance of the self. This reconnection process can be transformative, leading to what has also been studied and described as Post-Traumatic Growth, which includes qualities such as improved relating to others, an ability to perceive new possibilities, experience of personal strength and spiritual change, and a greater appreciation for life (Meichenbaum 2006; Tedeshi and Calhoun 1996, 2004). It is not enough for a teacher/clinician to be aware, however, of the need to reconcile these seemingly opposites. Some clients may initially feel "resistant" or disinclined to participate in mindful yoga.

Working with Resistance to Mindful Practices with Clients Who Have Suffered Trauma

> The greater the doubt, the greater the awakening; the smaller the doubt, the smaller the awakening. No doubt, no awakening.
>
> C.C. Chang

Depending on the clinician/teacher's own level of personal and professional experience with mindfulness practice, there are very few instances in which, skillfully rendered, these practices are contraindicated. However, given that mindfulness is still rather new to many people in the United States, a clinician who introduces mindfulness to his/her clients will likely encounter some confusion, and maybe even some resistance. This resistance may be even stronger in sub-cultures such as certain religious groups, more conservative regions of the country, or the military where there are stricter guidelines for acceptable behavior. Clients' objections may be that it is too "touchy feely," too "woo woo," or they worry they will seem weak or vulnerable. Some simply believe, "I can't do that." Others may be worried that they are going to release a floodgate of feelings and emotions that will prove overwhelming.

In my experience with clients, if I can "frame" the practices in a way that is relevant and accessible to the client, *and* if I can take a patient, creative, collaborative approach in offering the practices, it is almost always possible to find a practice or two that suits a given client. As a teacher, you need to be unruffled by the negativity and keep looking for the openings—sensing where the "wiggle room" is for this particular client. Of course, you are looking for a way to meet the client in a place that is within his/her "window of tolerance" (Siegel 1999). Most clients with trauma will not be able to sit in silence for very long without their minds "eating them alive." However, I have never experienced a deeper meditative stillness than at Walter Reed with some groups after 10–12 classes with me. The key is incremental change. In short, staying within the "Window of Tolerance" which facilitates baby steps that challenge the client just enough, but not too much. Siegel (1999) refers to the window of tolerance as a zone of autonomic and emotional arousal that is optimal for well being and effective functioning.

Neither hyper nor hypo arousal, it is the range in which "various intensities of emotional and physiological arousal can be processed without disrupting the functioning of the system" (Siegel 1999, p. 253). Over time, and not in a straight line progression, the window opens more and more which increases the zone so that information received from both internal and external environments can be integrated (Ogden and Fisher 2015).

While I was at Walter Reed I encountered almost every kind of resistance imaginable. The patients in this program arrived after trying every type of treatment the U.S. military had to offer and they were still in an extreme state of suffering. On the first day of the program at Walter Reed, I regularly met comments like the following:

- I can't do that.
- My head is too full of thoughts.
- That's against my religion.
- That's only for white women wearing spandex.
- That's only for gays.
- That's only for hippies.
- That's only for flexible people.
- That will hurt me.
- That's hocus-pocus.
- That's ridiculous.
- That's against my religion.
- That's a cult.
- I'm not a vegetarian.

I heard these objections so frequently that I developed a playful and nonconfrontive way to respond. I let students know that they had a right to their concerns, that I understood why they felt that way, and that I was not offering them a magic pill or panacea. Instead, hundreds of their fellow service members had come into the program with similar concerns, had given it a try, and found it to be very helpful in feeling less anxious, less depressed, less pessimistic, and less pain, increasing their ability to concentrate, sleep more hours and more soundly, and have better emotional balance. All I asked is that they give it a try (or two).

The clients' diagnoses ranged from acute PTSD, to Traumatic Brain Injury, to Medically Unexplained Physical Symptoms, to Military Sexual Trauma or Harassment, to chronic pain. There were a small percentage who were diagnosed with, and/or exhibited behavior indicating an underlying personality disorder, some had OCD, and a few had dissociative episodes. Many had histories of severe childhood trauma prior to entering the military. And there were those, male and female, who were survivors of sexual harassment and assault while on active duty.

Focusing on the natural functioning and regulation of the nervous system is a great way to explain and normalize why we practice mindfulness for students and clients. A practical, but not too technical explanation of the Sympathetic and Parasympathetic nervous system and how our bodies respond to traumatic or very stressful events makes their own experience much more understandable, normal, and not so personal. Using the example of when it rains outside is often helpful. When you are in the rain you get personally wet, however the rain is not personal. In the same way the central nervous system is not personal—it is geared to have an automatic reaction when danger is sensed. Meditation and yoga practice can provide the protection for when the central nervous system gets activated outside of one's awareness or control in order to retrain the body's response and manage the symptoms more effectively.

For example, I worked with a civilian woman who came to see me in my private practice who had also experienced trauma:

> Sylvia was referred to me by her therapist for mind-body skills instruction. Fifteen years earlier she had lost a brother and had developed and continued to suffer from severe anxiety. It affected her sleep, her physical health, and made her work life more difficult. She was on several kinds of medication to control her anxiety symptoms. Sylvia was a very smart, high achieving woman who was frustrated by the hindrances the anxiety put between her and her goals. During the first session Sylvia told me she wanted to learn to meditate in order to lessen her anxiety. After I had learned a little more about her and her goals for our work, we began a short, body-based, guided meditation. Immediately, her symptoms spiked and she felt panicky. I stayed composed, explained that there are many kinds of meditation, including moving meditation and that different people respond to different types of mindful practice. We then did some physical yoga postures to ground her in her lower body. She often used aerobic exercise to manage her symptoms so I reaffirmed that method and started teaching her to notice the feeling of energy in her body. She was able to tune in and stay focused on her physical sensations when I paused and repeatedly asked her to report on her experience—uncensored, as "there is no way you can do this wrong".
>
> Sylvia's anxiety was so intense that she often felt she would be overwhelmed by it. She responded most readily to things that helped her feel physically grounded and/or strongly drew her mental focus via physical sensation, for example, breath practices or chanting. She left most sessions feeling empowered rather than as if she was being chased by monstrous feelings. Sylvia came weekly to learn mindfulness in a variety of forms – we did physical asana, qi gong, Inner Resource meditation (drawn from Richard Miller's iRest yoga nidra), chanting and breath practices. We circled back to some things that had "worked" before, and when they didn't seem to be hitting the spot, I introduced new practices. Sylvia began a home practice of yoga postures and qi gong. She began reading about mindfulness.
>
> Within a year she decided to work with her psychiatrist to taper off her sleeping medications and other meds. She found herself able to respond more peacefully to challenges in her life. She got better at self-care and didn't judge and drive herself as relentlessly. About two years into our work together, Sylvia was able to sit in silent meditation for 10 min or so after we did some mindful physical movements together in our sessions. She was also able, some sessions, to engage in an iRest meditation dialogue (this is a one version of iRest) in which the instructor asks simple questions like "What sensation are you noticing now?" and "where do you feel that emotion in your body?" and "can you describe the sensation in your foot a little more fully?"). Her window of tolerance opened significantly through her courage and commitment to growth, and our patient, collaborative work, without an agenda or timetable.

Creating a Supportive Environment to Mindfully Reconcile Opposites

> When the other person is hurting, confused, troubled, anxious, alienated, terrified; or when he or she is doubtful of self-worth, uncertain as to identity, then understanding is called for. The gentle and sensitive companionship of an empathic stance…provides illumination and healing. In such situations deep understanding is, I believe, the most precious gift one can give to another.
>
> Carl Rogers

The thinking mind, already very active in most of us, is even more dominant with people who have trauma—and most of those thoughts are negative. When the system is stuck in flight/flight mode, our minds attempt to anticipate and preempt any and all potential threats (and even some that are not threats but the mind perceives them to be). Being "in our heads" is a way we try to protect ourselves. Though it is stressful to be thinking so much, it starts to feel normal to many people. Mindful practice may feel threatening to our clients' habitual attempt to stay in control by thinking. So how do we create a safe environment that encourages people to be vulnerable to try something different, to step out of their stressful comfort zone? What is the best environment to "reconcile opposites" so important to experiencing the benefits of mindful yoga? There are a number of suggestions that I have found to be helpful through my years of practice. They include creating a safe physical space, installing an inner resource with each student, modeling mindful curiosity and friendliness, preparing alternative plans, encouraging to make healthy choices, inoculating to prepare for inevitable emotional releases, directing mindful attention to the physical body, using voice and silences skillfully, refraining from surprises or unanticipated practices, working collaboratively with clients/students, approaching mindfulness practices as "experiments," allowing but never forcing playfulness, and finally, engaging in regular, personal, mindful practice. A brief explanation of each of these suggestions clarifies why they can lay the foundation for students/clients to increase their window of tolerance in mindful yoga and reconcile their own experiences of negotiating or reconciling opposites.

Creating a Safe Physical Space

When working in institutional settings, like hospitals or prisons, the instructor, may have little or no control of what is going on in and around the space in which to work. For example, I recently spoke to two colleagues who teach in prisons. One told me that her yoga class is held in a room close to the firing range where guards practice shooting and that the gunshots are constantly ringing in the ears of the students with complex PTSD.The other colleague described an open air space right in the middle of a chaotic prison unit with loudspeakers shouting bulletins, radios from the cells playing at top volume, and prison staff walking in and out of the area constantly. She said the environment made her so anxious the first few times, she could barely function.

Even though the instructor may not have complete control over the physical surroundings, there are ways to help make the mindfulness session physically "more safe." Think about the room that you are working in from the perspective of a hyperalert and hyperaroused person. When possible, make sure that the client(s) has the option of facing the door. Having one's back to the door can feel dangerous. Clients should be able to choose where to sit/stand/lie down in the room. Ask about having radios, etc., quieted during just the time of the class. If there are closets or cupboards in the room, it may help ease clients' minds to show them inside the cupboards in order to alleviate the worry about who or what may be lurking there. And you may want to keep the lights up, rather than dim the lights low. It may be stressful to traumatized people not to be able to see their surroundings for fear of anticipated danger.

Installing and Utilizing the Regular Usage of an Inner Resource

For some students/clients, this simple meditation is key to helping them feel more in control and able to regulate themselves. Many trauma modalities, such as EMDR, include the use of such a resource. Dr. Miller's iRest calls the resources, Inner Resource. As a mind-body practice, students are taught to access their Inner Resource using all of their senses and their imaginations. To find their Inner Resource, students are asked to bring to mind a scene in which they feel comfortable and at ease (Avoid the use of the word "safe" because so many of my students at Walter Reed told me that they had never felt safe in their lives. Asking them to find a "safe" place was both impossible and reinforced their sense of pessimism and that they were different than "normal" people). I give lots of options to seed their imagination—someone you love being with—a pet or a person, a place you love to be in nature, or an activity you love doing. It could be a memory, from current life, or even something totally imagined, something seen in a book or a movie.

Then I guide the students to see themselves in the scene and to look around at the sights, hear the sounds, taste the tastes, and notice the way being in the Inner Resource feels in their bodies. With every instruction, especially when the resource is just being installed, give plenty of time for students to really land in their bodies and feel their way.

As a mindfulness teacher, your job is to help the students access this state of simple well-being by utilizing all of their bodily senses—that is, NOT to make it conceptual, but embodied. In doing so, the body releases the same healthy hormones and responses as it would if one were actually in the situation one is imagining. The student learns to self-regulate by regularly practicing the access of this Inner Resource and can call upon it when feeling overwhelmed and triggered. For example:

> Tony, an Iraq war active duty service member suffers from PTSD and a Traumatic Brain Injury. His doctors had ordered an MRI several times and each time Tony would show up at the clinic for his test, get prepped, and as he was going into the chamber, his anxiety would become so intense, he would have to leave before completing the MRI. He told me, "I feel so defeated by my PTSD that I can't follow through with this simple procedure." Then Tony entered a PTSD program where iRest was being taught every day. At his fourth iRest session, Tony showed up beaming and reported that he had been able to complete the MRI he had scheduled the prior evening. He said that he drew upon his Inner Resource before and during the procedure, focusing on staying with that sense of comfort and ease in his body. "I feel victorious. I was in control of my PTSD. It was no longer in control of me."

In order to be readily available and effective as needed, students need to practice accessing an Inner Resource when they are not stressed or triggered; just as you have to lift weights daily to be able to lift a big weight in an emergency. Accessing Inner Resources can be utilized at the beginning of every mindfulness session with clients to reconnect them with it in order to use it anytime students begin to feel shaky, or out of control.

Modeling Mindful Curiosity and Friendliness

Always show up as curious and friendly, the two primary qualities of mindful attention. The more you can feel this way, the more clients can feel this way. No matter what the client's response to the mindful practice is, teachers respond in a curious and friendly manner. Nothing is off limits, wrong, or surprising. This teaches mindfulness more effectively than anything that can be said about it.

So what happens if someone has an abreaction, or someone walks in unexpectedly or there is a loud, unexpected sound? You can weave any and all of these things into your teaching seamlessly by modeling curiosity and friendliness.

For example, a car backfired outside the class where I was teaching a meditation session with a group of active duty service members with PTSD. The sound was like a gunshot and several of the students startled. I said something like, "Notice the unexpected sound outside the building. Now, be as curious as you can about the way your body and mind are responding right now. Notice your heart rate. Has it changed? Notice if any of your muscles tensed. If so, where do you notice the tension? How intense is it? Did your breath change in any way upon hearing the sound? How does it feel now?" After a few moments, depending on the intensity of the unexpected sound, the class can continue where it left off. Thus anything that happens, as long as it is not actually dangerous, is an opportunity to orient curious, friendly attention toward oneself and become more familiar with yet another state of being in this mind and body. Mindfulness is demonstrated as something that can be brought to any and all aspects of life, not just peaceful and calm states, as a helpful tool, a way to be in all the situations and circumstances that life brings.

Preparing Alternative Plans

Be prepared with a couple of practices to share. You may have a sense of what will suit the client. And then have 2–3 other practices you can offer. It is very common for trauma clients not to respond "by the book." The more readily you can normalize their response and offer them something else to try, the less likely your client will feel like he/she isn't getting it, or that this is just not going to work.

Encouraging Making Healthy Choices

Encourage clients to make good choices for themselves—including not to do as you suggest. It's extremely important when offering mind-body practices to trauma survivors to frequently reassert that they are in charge. I do this in a variety of ways. I mention before we begin any new practice that everyone responds differently. What is important is for the client to take good care of him/herself. That may mean letting me know at any time that this practice is not working today. I always tell the client a little about the practice we are going to try and I ask, "Is this something that you are up for today?" When the original trauma(s) happened, the client was likely in a situation where there were either no choices—being trapped or forced—or only bad choices. When we give the reins to the client and encourage them to make good choices, we are facilitating the healing of that aspect of the trauma and offering a chance to relearn how to care for one self. It is empowering and gives a sense of self-efficacy to say, "NO," as much as to say, "YES".

Inoculating to Prepare for the Inevitable Emotional Releases

Tell the client prior to any mindful practice that it is possible that the practice itself may elicit emotional material or emotional release. Part of the function of mindfulness is to reconnect us with what has been cast into the shadows or fragmented. It is normal if emotional material surfaces. The client can be reassured that you are there with them, no matter what. By preparing the clients, you are in a sense inoculating the clients against future emotional overload, which builds trust in your relationship with them. Mindfulness is not a panacea, nor an escape from themselves or life.

Directing Mindful Attention to the Physical Body

Focus on mindfulness in all practices. No matter what mindful practices you offer your clients, make sure you guide them with direct, simple inquiries about their immediate experience. Whether you are trying a new practice for the first time, or you are offering something you have taught them many times, ask questions to direct their nonjudgmental attention to their physical, somatic, kinesthetic sensations. For example:

> Ask: Where do you feel this in your body? What do you feel in your feet right now? Has your body temperature changed? Up or down? Where do you feel the most sensation? Where do you feel the least? Where is the body warmest? Where is the body coolest? Where do you feel tingling? Where do you feel numbness? Where is there tightness? Where is there openness?

Simply asking "what are you noticing" may be too open a question for many people with trauma. Asking specific body-based questions that there are no right/wrong answers for, helps develop mindful attention. Mindful attention to the body re-shapes the neural networks away from their orientation to thought and reorients people to living in their "felt sense," down below their necks. It sets up new habits of lived experience. According to the latest neuroscience, the cognitive capacities of the mind cannot be maximized without the emotional engagement systems being activated (van der Kolk 2014a, b). Combining activities that are top-down (to activate social engagement) with bottom-up methods (to calm physical tension in the body) (van der Kolk 2014a, b, p. 86) yields a greater ability to shift participants from "fight or flight" to being able to more effectively perceive danger and manage relationships. Tuning into one's felt sense offers the opportunity to notice and respond to this plethora of useful information, rather than overriding it with thoughts. This opens up many more options for clients in terms of self-care, noticing emotions before they are so intense they hijack actions, and helps facilitate the process of re-inhabiting and befriending the body. The more people are able to sense and feel, the less their thinking mind with its negativity bias will dominate their experience. The more people are out of their thinking minds, the more they are able to feel less judgment, less comparing, less competing, and as a result, less suffering.

Using Voice and Silence Effectively

Dr. Stephen Porges' Polyvagal Theory and other theorists in the neurobiology of attachment are emphasizing the importance of voice tone and prosody as strong signals, usually outside of awareness that humans read to determine the safety of the interpersonal relationship (Geller and Porges 2014). Consider how people talk to their dogs, or babies. Most of the time we talk in the higher register of our voices, we have a lilt to our voices, even almost a singing quality to the voice, a warm tone, and an even rhythm. When you are giving mindful instructions to your clients, be aware of the sound of your voice. Using the lowest registers of voice may not add to the feeling of safety and support that allows the client's healing process to progress. Record yourself leading a practice and then ask people who will tell you objectively how it "feels" to listen to you. Just as you want to understand the impact yourvoice has on class participants, it is important to also understand how silences are experienced.

Writer Anne Lamott describes well what can happen during silence, "My mind is like a bad neighborhood. I try never to go there by myself" (Lamott 1997). The thinking mind is often a "bad neighborhood," and it is really dangerous when trauma has been experienced. Leaving periods of silence is like asking someone to let their guard down and go into that bad place alone. Most people will need, not just prefer, to be anchored in the practice by your voice. Regular, kind, invitations to the present moment experience in the body, gentle reminders about coming back to the focus of the meditation, orient the client to their immediate experience, rather than being at the mercy of their mind. As the client's window of tolerance opens more widely, he/she will be able to tolerate longer periods of silence. Always keep your eyes open, even when practicing with a client. Stay tuned to his/her facial expressions, body language and movements. This will inform you how much verbal support is needed.

Refraining from Surprises or Unanticipated Practices

People with trauma are constantly trying to control their environments and control themselves and their chaotic, intense inner experience. As previously noted, doing mindfulness practices that take them out of their familiar and comfortable over-thinking habit, can feel very vulnerable, even out of control. Thus, it is very important to explain "the what" and "the why" of the practice you offer, before you start. Ask to see if they have questions or concerns before you begin. Even when you have been working with a client for a long time, it is best to mention to the client if you plan to add something or delete something. Routine and rituals feel safe. Knowing what you are going to do feels safe. Telling clients about even small changes in the process, builds trust and helps clients more readily move into the process.

Working Collaboratively with Clients/Students

In my experience, students love it when I don't know it all. When I rely on them to know and share with me their experience, whether it's good, bad or ugly. I tell them the first day that for this to be worthwhile, for them to have a chance at getting what they are looking for out of the work we do, we have to work together. And then I demonstrate that I really mean it by asking for not only what they experienced but if they have any ideas about how to modify what I've offered them to make it even better, or to avoid any unintended reactions they may have encountered. Unless I have some reason to think that what they come up with as a way to practice mindfulness is going to hurt them, I applaud their inventiveness and encourage them to try it out.

For example, one of my clients loves using imagery to regulate his anxiety. It's not really my thing, but it's my job to listen to what supports him, what he will actually practice on his own, and go with it. He brings in snippets of images, memories, and fantasies to almost every session and we talk about the important words for me to say in his meditation, as well as the important words for me NOT to say during the meditation. I need to "get" what about each scenario is important and soothing to him. Then and only then do we dive in and I lead him in a meditation completely based in his self-sourced imagery. I've given him complete permission to interrupt me at any time, during the meditation itself, or after, and tell me specifically what is or is not helpful. I also record the sessions for his home practice. We act as a creative team.

Approaching Mindfulness Practices as Experiments

Many people enter into learning something new with a fear of "getting it wrong" or "not being able to do it right." This conditioning is at odds with a truly curious and friendly approach to mindful practice. To counteract this largely unconscious straining to get the right answer or lie low so you don't get called out for doing it wrong, I like to approach mindful practice as an experiment. I explain to clients before we begin that while each practice I offer is intended to help them feel more balanced, calm, energetic, focused, or whatever their goal is, every practice is received differently for each practitioner each time. So a breathing practice, for example, that feels calming, even soporific for one person in the class can be agitating for another. That's why it is so important for each participant to tune into his/her experience and give me feedback on what they notice about the practice's effects. Depending on what they tell me about it, I might suggest a modification, or even suggest that they sit that one out for a while and try it again another day. To help them get a better gauge of the impact of each practice I suggest they do one, two or three self-assessments before and after the "experiment." I say: "Index 1 is the Anxiety scale. If 0 is no anxiety, just calm and alert and 10 is a panic attack, where do you place yourself right at this moment?" I invite their attention inside their neck, shoulders, back, belly, and they give themselves a number. I might even ask them to write it down, especially if there is someone with Traumatic Brain Injury in the room. I only ask the students to share their numbers if I have a clear sense that the group feels very comfortable with me and with each other.

"The next index is the Pain scale. If 0 is pain-free and 10 is excruciating, unbearable pain, where are you right now?". And finally, I may add, "The last is the

Thought Traffic Scale". If 0 is very few thoughts/cars on the road and there is lots of space between the thoughts/cars and 10 is gridlock traffic with several ambulances with screaming sirens going stuck in the jam: "What is happening in your mind right now? What number describes your thought traffic flow best right now?"

With these three questions people get a more precise sense of how they feel "before" the "experiment." If I ask them to tell me their answers, I can get a better sense of how each person in the room is on these important scales and I can adjust my lesson plan accordingly.

Once one or more scales are completed, we do the practice. Just as the practice is completed, before anything else, I ask several open-ended questions about their experience, primarily their felt sense in the moment. Then we re-take the scales. This method offers them a way of "gathering the data" from the experiment and quantifying their response to the practice without judging their "scores."

Finally, when I ask for numbers on the "after" scales, or just ask for a show of hands on how many went up on this scale, down, or stayed the same, it allows me to normalize all the "data." With a group of any size, or even two people, students quickly see that these practices are not a "one size fits all," and this is a relief. For every 4–5 hands that go up indicating they felt less anxious, or less pain, or lighter thought traffic, there are always one or two that say the opposite. And this frees up everyone to welcome his/her experience as it is—liberating everyone from the tyranny of doing it right—being able to be present with what is happening in the moment.

As a mindfulness teacher, this "experimental approach" offers me a lot of opportunities: I get a reading from the room and I am able to modify my plans for the group; I get to invite and demonstrate full acceptance of the diverse experiences students have; and I get to offer students choices about how and if to participate in a way that feels good for them; all of which creates more support, more trust, more mutuality, more freedom, and more welcoming in the room.

Allowing (But Never Forcing) Playfulness

It happens to be my nature, when I'm at my best, to be playful with people. And I find that playfulness is not, in many situations, an inappropriate stance to take with individuals who are in great distress. There is a way to be with people which allows their humor, their ability to see the absurd, even their light heartedness to have room to express itself without any pressure to be "cheerful," and without any denial of the darkness that brought them into the room. There are some movements from Qi Gong, meaning "energy work," that is a corollary to yoga, but stems from Chinese traditional medicine. Simple Qi Gong moves don't involve the same kind of "make this shape" directive that yoga postures connote, even when the teacher invites a noncompetitive attitude.

One such movement involves gentle jiggling of the body in a standing position with the knees bent. I first ask students to move their legs in a way that allows the bowl of their pelvis to jiggle as if it was full of Jello cubes: "You want to move in such a way that every single cube gets to mingle with every other cube at the party." Then you continue from the pelvis, adding the shoulders and arms, back, buttocks and finally every part of the body is jiggling loosely off the bones. It looks very silly and childlike, but for most people it feels good, freeing, and childlike. Almost no one can do it with a straight face. I always got such a kick of seeing these serious, muscled service members looking at me with complete disbelief as I demonstrated this and asked them to join me. Most would make the leap and everyone would have a good laugh at how ridiculous they felt. There was lots of gentle teasing and good fun; a shared moment of delight. After a minute or two, I'd slowly taper off the shaking and direct their attention to their rooted feet, their legs, and the countless sensations in their bodies. I would ask them to describe in a word or image what they sensed. "Fizzy," "bubbly," "tingly," "heat," "vibration," "pulsing," and "like a jellyfish" were common responses. This is a moment of mindfulness, a moment to explore sensation, generated by gentle movement, with curiosity and friendliness. A moment to be present in the body right now. From there, it was an easy segue to pointing them to the "fizzy" feeling as prana or qi as the life force, the invisible electricity that animates the body.

Another way I introduce mindfulness on the first day of class, or a first client session, is using small porcupine massage balls for foot massage. Many of the patients in the Walter Reed program were really worried that yoga was going to hurt them because they weren't flexible, or because they had a lot of injuries. We sat in chairs and I invited them (always their choice) to take off their shoes and socks and play with the sensations of these massage balls on their feet. We did all kinds of exploratory things with the balls while I asked open-ended questions about sensation in the moment. I kept redirecting their attention to their immediate experience when distractions arose. Not only did they feel relieved that yoga wasn't necessarily going to hurt them, it felt good and we got to examine the quality of the mind to move away from immediate experience and to reorient it. By using this kind of behavior, we are easily moving into a mindful experience.

Engaging in Personal, Regular, Mindful Practice

People can tell if what you offer them is something you are just recommending for them versus something you do for yourself and you are sharing from your own experience. Being authentic is one of the ways we as mindfulness instructors build trust. Having your own mindfulness practice is a way you can underline several important messages to your students/clients. First, this is so important, I do it for myself. Second, I am a human being just like you and we all need ways to care for ourselves. And third, mindfulness is not just for "weirdos" or "sick people," it's for all of us humans.

Your own practice will inform your skillful and facile use of mindfulness with your clients. Even if you haven't had exactly the response of every client to every practice, you know, for example, what it feels like to push yourself too hard in a breath practice and how quickly the body pushes back with a sympathetic response of increased heart rate, muscle tension, etc. So when you teach your client, you are not likely to forget to explain how important gentleness and patience is in breathwork. While you don't have to be a therapist to offer therapeutic mindful practices to clients/students with trauma, you do need to be a skilled mindful practitioner to do this kind of work effectively.

> Somehow, in a body experiencing very physical effects of depression and other multiple severe physical injuries, when I practiced yoga, I had less pain. In a world that felt like 24/7 chaos, like a battle zone at times, the mat gave me an anchor with which to align.
>
> Thank God for that 3x6 floor space because it was where I could simply breathe without suffocating.
>
> Taylor (2015, p. 28)
>
> U.S. Marine Veteran and Military Sexual Trauma Survivor

Conclusion

> I think, ultimately, healing comes through the body, and that the mind is informed, or comes to understand through the body.
>
> Dr. Richard Miller

The Warriors at Ease approach (WAE), as I've attempted to describe here, relies on a mindful yoga and meditation instructor who can skillfully bring the opposites into play. We train our teachers to meet students where they are, as they are, and help them find and access the opposite within themselves thereby, re-claiming "wholeness within." WAE also adopts a Public Health perspective in recognizing the importance of understanding the misconceptions and concerns that many people in U.S. culture, not just the military, have about yoga and meditation. We use secular, simple, practical language that frames the practices in terms of their practical outcomes, outcomes that are pertinent to the students. We strive to make what we offer accessible and relevant because we know that this is what makes skeptical people willing to overcome their discomfort or resistance and try something new.

And, most importantly, we train our teachers to be creative and flexible in their ability to create a safe container for students who have diminished capacity to be present in their bodies. As van der Kolk (2014a, b) states, "Self-regulation depends on having a friendly relationship with your body" (p. 97). Mindful yoga and meditation can offer a roadmap back to that friendly relationship, but only if the classroom is a safe space.

In conclusion, we come to a final pair of opposites. Some of the key leaders in the field of integrative medicine have described Talk Therapy as a "Top Down" approach that activates the social engagement of clients, a safe relational field for healing and growth. On the other hand, Yoga and Meditation are viewed as a

"Bottom-Up" method to regulate the Autonomic Nervous System and allow clients to self-soothe (van der Kolk 2014a, b, p. 86). I suggest that mindful yoga and meditation, when skillfully taught with an understanding of the need reconcile opposites within a consistent, supportive relational container, offers both.

References

Anderson, F. S., & Gold, J. (2003). Trauma, dissociation, and conflict: The space where neuroscience, cognitive science, and psychoanalysis overlap. *Psychoanalytic Psychology, 20*, 536–541.

Cozolino, L. (2010). *The neuroscience of psychotherapy*. New York: W.W. Norton & Company.

Davidson, R. J., & Begley, S. (2012). *The emotional life of your brain*. NY: Penguin.

Dickie, E. W., Brunet, A., Akerib, V., & Armony, J. L. (2011). Neural correlates of recovery from post-traumatic stress disorder: A longitudinal fMRI investigation of memory encoding. *Neuropsychologia, 49*(7), 1771–1778.

Doctor, R. M., & Shiromoto, F. N. (2010). *The encyclopedia of trauma and traumatic stress disorders*. New York: Facts on File.

Epstein, M. (2013). *The trauma of everyday life*. New York: Penguin Press.

Geller, S. M., & Porges, S. (2014). Therapeutic presence: Neurophysiological mechanisms mediating feeling safe in therapeutic relationships. *Journal of Psychotherapy Integration*, 24 (3), 178–192 (Washington, D.C.: American Psychological Association).

Herman, J. (1992). *Trauma and recovery*. New York: Basic Books.

Herman, J. (1997). *Trauma and recovery: The aftermath of violence—from domestic abuse to political terror*. (Reprint from original 1992 ed.). New York: Basic Books.

Harris, D. (2014). *10% happier: How i tamed the voice in my head, reduced stress without losing my edge, and found self-help that actually works - a true story*. NY: Harper Collins.

Jindani, F., Turner, N., & Khalsa, S. B. (2015). A yoga intervention for posttraumatic stress: A preliminary randomized control trial. *Evidence-Based Complementary Alternative Medicine, 2015*, 1–8. doi:10.1155/2015/351746

Johnston, J. M., Minami, T., Greenwald, D., Li, C., Reinhardt, K., & Khalsa, S. (2015). Yoga for military service personnel with PTSD: A single arm study. *Psychological Trauma: Theory, Research, Practice, and Policy, 7*(6), 555–562.

Kearney, D. J., McDermott, K., Malte, C., Martinez, M., & Simpson, T. L. (2012). Association of participation in a mindfulness program with measure of PTSD, depression and quality of life in a veteran sample. *Journal of Clinical Psychology, 68*(1), 101–116.

Kluepfel, L., Ward, T., Yehuda, R., Dimoulas, E., Smith, A., & Daly, K. (2013). The evaluation of mindfulness-based stress reduction for veterans with mental health conditions. *Journal of Holistic Nursing, 31*(4), 248–255.

Lamott, A. (1997). *My mind is a bad neighborhood I try not to go into alone*. http://www.salon.com/1997/03/13/lamott970313/

Lang, A. J., Strauss, J. L., Bomyea, J., Bormann, J. E., Hickman, S. D., Good, R. C., et al. (2012). The theoretical and empirical basis for meditation as an intervention for PTSD. *Behavior Modification, 36*(6), 759–786.

Levine, P. A. (2010). *In an Unspoken Voice: How the Body Releases Trauma and Restores Goodness*. Berkeley, CA: North Atlantic Books.

Levine, P. (2015). *Brain and body in search of a living past*. Berkeley, CA: North Atlantic Books.

Libby, D. J., Reddy, F., Pilver, C. E., & Desai, R. A. (2012). The use of yoga in specialized VA PTSD treatment programs. *International Journal of Yoga Therapy, 22*, 79–87.

Linehan, M. (2003). *Cognitive behavioral treatment of borderline personality disorder*. New York: Guilford Press.

Meichenbaum, D. (2006). Resilience and posttraumatic growth: A constructive narrative perspective. In L. G. Calhoun & R. G. Tedeschi (Eds.), *The handbook of posttraumatic growth: Research and practice* (pp. 355–368). Mahwah, NJ: Lawrence Erlbaum.
Miller, R. C. (2003). Welcoming all that is: Nonduality, yoga nidra and the play of opposites in psychotherapy. In J. J. Pendergrast, P. Fenner, & S. Krystal (Eds.), *The sacred mirror: Nondual wisdom and psychotherapy* (pp. 209–228). St. Paul, Minnesota: Paragon House.
Miller, R. (2005). *Yoga Nidra: A Meditative Practice for Deep Relaxation and Healing*. Boulder, CO: Sounds True, Inc.
Miller, R., (2015). *The iRest Program for Healing PTSD: A Proven-Effective Approach to Using Yoga Nidra Meditation and Deep Relaxation Techniques to Overcome Trauma.* Oakland, CA: New Harbinger Publications, Inc.
Nelson, C. A., & Carver, L. J. (1998). The effects of stress and trauma on brain and memory: A view from developmental cognitive neuroscience. *Development and Psychopathology, 10*(4), 793–809.
Northcut, T., & Kienow, A. (2014). The trauma trifecta of military sexual trauma: A case study illustrating the integration of mind and body in clinical work with survivors of MST. *Clinical Social Work Journal, 42,* 247–259.
O'brien, C., Gaher, R,M., Pope, C., & Smiley, P. (2008). Difficulty identifying feelings predicts the persistence of trauma symptoms in a sample of veterans who experienced military sexual trauma. *J Nerv Ment Dis, 196*(3):252–255. doi: 10.1097/NMD.0b013e318166397d.
Ogden, P., & Fisher, J. (2015). *Sensorimotor psychotherapy: Interventions for trauma and attachment*. New York: Norton.
Schore, A. N. (2003). *Affect regulation and the repair of the self.* New York: W. W. Norton & Company Inc.
Segal, Z. V., Williams, J. M., & Teasdale, J. D. (2012). *Mindfulness-based cognitive therapy for depression* (2nd ed.). New York: The Guilford Press.
Siegel, D. (1999). *The developing mind: How relationships and the brain interact to shape who we are*. New York: The Guilford Press.
Siegel, D., & Solomon, M. (2003). *Healing trauma: Attachment, mind, body, and brain*. New York: W. W. Norton & Company.
Stanovic, L. (2011). Transforming trauma: A qualitative feasibility study of integrative restoration (iRest) yoga Nidra on combat-related post-traumatic stress disorder. *International Journal of Yoga Therapy, 21,* 23–37.
Taylor, S. P. (2015). *Just roll with it: 7 battle tested truths for building a resilient life*. www.innovopublishing.com
Tedeshi, R. G., & Calhoun, L. G. (1996). The posttraumatic growth inventory: Measuring the positive legacy of trauma. *Journal of Traumatic Stress, 9,* 455–471.
Tedeshi, R. G., & Calhoun, L. G. (2004). *Posttraumatic growth: Conceptual foundation and empirical evidence*. Philadelphia, PA: Lawrence Erlbaum Associates.
Thomas, C. A. (2011). Healing trauma. In B. Boyce (Ed.), *The mindfulness revolution* (pp. 153–158). Boston: Shambhala by Random House.
van der Kolk, B. A. (1988). The trauma spectrum: The interaction of biological and social events in the genesis of the trauma response. *Journal of Traumatic Stress, 1*(3), 273–290.
van der Kolk, B. A. (2002). Posttraumatic therapy in the age of neuroscience. *Psychoanalytic Dialogues, 12*(3), 381–392.
van der Kolk, B. A. (2003). The neurobiology of childhood trauma and abuse. *Child and Adolescent Psychiatric Clin, 12*(2), 293– 31.
van der Kolk, B. A. (2004). Psychobiology of posttraumatic stress disorder. In J. Panksepp (Ed.) *Biological psychiatry,* 319–344 Hoboken, NJ: Wiley-Liss.
van der Kolk, B. A. (2006). Clinical implications of neuroscience research in PTSD. *Annals of the New York Academy of Sciences, 1071,* 277–293.
van der Kolk, B. A., & Najavits, L. M. (2013). Interview: What is PTSD really? Surprises, Twists of History, and the Politics of Diagnosis and Treatment. *J Clini Psychol, 69*(5) 516–522.

van der Kolk, B., Stone, L., West, J., Rhodes, A., Emerson, D., Suvak, M., & Spinazzola, J. (2014). Yoga as anadjunctive treatment for posttraumatic stress disorder: A randomized controlled trial. *J Clin Psychiat, 75*, e559–e565.

van der Kolk, B. A. (2014a). *The body keeps the score*. New York: Viking.

van der Kolk, B. A. (2014b). Yoga as an adjunctive treatment for posttraumatic stress disorder: A randomized control trial. *Journal of Clinical Psychiatry, 75*(6), 559–565.

Vujanovic, A. A., Niles, B., Pietrefesa, A., Schmertz, S. K., & Potter, C. M. (2011). Mindfulness in the treatment of posttraumatic stress disorder among military veterans. *Professional Psychology: Research and Practice, 42*(1), 24–31.

Weintraub, A. (2012). *Yoga skills for therapists*. New York: Norton.

Chapter 8
Beginning with the System: Using Meditative Dialogue to Help Couples Develop Compassion and Empathy for Themselves and for Each Other

Susan A. Lord

Introduction

Couples come to therapy for many reasons. Often they report a "stuck place" that they have repeatedly come to, and have not been able to move beyond. They say that they experience this as a "here we go again" centrifugal force of negative interaction that they feel incapable of escaping. It is a place of phantom pain; pain that, as with an amputated limb, continues to be present and enacted in the relationship despite the absence of the original circumstance. It may be pain that is, for example, related to family of origin issues, traumatic experiences, relational losses, emotional or physical illnesses, or even factors resulting from poverty and/or oppression. This stuck place may have to do with difficulty experiencing empathy and compassion for themselves and for others, as they have become caught up in struggling to have a voice or a sense of stability in interactions with intimate partners. It is a place where it seems that the same conflict is enacted over and over again in attempts to come to some solution or closure. It is a place where they may become flooded with feeling and lose the ability to reason. The couple may become hopelessly helpless and, if they are unable to disengage, tend to spiral down into negative interaction patterns.

Attaining a softening and flexibility in these interactions involves a certain interpersonal positioning and an investment in creating space for dialogue, a space in which each listens and speaks in order to understand and to move the conversation forward. According to Kabat-Zinn (1994), "mindfulness provides a simple but powerful route for getting ourselves unstuck, back in touch with our own wisdom and vitality" (p. 5). And, I would add, mindfulness can help couples get "unstuck" and back in touch with the wisdom and vitality of the relationship through enhanced empathy and compassion. While not all couples are able or

S.A. Lord (✉)
Department of Social Work, University of New Hampshire, Durham, USA
e-mail: susan.lord@unh.edu

T.B. Northcut (ed.), *Cultivating Mindfulness in Clinical Social Work*,
Essential Clinical Social Work Series, DOI 10.1007/978-3-319-43842-9_8

willing to participate in mindfulness practices, these practices can become a source of great solace and strength, and a huge resource for those who are open to them.

One of the ways mindfulness practices can become a resource for couples to use within the therapeutic session is in the form of "Meditative Dialogue". Meditative Dialogue is a term that I have developed to describe a process of collaborative interaction that "combines meditative practices of sitting and listening to the space between the breaths with postmodern collaborative practices of "not-knowing"" (Lord 2007, p. 334). This chapter offers an overview of selected literature on the use of mindfulness and couple's therapy. It describes a simple and innovative Meditative Dialog practice which can help couples to develop compassion and empathy for themselves and for each other as they work to strengthen and heal their relationships from the inside out.

What Is Mindfulness?

In order to understand meditative dialogue, it is important to understand what is meant by mindfulness, as there are many different definitions, just as there are different types of mindfulness and meditation, as evident in the chapters in this text. Mindfulness can be defined as a state of being, cultivated through a meditation or a contemplation practice that encourages presence, openness, compassionate acceptance, witnessing, and nonjudgment (Bishop et al. 2004). Germer defined mindfulness as "moment-by-moment awareness" (2005, p. 6). Kabat-Zinn (2003) offered a succinct definition of mindfulness, "mindfulness is the awareness that emerges through paying attention on purpose, in the present moment, and nonjudgmentally to the unfolding of experience moment to moment" (p. 145). While mindfulness has been practiced for hundreds of years, recent clinical, empirical and neurological studies have been "rediscovering" its many benefits.

Recent literature on the neurological impacts of mindfulness practices suggests that mindfulness offers great promise for facilitating change processes in therapy with couples. In her 2014 paper "The Mindful Couple," Judith Siegel writes about the capacity of couples to "incite and enrage" one another, and also to calm, soothe and "restore emotional balance" to each other and to their shared system (p. 282). She discusses the ways in which mindfulness interventions can help to "establish safety in the treatment process and allow the couple to productively explore and discuss problems and stressors" (p. 284). Siegel also emphasizes mindful breath work as an intervention that helps to slow things down, calm amygdala activity, and decrease hyperarousal and rumination that might interfere with productive and meaningful communication.

Tang et al. (2015) offer a comprehensive review of the current state of research on mindfulness meditation. Specifically, the authors examine how mindfulness meditation helps with focus, emotion regulation and self-awareness. Although the authors acknowledge that understanding the "mechanisms that underlie the effects of meditation is therefore still in its infancy…there is emerging evidence that mindfulness meditation might cause neuroplastic changes in the structure and function of brain regions involved in regulation of attention, emotion and self-awareness" (Tang et al. 2015, p. 10). Roberts (2007), in his article reviewing research on the interface between neuroscience and psychotherapy, suggests that traditional verbal methods of couple's therapy need re-thinking, "Mindfulness practices can help calm the amygdala and foster living more in the present by reducing the intrusion of past negative memories" (p. 14). He recommends the use of nonverbal techniques, understanding more about how the brain impacts each partner, and using mindfulness techniques to create new experiences during sessions.

Richard Davidson and his colleagues at the University of Wisconsin-Madison studied the effects of compassion meditation on the brain (Davidson and Lutz 2008; Lutz et al. 2008; Slagter et al. 2011). They found that "expert" meditators, Buddhist monks who had meditated for 10,000–50,000 hours in a variety of traditions, including compassion meditation, exhibited high levels of activation in the insula, an area said to be important in detecting emotions, and in the temporal parietal lobes, particularly in the right hemisphere, an area that has been linked to processing empathy. Their findings support their hypothesis that people can cultivate compassion and empathy through practicing compassion meditation, which may be able to "enhance emotion sharing, as well as perspective taking" (Lutz et al. 2008, p. 4).

A 2011 study at Massachusetts General Hospital in Boston found that meditators were able to increase the density of gray matter in the hippocampus of the brain, as well as in other areas related to memory, self-awareness, empathy, and learning (Holzel et al. 2011). The authors concluded that participation in an 8-week MBSR course developed by Kabat-Zinn (1994) increased gray matter concentration in the brain regions that were "involved in learning and memory processes, emotion regulation, self-referential processing, and perspective taking" (Holzel et al. 2011, p. 36). Meditation practices were also found to result in "enduring changes in brain structure that could support improved mental functioning" (Holzel et al. 2011, p. 42).

In addition to studies examining neurological changes as a result of practicing mindfulness, there is a great deal of work exploring acceptance and nonjudgment of oneself and of others. Mindfulness practices aim to facilitate self and other awareness, empathy, compassion, and a focus on the present moment, all of which can help with issues that arise in intimate relationships. In their 2007 randomized controlled study on the use of mindfulness practices in couples work, Carson, Carson, Gill, and Baucon looked at the effects of a couples-based mindfulness intervention, modeled on Kabat Zinn's mindfulness program, on relationship satisfaction using pre- and post-tests that included a Quality of Marriage Index, a Global Distress Scale, an Exciting Activities Index, an Acceptance of Partner Index, and an Individual Relaxation Index. They found that couple relationships grew stronger through relaxation, acceptance, and "mutual engagement in exciting, self-expanding activities" (Carson et al. 2007, p. 518). Mindfulness practices have been shown to increase empathic concern and perspective taking in intimate relationships (Wachs and Cordova 2007). Gambrel and Keeling (2010) also identified mindfulness as an intervention in marriage and family therapy that has been shown to improve relationship satisfaction, develop empathy, and improve physical, emotional, and mental health.

Additional literature on couple work emphasizing the use of mindfulness in the development of empathy and compassion has focused on: researching evidence based practices that aimed to increase couples' communication skills, helping with attunement, and developing empathy and compassion (Angera and Long 2006; Atkinson 2013; Baer and Krietemeyer 2006; Gottman 2011; Jones et al. 2011; Neff and Germer 2013), enhancing intimate relationship skills through mindfulness practices (Barnes et al. 2007; Beckerman and Sarracco 2011; Burpee and Langer 2005; Carson et al. 2007; Christensen et al. 2004; Gambrel and Keeling 2010; Gehart 2012; Jacobson et al. 2000; McCollum 2011; Nanda 2013; Napoli 2011; Pruitt and McCollum 2010; Wachs and Cordova 2007), and developing capacities for empathy and compassion by the use of mindfulness (Bell 2009; Block-Lerner et al. 2007; Csaszar and Curry 2010). All of these results support mindfulness practices as offering promising results for the development of empathy and compassion in couple work. They can help to facilitate awareness, acceptance, openness and nonjudgment in the present moment, all of which can help with intimate relationship issues.

It is clear that there is a great deal of interest in understanding how mindfulness can facilitate the development of empathy and compassion in couple work, however, what is less clear is how mindfulness can be used in session with both members of the couple present. Surrey (2005) has written about what she calls "co-meditation" in sessions with clients. She describes the co-meditation process as deepening and enlarging the therapy process, "it begins to show a quality of growth consistent with the broader goals of mindfulness" (p. 95). My work on Meditative Dialogue helps to fill the gap of how mindfulness can be used with a couple during the therapeutic hour (Lord 2007, 2010).

The Space in Between: Sacred Space

One of the elements critical to the use of Meditative Dialogue in couple's therapy is the intentional co-creation of what I call "sacred space" by the couple and therapist during the session (Lord 2010). Sacred space is space that is safe and secure. It is co-created in the middle of the room by the therapist and the couple. This sacred space may hold spiritual energies and become an alchemical crucible that can withstand and metabolize whatever may come. It may be the only space that the couple has had that is emotionally and physically safe and is uniquely theirs.

In his book *Playing and Reality* (1971), Winnicott spoke of transitional space or potential space as important to the process of creativity and to change processes.

He described transitional space as an intermediate realm of experience in which inner and outer realities are separate-yet-related. Potential space is that intermediate area of experience where creativity is said to occur. The sacred space in between for couples can be said to be a transitional or a potential space where new experiences can be created.

I have been fascinated by the energies of the space that is cultivated in between as I work with clients to change and heal their relationships. In my work with couples I think of myself as a facilitator of process and as a coach to their interactions. We are each differently empowered, and the work occurs in this co-created space in between us. Nobody is *performing* the "work" of the therapy, all of us are cultivating the energies and fanning the flames of the crucible that we tend and develop. Wisdom arises from the space in between, and the process of sitting together in silence and "just being" seems to alter our very chemistry and helps position us for meaningful dialog. Before we can begin any dialogue, we work to develop the sanctity of this co-created space in between. And so, the process of sitting and meditating together during each session becomes a ritual to create a safe and sacred space from which to bring forth agency and talk about what really matters.

Meditative Dialogue

Meditative Dialogue is a structured collaborative dialogical practice that I use at the beginning of each session as a way of inviting couples who are open to experiential and mindfulness practices into the room. It helps them to become fully present and engage in interaction from a place of deep connectedness with themselves and with each other. It encourages the development of one's abilities to deeply listen to the wisdom of one's inner dialog and to the wisdom that arises from the carefully tended intimate space in between each other in couple's therapy. It helps to move partners to a position of curiosity and openness, increasing self-compassion, and compassion and empathy for each other. The process of sitting and meditating in the presence of one's partner promotes an experience of what clients have described as a grounding and "molecular or cellular rearrangement" that helps them to position themselves differently as they negotiate the stuck places in their relationships.

Although not all couples are able to immediately sit and meditate together in the therapy session, it is a skill that can be learned, and those who are open to it can gradually move to a place of sitting in silence and cultivating empathy and compassion. Once clients have indicated an interest in meditative dialogue, we discuss the practice of meditation and, if they have not meditated before, I instruct them very simply about: checking in somatically and relaxing and grounding themselves; breathwork—taking long slow and deep belly breaths, observing their thoughts as they pass through, focusing on a meaningful phrase or a mantra that they find useful, repeating it on the in-breath and again on the out-breath; and sitting in silence for a period of time. Although it can be difficult in the beginning for a couple to focus and to sit in the room with their eyes closed, it becomes a practice that they come to value and request.

Empathy and Compassion

Empathy

Empathy, generally conceptualized as the ability to "put oneself in another's shoes" or, in the Native American tradition, to "walk in their moccasins," is a highly complex concept. Essentially one can never truly "understand" another human being, even, or perhaps especially, couples who may have been in relationship for as many as sixty plus years. Longevity of a relationship does not ensure knowledge of self or of the other.

Decety and Jackson (2006) described empathy as "the capacity to understand and respond to the unique affective experience of another person" (p. 54). They identified three components of empathy: (1) an affective response that often includes sharing another's emotional state, (2) an ability to cognitively understand the other's perspective, and (3) an ability to self-regulate and avoid confusion between one's own and another's feelings. The third characteristic, an ability to self-regulate and avoid confusion, tends to be a major focus of work with couples, as they often have difficulty separating out what is happening within and outside of themselves in intensely heated moments. Self-awareness is of paramount importance in this process, and a lack of self-awareness contributes to difficulties in understanding the feelings of one's partner and being able to offer empathy (Decety and Meyer 2008).

Jacobs (2013) speaks of an empathic attunement that goes beyond that described by others, and is developed through a process of moving beyond careful and attentive listening and beyond being able to imagine oneself into another's experience. He said that in order to be able to be empathic with another, one has to embrace the chaos and complexity of not knowing what would arise in the interaction, along with an openness to "creations on the part of the analyst" (p. 166). These included the analyst's own unbounded reveries, fantasies, memories, intuitions, daydreams and dreams. He spoke of a co-created process between analyst and client in which a conduit was opened between the two through which both conscious and unconscious communications could flow. This required a certain state of mind, and an evocative form of listening through which there was an experiential understanding of what was being communicated. This kind of listening called forth openness and curiosity on the part of both analyst and client, and a sense of wonder as to what would be communicated verbally and nonverbally, consciously and unconsciously. This sense of wonder, deep listening and openness to the unknown is a goal of the Meditative Dialogue process. Many of the skills of a good therapist are human interaction skills that a couple might do well to cultivate: kindness, curiosity, openness, nonjudgment, acceptance, empathy, compassion, and listening evocatively.

Daniel Siegel coined the acronym COAL to describe qualities enhanced by mindfulness practices (2007). Curiosity, openness, acceptance and love are all ways of being in relationship with ourselves and with one another that have the capacity to effectively shape our lives and our lived experiences. They are particularly useful ways of being as we strive toward honest and meaningful compassionate dialogue in couple's work.

Compassion

Compassion is said to begin with empathy and move beyond awareness of another, to a desire to alleviate the other's suffering (Gehart and McCollum 2007; Germer 2009). Although suffering is said to be a part of the human condition, Germer emphasizes the importance of surpassing acceptance of that suffering in order for emotional healing to occur. He also talks about self-compassion, saying that we must "turn toward" emotional pain rather than avoid it, and work actively to ease our pain through self-compassion. By "turning toward" pain, Germer is encouraging what Kabat-Zinn has termed "full catastrophe living"—embracing the richness of life, including "all of its dilemmas, sorrows, tragedies, and ironies" (1990, p. 5). Germer states that it is critical to accept one's self: "Self-compassion is a form of acceptance. Whereas acceptance usually refers to what's happening to us—accepting a feeling or a thought—self-compassion is acceptance of the person to whom it is happening. It is acceptance of ourselves while we are in pain" (2009, p. 35). Through accepting one's self and embracing the fullness of all that life has to offer, one can become more present and open to oneself and thus more available to another. "Mindfulness meditation may also cultivate compassion less directly by the continued practice of suspending judgment, which may extend beyond the present moment to inform practitioners' feelings toward themselves and others" (Kozlowski 2013, p. 94). Compassion, I would add, also involves acceptance of others while they are in pain, a positioning that is crucial to intimate relationships.

Positioning, Otherness, and the Capacity to Be Alone in the Presence of Another

Positioning, a sense of otherness, and having the capacity to be alone in the presence of another are all components of healthy couple relationships. All three of these components can be cultivated and become enhanced through engaging in the Meditative Dialogue process in couple's therapy.

Positioning

In the pursuit of empathy and compassion, positioning is everything. According to Rober, "positioning implies a spatial metaphor linking a voice with a point of view from which one observes reality. Each point of view gives one a perspective, but at the same time it has inherent limitations…" (2015, p. 109). In couple work, it then becomes useful to not only cultivate a positioning of empathy and compassion in the therapist, but also in each partner in the couple. As they are so familiar to each other, they may be in the habit of assuming that they know what the other means, feels, and thinks. In many ways they may be able to predict or call forth a response from the other, having turned away from the other as subject and begun to experience the other as an object of projection. They *know*, with an inviolable certainty, what is going to happen.

I often will ask couples, "How do you know what you know?" in an attempt at helping them to position themselves in embodied and open ways of knowing. I encourage them to check in with their physical selves, and I am interested in ways of knowing that move beyond intellect and include somatic awareness, emotions, and spirituality. The reparative act of deliberately positioning oneself to listen evocatively with curiosity and openness requires a certain form of courage, a willingness to leap off from the "known" into the cyclone of not knowing. It also requires a trust and faith in the process of dialogue, and in the very fabric of the relationship.

Otherness

Lyman Wynne coined the term "rubber fence" to describe the boundary that families construct around themselves to keep themselves in and keep others out, thus preserving the integrity of the whole (Simon et al. 1985). In a sense, an intimate relationship requires a rubber boundary around the external perimeter of the couple so that the couple is able to safely and resiliently withstand the work that must be done from the inside out. Each person in the couple must be willing to lose his/her bearings and launch into the unknown with curiosity, openness, acceptance and love as he/she listens to understand, and to propel things forward to territories unknown in new and unfamiliar ways. This boundary not only preserves the integrity of the couple, but also helps to create a safe environment within which a sense of one's partner as "other" can be preserved.

One of the most difficult and intriguing ongoing challenges about being a member of a couple is holding onto a strong sense of separateness and self, a sense of what I call *otherness*. Often partners speak of losing their identities when they are in a couple. They talk about needing to give up their sense of self for the greater good of the partnership. Much of relationship has to do with compromise and negotiation. Common goals and ways of being generally bring people together and may become lost over time as individuals grow and change. Relationships are ideally about creating and maintaining a safe haven, a partnership of mutual respect and trust, a feeling of being supported and challenged to develop and live from one's authentic self, and a willingness to flexibly grow and change together and apart over time within the larger boundaries of the relationship.

In my work with couples, the beginning phase of treatment tends to be about helping them to remember who they are and what brought them together. What attracted them to one another? One of the truths of many couples is that over time they begin to treat one another in ways that they would never dream of treating others. They lose sight of themselves and each other, and may regress to much younger versions of themselves in their interactions.

Couples move through developmental phases together, within the relationship and as individuals. Their choice of partner may have to do with what they are trying to work out in their own development. While some may go through many phases in one relationship, others may move through an evolution of self in several relationships. I recently ran into an acquaintance I hadn't seen in years who told me that she had just gotten married for the third time. I laughingly said that she seemed to have entered the realm of the perpetually hopeful, and she quickly responded, "No: good, better, best."

The Capacity to Be Alone in the Presence of the Other

One important aspect of maintaining a solid sense of self and of wonder with one's partner is the cultivation of that sense of otherness. Winnicott (1958) spoke of the importance of the capacity to be alone in the presence of another as a sign of maturity. He said that sitting in silence in the presence of another and "just being" was a process that could help to develop a strong sense of self or "I-ness" that he thought was critical to authenticity and enlivenment. "After being—doing and being done to. But first, being" (Winnicott 1971, p. 99).

Out of the ability to be alone in the presence of one's partner comes what I would call *true dialogue*, dialogue that is an authentic expression of each partner and consists of listening and speaking to understand and move the conversation forward.

Dialogue

Dialogue in Couples Work

Dialogue, from the Greek *dia*, translated as *through*, and *logos*, meaning *word*, refers to "social exchange and the generation of meaning and understanding through it"

(Anderson 2007, p. 34). Dialogue is a relational activity that involves listening, hearing, and speaking with the intention of learning, trying to understand, and respectfully inviting conversation toward an improved relationship. It encourages multiple voices and opinions, and an honoring of difference and otherness.

So often the difficulties that couples encounter have to do with defending a position or a way of being, listening to promote a certain sensibility rather than listening to understand the other, or attempts to change or control the other in order to fit them into an idea of how things should be. Compounding these difficulties, couples generally come to therapy having developed years of patterns of interaction and preconceived notions or frames for how things are going to go or how much change is possible. The phrase "familiarity breeds contempt" is an apt one, as we work to untangle the snarls of negative wiring and interactional patterns. It is important in the beginning of becoming a couple, and throughout the life of the couple, to approach each interaction with "beginner's mind," for "in the beginner's mind there are many possibilities, but in the expert's there are few" (Suzuki 2011, p. 21).

Creating Space for Dialogue and a Sense of Other

Peter Rober asks a critical question in his article on how to create space for dialogue in couple work. He states that in couple work there is so often tension and conflict, even violence: "How can dialogical space be created in the therapy session, in such a way that there is room for growth and understanding?" (2015, p. 110). Dialogical space is defined as space in which there is a free and spontaneous flow of communication "in which mutual understanding and intimacy can grow" (p. 110). According to Rober, there is a constant tension between expression and nonexpression in relationships, and what is actually said or not said is not the final outcome of a process, but rather a momentary freeze frame of this tension, uniquely shaped by the dialogical context. A positive aspect of this tension is that the process continues and the outcome can be radically changed with attention to developing and sustaining dialogical space that is compassionate, empathic and open.

Talking With, *Rather Than* At *or* To

The goal, then, is to cultivate dialogue in which there is a sense of wonder, of discovery. The goal is to stand next to one another and to try to see what the other sees, a goal that begins with loving the other. One doesn't fall in love with another because they are *like* you, an other is never like you, and always different from you. In a sense love means something like, "I cannot know you, I will never be able to know you." The acceptance that the other is unknown can breathe life and curiosity into the relationship. All of our relationships, particularly our most intimate relationships, begin with that premise and need to remain so.

Dealing with the challenge of the otherness of one's partner is an ongoing project that continues throughout the whole of life. It is never finished because a tension between expression and nonexpression is always present. Not knowing, with a curiosity about not knowing, represents a paradox of staying in the moment in order to be able to hear the other, while also realizing we can never truly know the other. Transparency and authenticity are of paramount importance in the pursuit of talking with an other. The Open Dialogue approach offers a good example of this in a grounded and embodied way.

Open Dialogue

The Open Dialogue approach, which originated in Finland as an alternative approach to healing psychosis, "emphasizes creating a common language, holding multiple voices, and embodying a stance of 'being with'" (Olson et al. 2012, p. 421). Olson and colleagues speak of the importance of the activity of listening in the beginning phase of dialogue, and of making room for everybody's voice democratically so that everyone is able to have their say and the interaction occurs relationally in the space between people.

Seikkula and Trimble (2005) described an "embodiment of love" that developed in their work with clients through dialogical interaction, which they said marked "moments of healing" (p. 473). "The feelings of love that emerge in us during a network meeting are neither romantic nor erotic. They are our own embodied responses to participation in a shared world of meaning co-created with people who trust each other and ourselves to be transparent, comprehensive beings with each other" (p. 473). This embodiment of love is palpable in the Meditative Dialogue process. It is particularly powerful in couple work, as the couple is tending to the very fabric of their relationship and investing in developing skills for continuing to fuel the fire of their intimate connection into the future.

Meditative Dialogue Guidelines

Meditative Dialogue softens structures and patterns of communication, opening flexibility, curiosity and creativity in couple therapy. Through the process of meditating together and following the guidelines it appears that the relationship becomes more important to each partner than the small self or ego. Each is able to experience being alone in the presence of another. Perspective opens, the lens is pulled back and there evolves a harmony, unity, oneness and openness to possibility. The act of participating together in Meditative Dialogue, of committing to the process and to the vulnerability of sitting in silence with eyes closed, and speaking from a place of deep listening, makes it possible for a different kind of conversation to occur between partners. Hearing one another and creating a new frame for the relationship, developing new meaning together, changes the dynamic so that the interaction feels alive and always characterized by "beginner's mind." In our work together, the process of following structured guidelines encourages each of us to tune in to energies beyond the manifest dialog within, without, and between:

1. Focus on the breath, body sensations, and on the space in the middle of the room.
2. Reflect, contemplate, and pause.
3. Listen deeply.
4. Allow speech to arise from silence.
5. Experience the space.
6. Notice assumptions.
7. Notice reactions and judgments.
8. Give the process full attention.
9. Say only what really wants or needs to be said.

We begin each session in silence with a ten minute meditation, which quickly moves the members of the couple and the therapist to deeper levels of concentration and openness. We sit facing one another with our eyes closed. When we are ready, we open our eyes, speech arises from the space in between, and dialogue ensues. As we engage in this process together over time, there is a deepening of connection of inner and outer worlds and we give voice to our inner conversations, venturing into unknown territories and using breath and somatic awareness to ground our interactions. "Somehow the shared communion and the shared fanning of the flames of meditation heighten the energy and sense of possibility in the room as we work together on the material that arises from the space in between" (Lord 2010, p. 279). As needed, we also may use the Meditative Dialogue guidelines at different times during sessions to slow things down and connect with ourselves and with the space in between.

This is a space of wisdom and of openness to listening to understand and promote one's life and that of one's partner. The process of meditating together can increase intimacy, and open the couple to an elevated sensory awareness that can access creativity, love, and profound change processes that move them to new and previously inaccessible levels of interdependence and authenticity.

Illustration

John and Rachael were a couple in their late thirties who began therapy following a crisis in which Rachael, who had been previously diagnosed with Bipolar Disorder, had made a suicide attempt by overdosing on her medications, and had been hospitalized. Both John and Rachael had significant trauma histories, and both were professionals in the mental health field. They shared a practice with several other mental health professionals, and were reportedly viewed by outsiders as having a "perfect marriage." They had a son, age 13, and said that they were concerned about how he viewed their marriage, as he had observed many of their frequent conflicts. They said that they wanted to improve their marriage so that it could become a model for their son's future relationships. In the beginning they made no mention of wanting to improve their relationship for themselves or for each other. They seemed interested in the view of their marriage from the outside in, and consequently much of our beginning work had to do with a focus on inhabiting their marriage and learning to live from the inside out.

When they began they said that they were having trouble communicating and connecting with each other. They had been together since college, and Rachael and John's recurring argument centered on his needing to have clarity as they discussed things, and her "going from zero to one hundred the minute we begin to discuss anything." Both agreed that they could use some help with listening to understand rather than listening to make a point.

Each appeared to be extremely intelligent and highly verbal. John tended to be more even-tempered and rational, while Rachael described herself as extremely emotional. In our first session together I asked them to not speak, as the flurry of words seemed to be getting in the way of our therapeutic process. Borrowing from Linehan's model of Dialectical Behavioral Therapy, we decided to use nonverbal and embodied, or physical practices in our work together in order to help them to cultivate "wise mind" (1993, p. 215) in their interactions with each other. I asked them to sit in silence facing each other and just look at each other. Both seemed to soften as they looked at one another, and Rachael began to cry, saying, "I miss you." He responded a bit defensively that he was "always here," and we talked about presence, and how easy it is to show up and not be there in spirit. We moved from there into the Meditative Dialogue process, as it seemed to be a perfect vehicle for cultivating an embodied way of slowing things down and "being" together without words. We took five minutes and followed the guidelines, closing our eyes, focusing on the breath and sitting in silence. When the time was up, we opened our eyes and waited for the dialogue to arise from the space in between.

Rachael and John had developed a very clear intellectual sense of what went wrong in their interactions and didn't seem to have any idea about how to change things. They had been together for eighteen years, and had, in a sense, grown up together in their marriage. While they clearly loved each other and were committed to their relationship, there were some major issues and patterns that had developed and needed to be changed.

One of the glaring issues in their relationship was that they had stopped being present to each other, and had stopped listening to each other. Both were extremely self-critical and had difficulty looking outside of their self-loathing to be able to position themselves to listen to the other. Their trauma histories had impacted their abilities to experience the world from the inside out, as they were both in the habit of hypervigilantly scanning the environment to be sure that they were relatively safe. They needed help with remembering who they were to themselves and to each other. They needed to be reminded that they were safe. In addition to this, John had developed a pattern of dismissing Rachael, and didn't really listen as she spoke. Rachael's response was to become extremely emotional; she would become flooded with feeling and would be unable to continue in a rational way, which would result in John "shutting down."

Though both John and Rachael had trauma histories, they had participated in many experiential workshops and appeared open to the process of Meditative Dialogue. We sat in a small circle of three and began each session with a ten minute meditation. We began with a body scan, then began focusing on our breath and each of us would focus on the mantra we had consensually adopted, "I am." When we opened our eyes we would wait for the conversation to arise from the space in between.

Rachael began, "I feel that you don't take me seriously since my suicide attempt. That you no longer see me as your partner, but as a burden—one more thing that you have to be responsible for and take care of." John nodded, "I do feel afraid of losing you. And it's hard for me to feel that you are able to be my partner because of it. I've taken care of people all of my life. That's what I know how to do. I'm good at it." They went on to talk about patterns that they had had for years, in which he had not been able to take her seriously, and she had felt dismissed.

When John was growing up his parents ran a group of nursing homes and he was enlisted as a worker for them from the age of fifteen. He had three younger sisters, and a mother who suffered from depression and was largely absent. All of the women had leaned on John in many ways, and his father had reportedly molested each of his sisters. He had been the whistle blower, and became their protector, as well as his mother's caregiver after she and his father divorced.

He said that he had been attracted to Rachael's depression, and had in fact thought that he could "save her." He had not learned of her incest history until her hospital admission following her suicide attempt. His own history of having had to take care of his sisters who had been survivors of incest complicated things. He felt overwhelmed and burdened by this added information, and had experienced a sense of extreme hopelessness when he learned of her history.

Following the first Meditative Dialogue process, both spoke of a sense of things having been rearranged inside of them "on a molecular level". It was, they said, as if their cells had been reorganized. They said that things seem brighter, clearer, and they felt more aware of the love that they had for each other, and of a wish to work on things and move forward to a more enlivened marriage. They began a practice of meditating together outside of sessions which, they said, helped them to feel connected to each other, paradoxically, in a "more separate way." Over time John was able to move to a place of having more empathy and compassion for Rachael, and began to value the wisdom that she had to offer, while Rachael developed a greater sense of compassion for herself and for John as she was able to understand more of his story and motivations. Each spoke of having a clearer sense of the other as other, which helped them to come together in a more intimate way. As they had developed more compassion for themselves and their own pain, each was able to approach the other from a place of wholeness and offer compassion to the other rather than desperately seeking compassion from the other.

Implications for Practice: The Future of Meditative Dialogue

To date there is much clinical practice-based evidence that Meditative Dialogue is effective in couple work. Workshops have been offered nationally and internationally to introduce the process to others, and clinicians have begun using it in their practices and have offered anecdotal evidence of its effectiveness. While the evidence has been based on outcome feedback from clients, there has been no formalized research or training offered as yet. Longitudinal qualitative research is needed which could examine the experiences of couples who have practiced Meditative Dialogue in session. With all of the recent discoveries in neuroscience, it would be helpful to examine pre- and post-tests of the changes in the brains of couples who have practiced Meditative Dialogue over time. There is much evidence that meditation helps to develop the centers of the brain having to do with compassion and empathy (Davidson and Lutz 2008; Holzel et al. 2011; Lutz et al. 2008; Slagter et al. 2011), and also calms amygdala activity, decreasing hyperarousal (Siegel 2014).

Conclusion

Meditative Dialogue offers an innovative way for couples to quickly position themselves for meaningful conversations that work to increase empathy and compassion for self and other, and offers healing from the inside out in intimate relationships. It helps partners to become curious, open, accepting and loving in their interactions as they dip into the energies cultivated in the space in between. They learn to fan the flames and nurture the fabric of their relationships in ways that can help to sustain them over time. The Meditative Dialogue process invites engaged and activated presence into relationships and cultivates embodied authentic experiences in one's life. It helps to develop compassion and empathy in relationships and improves acceptance, collaboration, nonjudgment, and flexibility.

For Rachael and John, engaging in the Meditative Dialogue process together in couple therapy helped them to slow down, get out of their heads, and develop more compassion for themselves. This, in turn, helped them to be able to connect from a more separate and centered position and to freely offer compassion and empathy to each other, improving their marital relationship from the inside out.

References

Anderson, H. (2007). Dialogue. In H. Anderson & D. Gehart (Eds.), *Collaborative therapy: Relationships and conversations that make a difference* (pp. 33–41). London: Routledge.

Angera, J., & Long, E. (2006). Qualitative and quantitative evaluations of an empathy training program for couples in marriage and romantic relationships. *Journal of Couple and Relationship Therapy, 5*(1), 1–26.

Atkinson, B. (2013). Mindfulness training and the cultivation of satisfying, secure couple relationships. *Couple and Family Psychology: Research and Practice, 2*(2), 73–94.

Baer, R. A., & Krietemeyer, J. (2006). Overview of mindfulness- and acceptance based treatment approaches. In R. A. Baer (Ed.), *Mindfulness-based treatment approaches: Clinician's guide to evidence base and applications* (pp. 3–27). Burlington, MA: Elsevier.

Barnes, S., Brown, K. W., Krusemark, E., Campbell, W. K., & Rogge, R. D. (2007). The role of mindfulness in romantic relationship satisfaction and responses to relationship stress. *Journal of Marital and Family Therapy, 33,* 482–500. doi:10.1111/j.1752-606.2007.00033.x

Beckerman, N. L., & Sarracco, M. (2011). Enhancing emotionally focused couple therapy through the practice of mindfulness: A case analysis. *Journal of Family Psychotherapy, 22*(1), 1–15. doi:10.1080/08975353.2011.551082

Bell, L. G. (2009). Mindful psychotherapy. *Journal of Spirituality in Mental Health, 11,* 126–144. doi:10.1080/19349630902864275

Bishop, S. R., Lau, M., Shapiro, S., Carlson, L., Anderson, N. D., Carmody, J., et al. (2004). Mindfulness: A proposed operational definition. *Clinical Psychology: Science and Practice, 11,* 230–241. doi:10.1093/clipsy.bph077

Block-Lerner, J. J., Adair, C. C., Plumb, J. C., Rhatigan, D. L., & Orsillo, S. M. (2007). The case for mindfulness-based approaches in the cultivation of empathy: Does nonjudgmental, present-moment awareness increase capacity for perspective-taking and empathic concern? *Journal of Marital and Family Therapy, 33*(4), 501–516.

Burpee, L. C., & Langer, E. J. (2005). Mindfulness and marital satisfaction. *Journal of Adult Development, 12*(1), 43–51.

Carson, J. W., Carson, K. M., Gil, K. M., & Baucom, D. H. (2007). Self-expansion as a mediator of relationship improvements in a mindfulness intervention. *Journal of Marital and Family Therapy, 33*(4), 517–528.

Christensen, A., Sevier, M., Simpson, L., & Gattis, K. (2004). Acceptance, mindfulness, and change in couple therapy. In S. Hayes, V. Follette, & M. Linehan (Eds.), *Mindfulness and acceptance: Expanding the cognitive-behavioral tradition* (pp. 288–311). New York, NY: Guilford Press.

Csaszar, I., & Curry, J. (2010) Loving kindness meditation: A promising practice for reducing stress and increasing empathy. *VISTAS Online, 86,* 1–11. Retrieved from http://counselingoutfitters.com/vistas/VISTAS_Home.htm

Davidson, R., & Lutz, A. (2008). Buddha's brain: Neuroplasticity and meditation. *IEEE Signal Processing Magazine, 25*(1), 174–176. doi:10.1109/MSP.2008.4431873

Decety, J., & Jackson, P. L. (2006). A social-neuroscience perspective on empathy. *Current Directions in Psychological Science, 15*(6), 54–58. doi:10.1111/j.0963-7214.2006.00406.x

Decety, J., & Meyer, M. (2008). From emotional resonance to empathic understanding: A social developmental neuroscience account. *Cognitive Therapy and Research, 20,* 1053–1080.

Gambrel, L., & Keeling, M. L. (2010). Relational aspects of mindfulness: Implications for the practice of marriage and family therapy. *Contemporary Family Therapy: An International Journal, 32*(4), 412–426. doi:10.1007/s10591-010-9129-z

Gehart, D. R. (2012). *Mindfulness and acceptance in couple and family therapy.* New York, NY: Guilford Press.

Gehart, D. R., & McCollum, E. E. (2007). Engaging suffering: Towards a mindful revisioning of family therapy practice. *Journal of Marital and Family Therapy, 33*(2), 214–226.

Germer, C. K. (2005). Mindfulness: What is it? What does it matter? In C. K. Germer, R. D. Siegel, & P. R. Fulton (Eds.), *Mindfulness and psychotherapy* (pp. 3–27). New York, NY: Guilford.

Germer, C. K. (2009). *The mindful path to self-compassion: Freeing yourself from destructive thoughts and emotions.* New York, NY: Guilford.

Gottman, J. M. (2011). *The science of trust: Emotional attunement for couples*. New York, NY: Norton.

Holzel, B. K., Carmody, J., Vangel, M., Congleton, C., Yerramsetti, S. M., Gard, T., et al. (2011). Mindfulness practice leads to increases in regional brain gray matter density. *Psychiatry Research: Neuroimaging, 191*(1), 36–43.

Jacobs, T. J. (2013). *The possible profession*. New York, NY: Routledge.

Jacobson, N. S., Christensen, A., Prince, S. H., Cordova, J., & Eldridge, K. (2000). Integrative behavioral couple therapy: An acceptance-based promising new treatment for couple discord. *Journal of Consulting and Clinical Psychology, 68,* 351–355. doi:10.1037/0022-006X.68.2.351

Jones, K. C., Welton, S. R., Oliver, T. C., & Thoburn, J. W. (2011). Mindfulness, spousal attachment, and marital satisfaction: A mediated model. *Family Journal, 19*(4), 357–361. doi:10.1177/1066480711417234

Kabat-Zinn, J. (1990). *Full catastrophe living: Using the wisdom of your body and mind to face stress, pain and illness*. New York, NY: Delacorte Press.

Kabat-Zinn, J. (1994). *Wherever you go there you are: Mindfulness and meditation in everyday life*. New York, NY: Hyperion.

Kabat-Zinn, J. (2003). Mindfulness-based interventions in context: Past, present, and future. *Clinical Psychology: Science and Practice, 10*(2), 144–156.

Kozlowski, A. (2013). Mindful mating: Exploring the connection between mindfulness and relationship satisfaction. *Sexual and Relationship Therapy, 28*(1–2), 92–104. doi:10.1080/14681994.2012.748889

Linehan, M. (1993). *Cognitive behavioral treatment of borderline personality disorder*. New York, NY: Guilford.

Lord, S. (2007). Meditative dialogue: A tool for engaging students in collaborative learning processes. *Journal of Family Therapy, 29*(4), 334–337. doi:10.1111/j.1467-427.2007.00396.x

Lord, S. (2010). Meditative dialogue: Cultivating sacred space in psychotherapy—An intersubjective fourth? *Smith College Studies in Social Work, 80*(2), 269–285. doi:10.1080/00377311003754187

Lutz, A., Brefczynski-Lewis, J., Johnstone, T., & Davidson, R. J. (2008). Regulation of the neural circuitry of emotion by compassion meditation: Effects of meditative expertise. *PLoS ONE, 3* (3), 1–5. doi:10.1371/journal.pone.0001897

McCollum, E. E. (2011). Could EFT have saved the Buddha's marriage? A reflection on Beckerman and Sarracco. *Journal of Family Psychotherapy, 22*(1), 16–21. doi:10.1080/08975353.2011.551088

Nanda, J. (2013). Mindful relationships. *Sexual and Relationship Therapy, 28*(1–2), 120–131. doi:10.1080/14681994.2012.758838

Napoli, M. M. (2011). React or respond: A guide to apply mindfulness for families and therapists. *Families In Society: The Journal of Contemporary Social Services, 92*(1), 28–32.

Neff, K. D., & Germer, C. K. (2013). A pilot study and randomized controlled trial of the mindful self-compassion program. *Journal of Clinical Psychology, 69*(1), 28–44. doi:10.1002/jclp.21923

Olson, M., Laitila, A., Rober, P., & Seikkula, J. (2012). The shift from monologue to dialogue in a couple therapy sessions: Dialogical investigation of change from the therapists' point of view. *Family Process, 51*(3), 420–435. doi:10.1111/j.1545-5300.2012.01406.x

Pruitt, I. T., & McCollum, E. (2010). Voices of experienced meditators: The impact of meditation practice on intimate relationships. *Contemporary Family Therapy, 33,* 135–154. doi:10.1007/s10591-009-9112-8

Rober, P. (2015). The challenge of creating dialogical space for both partners in couple therapy. *Australian and New Zealand Journal of Family Therapy, 36,* 105–121.

Roberts, T. W. (2007). Brain biology and couple therapy. *Journal of Couple & Relationship Therapy, 6*(1/2), 5–16.

Seikkula, J., & Trimble, D. (2005). Healing elements of therapeutic conversation: Dialogue as an embodiment of love. *Family Process, 44,* 461–475.

Siegel, D. J. (2007). *The mindful brain*. New York, NY: WW. Norton & Co.

Siegel, J. P. (2014). The mindful couple. *Clinical Social Work, 42,* 282–287. doi:10.1007/s10615-014-0489-y

Simon, F., Stierlin, H., & Wynne, L. (1985). *Language of family therapy: A systemic vocabulary and source book.* Ann Arbor, Michigan: Family Process Press Series.

Slagter, H. A., Davidson, R. J., & Lutz, A. (2011). Mental training as a tool in the neuroscientific study of brain and cognitive plasticity. *Frontiers in Human Neuroscience, 5,* 1–12.

Surrey, J. L. (2005). Relational psychotherapy, relational mindfulness. In C. K. Germer, R. D. Siegel, & P. R. Fulton (Eds.), *Mindfulness and psychotherapy* (pp. 91–110). New York: Guilford Press.

Suzuki, S. (2011). *Zen mind, beginner's mind.* Boston: Shambala Publications.

Tang, Y. Y., Holzel, B. K. & Posner, M. I. (2015) The neuroscience of mindfulness meditation. *Nature Reviews Neuroscience* 1–13. AOP, published online 18 March 2015. doi:10.1038/nrn3916

Wachs, K. K., & Cordova, J. V. (2007). Mindful relating: Exploring mindfulness and emotion repertoires in intimate relationships. *Journal of Marital and Family Therapy, 33*(4), 464–481.

Winnicott, D. W. (1958). *Through paedeatrics to psychoanalysis.* New York, NY: Basic Books.

Winnicott, D. W. (1971). *Playing and reality.* New York, NY: Basic Books.

Chapter 9
Beginning with the Symptom: Incorporating Mindfulness in the Treatment of Substance Misuse

Jenifer Talley

"I don't like how I feel—I feel bad and I hate it. I know alcohol will make me feel better." "I feel ashamed about looking for relief from alcohol so I keep drinking and then I don't have to feel anything." Sentiments like this are commonly expressed by those seeking treatment for substance use disorders and highlight a universal theme—"feelings are bad, I don't like them and I know what I can do to escape and feel different". Rather than slowing down, noticing these layers of reactivity, there tends to be a focus on seeking immediate relief from distress and a struggle to engage in more adaptive ways of coping. For many clients, emotional resources appear to narrow with time and there is an increasing reliance on external factors to serve self-soothing and self-regulatory functions. Over time, self-efficacy may decrease and there is less confidence in one's capacity to manage distress and adapt to circumstances without misusing substances or engaging in other maladaptive behaviors such as overeating. Consequently, interventions designed to increase one's ability to contain difficult emotions and reduce impulsive reactivity are very important. Mindfulness is one such intervention that can enhance the capacity to stay in the moment and build resources to better tolerate discomfort and distress, particularly when used within a harm reduction model. Mindfulness Based Relapse Prevention (MBRP; Bowen et al. 2010) will be discussed as an effective way to intervene with clients to address the many biopsychosocial factors contributing to substance misuse. A clinical illustration will demonstrate how this integration of mindfulness pragmatically translates into collaborative work with a woman with lifelong substance use issues and histories of multiple traumas.

Researchers and clinicians have found that substance use can serve many vital functions such as modulating emotions and helping people cope with stressors, but overly relying on substances in this way is not ideal and can lead to difficulties in a

J. Talley (✉)
Psychology Department, The New School for Social Research, New York, USA
e-mail: jtalley@cfol.org

J. Talley
The Center for Optimal Living, New York, USA

T.B. Northcut (ed.), *Cultivating Mindfulness in Clinical Social Work*,
Essential Clinical Social Work Series, DOI 10.1007/978-3-319-43842-9_9

variety of domains. Many have voiced the need to focus on the role of underlying psychological factors in the development and maintenance of substance use issues to inform clinical interventions (e.g., Murphy and Khantzian 1995; Tatarsky 2007; Wurmser 1993). Specifically, Wurmser (1993) observed that people with substance use issues often struggle with adaptive emotion management skills, overly rely on avoidance and dissociation, and opt for action-oriented responses to distress and seek relief through external sources (e.g., substances, risky behaviors). Biological, psychological, and social/relational factors are associated with substance use disorders and should be considered in the assessment and treatment process as well. Murphy and Khantzian (1995) describe how substance use issues and other risky behaviors emerge out of self-regulation deficits across four domains of functioning. These domains include emotion regulation (i.e., identifying and modulating emotions), interpersonal relationships and conflict management, identity and self-esteem, and self-care (Murphy and Khantzian 1995). Marlatt's research led to the development of a model of understanding and preventing relapse on substances or other problematic behaviors based on principles of cognitive behavioral therapy that addresses the intersection of individual and environmental risk factors (Marlatt and Witkiewitz 2005). More recently, Marlatt's relapse prevention model has been adapted to include a focus on mindfulness practices (Bowen et al. 2010).

Many people who seek treatment are not ready to stop using substances and experience intense ambivalence about the nature of their relationship to these substances. On the one hand, substances offer quick relief from distress, but may also have led to significant disruptions in relationships, work, health, and day-to-day functioning. This is characteristic of the pre-contemplation or contemplation stages of change where individuals may not be fully committed to change and experience ambivalence about the nature of their relationship to a particular substance or problematic behavior (Prochaska et al. 1992). They may acknowledge the consequences of their use but may not feel confident in their capacity to change or may not be ready to commit to taking steps towards change, particularly if abstinence is seen as the only option.

The narrative in American culture tends to be more associated with the disease model and 12-step approaches than one that is more nuanced and considers the complex interplay of individual and social factors in the development of substance use issues (Davis and Rosenberg 2013; Van Amsterdam and van den Brink 2013). This can be attributed to the long history and widespread availability of Alcoholics Anonymous (AA) and other 12-step approaches which rely on lay leadership who themselves are members of the program. Research findings about 12-step approaches have been mixed, and sometimes contradictory, which makes sense given the strict requirements for anonymity of participants. In a review of the literature on AA's effectiveness, Kaskutas (2009) cited several studies and noted that those who regularly attend AA meetings are twice as likely to report abstinence and approximately 50% of those who participated in only AA or other 12-step meetings endorsed abstinence after 1, 3, and 8 years compared to one-fifth of those who did not attend meetings. The findings suggest that AA and other 12-step programs are effective for those pursuing abstinence as their goal, and those who are motivated to commit to being a member of these programs. AA and other 12-step programs are considered effective through their emphasis on maintaining abstinence, acknowledging the nature of one's condition, relapse prevention strategies, and by providing a path toward spiritual growth. In addition, the focus on fellowship and socializing provides opportunities for members to connect to one another and build new relationships.

Unfortunately, there continues to be a bias in our culture that assumes abstinence is the only acceptable goal or outcome in treatment and that substance use issues stem from compromised morals, certain personality types or a lack of willpower (Broyles et al. 2014). It is common to hear clients describe feelings of anxiety and shame about disclosing to others that they are struggling with substance use issues and are working on moderating or stopping use. There is a sense that one might be judged or misunderstood for this type of disclosure and possibly blamed for displaying symptoms of a substance use disorder. It is important to "meet clients where they are" in terms of their level of motivation and readiness for change (Denning and Little 2012; Washton and Zweben 2008). Allowing clients to choose their own treatment goals is associated with better outcomes in terms of treatment retention and reductions in risky use (Davis and Rosenberg 2013; Van Amsterdam and van den Brink 2013). However, the historical emphasis on abstinence as the only acceptable goal can interfere with some clients seeking help. For instance, Davis and Rosenberg (2013) studied a sample of members of a national association of addiction professionals and found that two-thirds to three-quarters of the respondents would not allow their clients to work toward non-abstinence as either an intermediate or final outcome goal in treatment. The reasons for not allowing clients to pursue non-abstinence included not wanting to "send the wrong message," "non-abstinence is not effective," and "allowing non-abstinence is not consistent with treatment philosophy" (Davis and Rosenberg 2013). Proponents of the disease model believe that due to having the disease of addiction, which is characterized as a chronic relapsing condition, an individual must admit powerlessness over this illness and completely abstain from all substances in order to avoid losing control.

Rather than conceptualizing substance use issues as an all-or-nothing dichotomy, a more useful framework is to view substance use issues as occurring on a continuum of risk and severity (Tatarsky 2007; Washton and Zweben 2008). Harm reduction psychotherapy acknowledges the multiple personal and social meanings and functions of substance use and does not require an a priori commitment to abstinence (Denning and Little 2012; Khantzian 1985; Marlatt et al. 2012; Tatarsky 2007). This approach may ultimately lead to abstinence, but it is not a prerequisite for embarking in the treatment process. Understanding people's unique relationship to a substance or problematic behavior, the context associated with their use, along with the reasons why they may be considering change, is a crucial foundation from which to begin the therapeutic process.

Mindfulness is uniquely suited to this approach as it allows for a nonjudgmental observation of the patterns associated with substance misuse such as wishing to escape from harsh self-critical thoughts, an inability to tolerate frustration or discomfort, or as a habitual response to cravings. The integration of mindfulness with harm reduction empowers clients to make choices about the relationship they wish to have with a certain substance or behavior without a presumption that abstinence is the ideal or only acceptable outcome. Additionally, practicing mindfulness may aid the development of emotion management and distress tolerance skills that can gradually replace one's reliance on substances or problematic behaviors as a way to cope. Useful applications of mindfulness in the treatment of substance misuse can include developing the capacity to observe and "unwrap" cravings, along with practicing "urge surfing" when experiencing a craving (Tatarsky 2007; Bowen et al. 2010). By shifting the relationship to cravings and learning how to be curious about what is being communicated through them opens up a space where we can respond more effectively so as to minimize harm and promote self-care. In order to understand how mindfulness can facilitate this process, it is important to first consider the relationship between substance use and difficulties in self-regulation impacted by biopsychosocial influences.

Understanding Substance Misuse

Considering that substance use issues and other problematic behaviors often result from attempts to cope with overwhelming emotions, trauma, relational conflict, and other difficult life circumstances such as being a member of a marginalized or stigmatized group, one of the tasks in the treatment process is to promote the development of more adaptive self-regulatory capacities. In addition, adopting a biopsychosocial lens allows us to account for the impact of biological factors, psychological influences, and social/environmental issues in the development and maintenance of substance use issues. By understanding the reciprocal and bidirectional influences occurring at multiple levels (social and personal), we can begin to understand the meaning and function underlying substance misuse and work to develop individualized interventions in collaboration with our clients.

Trauma

A history of trauma is often associated with problematic substance use and other risky behaviors. The Adverse Childhood Experiences Study (Dube et al. 2003) measured the association between drug use and 10 types of adverse childhood experiences (e.g., emotional, sexual, and physical abuse, neglect, household dysfunction, parental substance use) among a large sample of adults in a primary care clinic. The presence of adverse childhood experiences increased the rate of drug use initiation in early adolescence by 2–4 times and increased the probability of lifetime drug use as well. These findings speak to the profound impact of stress in the developmental course of substance use disorders and how experiencing trauma can hinder the development of adaptive ways of managing distress and self-regulating (Maté 2010). Many studies have documented the connection between trauma and substance use disorders and approximately half (46.4%) of those who meet criteria for post-traumatic stress disorder (PTSD) also meet criteria for a substance use disorder (Pietrzak et al. 2011). It is estimated that among individuals seeking treatment for a substance use disorder, between 30 and 60% have a lifetime prevalence rate of PTSD (McCauley et al. 2012). Mounting evidence supports an integrative approach that addresses symptoms of trauma and substance misuse concurrently and is consistent with the self-medication hypothesis that views substance use as an attempt to manage overwhelming affect states (McCauley et al. 2012; Ruglass et al. 2014).

When we consider the prevalence of trauma among those who experience issues with substances, it is important to consider the possibility of dissociation and disconnection from emotional, cognitive, and somatic states. Many individuals who experience trauma, particularly early in life, report difficulties in recognizing, labeling, and appropriately responding to emotions. If one grows up in an environment that is unsafe and where one's emotional reactions are invalidated, it is not uncommon to see issues with emotion regulation (Linehan 2014). There is an interaction between an individual's unique disposition and the environment that could set the stage for subsequent vulnerabilities in identifying, modulating, and responding to emotions. This also has implications for the development of one's sense of self and identity along with interpersonal relationships. Emotions communicate valuable information if one has the capacity to pay attention and garner resources to respond appropriately. Many people are unaware of the connection between their emotions, thoughts, somatic experiences, and behaviors. This has implications for people who are misusing substances and who engage in risky and problematic behaviors as they might not be aware of the nature of their habitual responses leading up to the use and/or behaviors. Mindfulness, with its emphasis on building the capacity to be in the moment and observe unfolding thoughts, emotions, and sensations, can be useful in helping people move from "autopilot" or increased reactivity toward more equanimity during times of distress (Brown et al. 2007).

Sociopolitical Influences

With many substances continuing to be criminalized, we will encounter clients who have been impacted by the criminal justice system due to their substance use and/or substance-related involvement. Young men of color are particularly vulnerable to being involved with the criminal justice system, and are disproportionately arrested for drug-related crimes when compared to other racial groups. Criminal involvement is predictive of later issues with employment and education due to limited opportunities following incarceration and the barriers that exist for people with a criminal history. In addition, being part of the criminal justice system may expose youth to a social network that reinforces criminal behavior and is predictive of later criminal involvement (Hart 2014). Involvement with the criminal justice system places an individual at a greater risk for poor health outcomes and is associated with an increased likelihood of developing a substance use disorder. This may be exacerbated by health disparities for racial and ethnic minority groups that exist prior to involvement with the criminal justice system due to structural and interpersonal racism (Binswanger et al. 2012; Witkiewitz et al. 2013).

Females tend to experience higher lifetime prevalence rates of mood and anxiety disorders than males and are more likely to be victims of childhood sexual abuse, which increases the risk of developing substance use issues later in life (Back et al. 2006; Greenfield et al. 2010). Some studies have found that females are more likely to drop out of treatment and that minority women in particular have higher dropout rates (Mertens and Weisner as cited in Witkiewitz et al. 2013). Most of the existing studies of substance abuse treatment have been conducted with primarily white male clients so it is important to reflect on the applicability of the findings to diverse and underserved populations (Miranda et al. as cited in Witkiewitz et al. 2013).

Sociocultural narratives about people with substance use issues may exacerbate feelings of shame and guilt, along with a sense that one is part of a marginalized group. Additionally, stigma and shame may then impact help-seeking behaviors due to concerns about being identified as part of a group with negative associations in mainstream culture. Concerns about acknowledging illicit behavior may also pose a barrier to seeking treatment. This is particularly relevant when we consider that mothers and caregivers who engage in substance misuse may not pursue treatment due to fears of losing custody of children or being stigmatized for disclosing their substance use. Our culture would benefit from shifting to a mindset that "radically accepts" the fact that people do and will continue to use substances. Instead of adopting a punitive and disempowering stance, we need to consider the whole person and the unique factors implicated in their relationship to substances so that we can offer appropriate interventions (Hart 2014; Rothschild 2015).

The role of language is also important to consider as we may be inadvertently conveying a bias through our use of certain terminology (e.g., "addict," "junkie"), which may be associated with implicit assumptions about substance users. Rather than focusing on pathology, it has been recommended that we use "recovery-oriented language" focused on healing and resilience that affirms individuals' worth and dignity (Broyles et al. 2014). Terms like, "people with substance use issues" along with "substance misuse" and "substance use disorders" are considered to be less stigmatizing (APA 2013; Broyles et al. 2014). This is particularly important when we acknowledge those who are more ambivalent about seeking help or who are in the early stages of recovery who may feel demoralized or struggle to maintain motivation if they have to ascribe to that type of label and mindset. On the other hand, there are some who find it useful to label themselves an "addict" and we should be open to how clients wish to define themselves and how they view their relationship to substances and the recovery process.

Putting It Together

As mentioned previously, factors such as lower levels of distress tolerance, increased susceptibility to experiencing negative affect, difficulty modulating reactions to cravings, and limited coping resources are associated with an increased likelihood of developing substance use issues and predict increased relapse rates (Hsu et al. 2013). Exposure to stressors and trauma in childhood affect the development of adaptive self-regulatory systems and may lead to ongoing difficulties managing stress later in life. Specifically, there is more reactivity to stressors along with deficits in managing overarousal, modulating emotional reactions, disengaging from self-critical thoughts, and anticipating long-term consequences (Maté 2010). In addition, feeling disconnected and isolated from social networks, and having experienced numerous negative sociopolitical situations may drive substance misuse and other risky behaviors (Hart 2014). These findings are in line with the self-medication hypothesis, which acknowledges the impact of limitations in emotion regulation, identity and self-esteem, difficulties negotiating relational conflict, and self-care deficits as contributing to the development of problematic substance use (Khantzian and Albanese 2008). Substance use often operates as a negative reinforcer in that it allows individuals to escape from or avoid the experience of discomfort or distress.

A theme that often emerges in this type of work is how clients relate to pain and suffering. Frequently, there is a narrative about the experience of pain that exacerbates and prolongs its duration, which leads one to feel helpless and inadequate in terms of being able to manage it. It is often useful to discuss the importance of developing ways to "find ease in discomfort;" a way of softening around the experience of pain and discomfort so as to not inadvertently increase suffering.[1] On the other hand, there are instances where substance use is an attempt to extend a pleasurable state and may be used during times of celebration and joy. As such, substance misuse may be conceptualized as a maladaptive attempt at managing discomfort and negative emotions while attempting to prolong experiences of pleasure.

Deficits in inhibitory control and poor decision-making, along with increased reactivity and decreased self-efficacy are associated with problematic substance use (Witkiewitz et al. 2012). Neurobiological correlates of addictive behaviors include alternations in the prefrontal cortex and the mesocorticolimbic system (i.e., the reward system) which impact one's ability to modulate responses to reward-based cues and engage in cognitive behavioral processes such as inhibiting responses to cravings/triggers and anticipating consequences (Witkiewitz et al. 2012). Structural deficits (i.e., reduced volume of grey matter) have been identified in the brain reward system of individuals who are prone to relapse (Durazzo et al. as cited in Witkiewitz et al. 2012).

Positive and negative feedback loops may be established with repeated instances of engaging in substance use in response to distress. Specifically, this can lead to biased information processing wherein memories associated with use and anticipatory relief-based beliefs are more salient and result in increased motivation to seek relief

[1]See Kabat-Zinn's (1990) work on MBSR for more extensive discussion on this topic as well as other chapters in this text.

through substance use or other behaviors (Witkiewitz et al. 2012; Brewer et al. (2010); Brewer et al. 2013). Essentially, a chain of events arises where an individual experiences an intense affective response to stimuli (either internal or external) that is associated with a craving and based on learning and habit, reacts to this experience by seeking relief through substance use or another behavior. With time, these pathways are strengthened and one's repertoire of coping resources becomes narrower. This suggests a lack of flexibility and diversity of response options when confronted with stressors or intense cravings associated with substance use.

Mindfulness appears to be useful in helping people find a different way to relate to and be more accepting of their positive and negative experiences by slowing down these feedback loops. By teaching clients how to nonjudgmentally observe the habitual patterns associated with substance use and develop a more accepting and kind stance toward discomfort, they can build additional resources to reduce risky and harmful behaviors. Mindfulness can aid in reducing the emotional intensity and motivation to self-medicate that we often encounter among those with substance use issues (Brewer et al. 2013; Hsu et al. 2013; Witkiewitz et al. 2012).

Role of Mindfulness in Addressing Substance Misuse

Building on the relapse prevention (RP) model for treating substance misuse (Marlatt and Gordon 1985), mindfulness-based relapse prevention (MBRP) focuses on how one relates to experiences (cognitively and affectively) and emphasizes the development of acceptance skills (Bowen et al. 2010, 2014). RP uses a cognitive behavioral framework for helping clients develop skills to identify and manage triggers associated with substance use, reframe self-critical thoughts in response to a slip or resumption of use, observe expectancies about use, increase self-efficacy, and address lifestyle imbalances (Larimer et al. 1999). Strategies to address lifestyle imbalances include relaxation training, reducing stressors, and increasing pleasurable activities, improving time management, and incorporating practices such as meditation and mindfulness (Marlatt and Witkiewitz 2005). In addition, RP focuses on how clients may be impacted by the "abstinence violation effect," a process where an initial lapse or slip in substance use may lead to an influx of negative self-statements, feelings of hopelessness, increased substance use, and avoidance of engaging social support networks (Larimer et al. 1999). For instance, a client who has been working on abstaining from alcohol may resume use following a stressful altercation with a significant other. In response to the lapse, the client may think, "I am never going to be able to stop drinking, this is pointless, I am a failure and I'll always be an addict." This appraisal of the lapse may lead to an increase in alcohol use due to feelings of hopelessness and shame. Helping clients reframe this process and shift how they relate to a slip is an important aspect of the RP model and is also infused within the MBRP protocol.

MBRP also incorporates elements of mindfulness-based stress reduction (MBSR; Kabat-Zinn 1990) and mindfulness-based cognitive therapy (MBCT; Segal et al. 2002).

Empirical studies of MBRP indicate that it is effective in reducing substance use, cravings, increases present-moment awareness, and decreases reactivity to cues associated with substance use (Bowen et al. 2014; Zgierska et al. 2009). Given that negative affect is often associated with cravings and substance misuse, MBRP aims to help clients enhance their capacity to experience intense and negative emotions by developing an attitude of curiosity, compassion, and acceptance.

The practices of MBRP offer clients a systematic way of building awareness of internal states and the external environment by learning how to focus and shift one's attention. This is done through the use of formal mindfulness practices (e.g., focusing on sensations of breath, body scan) and by incorporating mindfulness in everyday life. There is a shift from being in a state of "auto-pilot" characterized by less awareness to one of being more attentive and attuned to moment-to-moment experiences and one's reactions to those experiences. Being able to notice cravings along with the thoughts, emotions, and behavioral reactions that accompany them is an important part of the process. As clients slow down and pay attention to their habitual patterns of reactivity with less judgment and more acceptance, they see that there are options in how they relate to their experiences, particularly discomfort (Bowen et al. 2014). This then allows for an inquiry process where we can gain a better understanding of what important needs are being met through substance use and consider alternative and more adaptive ways of responding (Bowen et al. 2014; Tatarsky 2007).

With time, a habitual and aversive reaction to anxiety that had been met with increased alcohol use may include a brief mindfulness practice such as the SOBER Breathing Space (see Appendix 1), whereby clients go through a process of slowing down, observing, and describing their experiences and shift their focus to their breath, expand their awareness, and respond mindfully and skillfully to that craving based on what is needed in the moment (Bowen et al. 2010, 2014). This type of practice is a starting point for shifting a pattern of immediately responding to distress by seeking relief through a substance. A client might begin by noting increased tension in the body, a sense of anxiety and dread, self-critical thoughts, and then choose to practice the SOBER Breathing Space to allow for these feelings to be present before evaluating how to respond skillfully and effectively in the moment. Given that clients often report being unaware of what immediately precipitates a craving or an action-oriented response associated with substance use, it is useful to offer this practice as a way of helping them make contact with what they are experiencing along with the narrative that is associated with the experience. There is the initial experience, a reaction or judgment, and then an urge to use. If we can help clients slow down the chain of events and start to pay attention to how they are judging their experiences and underestimating their own capacity to tolerate discomfort, we are on the road to helping them develop a greater repertoire of responses.

Interestingly, Witkiewitz et al. (2013) compared outcomes of MBRP and RP between non-Hispanic white and racial or ethnic minority women in a randomized clinical trial. They found that racial or ethnic minority women who received MBRP evidenced fewer drug use days than non-Hispanic white participants at the 15-week follow-up and were more likely to complete the follow-up assessment. Racial and ethnic minority women who received RP demonstrated a higher score on the medical problems subscale of an addiction severity measure relative to baseline (40% increase) compared to an 85% decrease in the those scores for racial or ethnic minority women who received the MBRP intervention. Although more research needs to be conducted to assess what mechanisms contribute to improved outcomes for racial or ethnic minority women who received MBRP, the authors speculated that the personalized and experiential focus of MBRP in comparison to the more didactic nature of RP may have allowed participants to individually tailor how they implemented the treatment in everyday life rather than learning more general coping skills in the RP group. In addition, they hypothesized that the compassionate, acceptance-based approach of MBRP might have resonated more with racial or ethnic minority clients who may have encountered discrimination and racism (Witkiewitz et al. 2013). Taken together, these findings suggest direct experience with mindfulness that emphasizes cultivating compassion, self-care and increased acceptance, may yield more positive effects for racial or ethnic minority women and these findings may be particularly relevant in terms of improvements in medical conditions. Given that racial or ethnic minority women experience more health disparities and medical issues in general and as a consequence of substance use, these findings are very promising and further research is warranted.

It would be remiss to not include a discussion of the importance of the clinician's own mindfulness practice and how it is an essential starting point in this process. Without firsthand experience with meditation and mindfulness, it is difficult to imagine how one would demonstrate the practice to others. Drawing on the intentions of the practice and adopting a stance that is open, accepting, and compassionate has tremendously helped my clinical work and has been useful during times of increased stress. Working with clients who engage in risky behaviors and display difficulties with self-regulation makes for an interesting and often eventful day, but may also contribute to stress and burnout. Establishing a regular practice and a commitment to being attuned to our moment-to-moment experiences (both inside and outside the office) in a kind and compassionate way can help mitigate the impact of stressors. I often rely on my own experiences with mindfulness while guiding clients and share instances where I have struggled with it and when I have been able to use it to manage challenging circumstances. These disclosures are always tempered with my understanding of the clients' experiences with trauma and boundary violations. Selectively sharing my own experiences (and struggles) offers clients a more tangible, practical, and accessible way to understand the practice and may inspire them to begin to experiment with it on their own.

Practical Application and Case Examples

My approach to working with clients with substance use issues is informed by the work of Tatarsky (2007), Denning and Little (2012), Herman (1992), Linehan (1993, 2014), Najavits (2002) and incorporates elements of both MBCT (Segal et al. 2002) and MBRP (Bowen et al. 2010). Although MBCT and MBRP were designed to be implemented in groups, I often integrate practices from those protocols in my work with individual clients in addition to using them in group settings. I will outline the general process I use when working with clients and will share examples of specific mindfulness exercises I use in my work. This description of the pragmatics of practice includes developing skill awareness and change, working with cravings and urges, accepting ambivalence, setting goals, and coping with trauma. A description of a case will be provided at the end of this section to illustrate my approach. Additional resources I share with clients are included in Appendix 2.

The quality of the alliance and rapport we establish with clients is an important element of any good clinical practice and is an essential factor when working with substance users. The strength of the therapeutic relationship is a crucial foundation from which the change process develops. Drawing on principles of motivational interviewing, with its emphasis on active listening, expressing empathy, and eliciting feedback, clients are given the opportunity to reflect on the nature of their use along with describing the changes they would like to make (Miller and Rollnick 2013; Tatarsky and Kellogg 2010). The nature of the relationship is collaborative, supportive, and affirming of small incremental goals that reduce harm. Rather than arguing for change, the clinician's role is one of a collaborator and an ally in the process of change. The client is viewed as the "expert" and treatment goals and strategies are negotiated based on the client's definition of the problem and an exploration of ambivalence about change that acknowledges reasons for both changing and for maintaining the status quo. In addition, we consider whether the client feels it is important to make changes, how ready they feel to begin to address their concerns, and how confident they are about their capacity to make changes (Miller and Rollnick 2013). What is unique about this approach is that clients are invited to express both sides of their ambivalence and encourage a dialogue with the parts of the client who are more reluctant to change and who may wish to continue to use (Rothschild 2010).

By introducing mindfulness early in the treatment process, clients become more aware of the antecedents and consequences associated with substance use and other risky and problematic behaviors which then guides the establishment safe use parameters to decrease harm. By inviting clients to participate in the treatment process in this way, their autonomy is honored and they ultimately feel empowered to make positive changes (Tatarsky 2007). Exploring the nature of the relationship to the substance or behavior and the benefits they feel they derive from it along with their reasons for wanting to change is often a useful starting point. This offers insight into the function and meaning of the use and helps us formulate hypotheses about the role that substances play in managing overwhelming emotions, negotiating relational conflicts, and bolstering one's sense of self and self-worth (Murphy and Khantzian 1995). We also focus on the role of stigma, trauma, and shame and its impact on continued use, relationships, one's identity, and aspirations for the future. Groups and individual sessions often begin with a "check-in practice" (see

Appendix 3) designed to bring awareness to present moment experiences and focuses attention on the body, thoughts, emotions, and breath.

Skills for Awareness and Change

Assessment is an ongoing element of the treatment process (Denning and Little 2012) and allows for a better understanding of the biopsychosocial factors associated with use. Treatment goals and strategies for change are collaboratively explored and negotiated based on the information gathered in our ongoing assessment. Clients are asked to observe their substance use patterns during the week, what contributes to cravings, how cravings are responded to, and experiences that lead to feelings of distress and subsequent misuse. As we consider this information together, clients begin to develop short- and long-term goals that are attained incrementally at their pace. By establishing a "hierarchy of needs," clients take ownership of this process and feel more invested in committing to the goals we establish together (Denning and Little 2012; Miller and Rollnick 2013; Rothschild 2015). When relevant, psychoeducation about the physiological implications of certain substances can lead to a consideration of additional goals and treatment options to include consultation with a medical provider and/or addiction psychiatrist.

Clients are also encouraged to describe their use patterns by focusing on identifying the "drug, set, and setting" factors that are unique to them (Denning and Little 2012). For instance, under the "drug" category, clients specify their use patterns in detail (e.g., type of substance/behavior, frequency and quantity, route of administration), for "set," we consider the personal variables that differ for each client (e.g., mood and anxiety issues, sleep/eating patterns, reasons for substance use, coping skills), and under "setting," we identify the contexts associated with use (e.g., drinks alcohol when in the company of groups, or isolates when drinking). By mapping out the variables associated with use, clients can then identify what feels like a reasonable first step toward making a change. The assumption is that if we initiate change across one of those domains, it will have an impact on the others (Denning and Little 2012). If we identify anxiety as a factor that leads one to overdrink, we may decide to implement relaxation skills training and cognitive behavioral strategies to address the symptoms of anxiety and establish moderation practices (e.g., drinking water, not drinking on empty stomach, maintain safe blood alcohol levels) to limit one's intake according to their goals (Rotgers et al. 2002; Witkiewitz and Marlatt 2006). All of this is done with an experimental attitude where clients are not set up to expect perfection or a certain outcome, but rather, to experiment with different strategies and techniques to see which ones are the best fit for them. Clients are encouraged to report back the results of their experiments so we can continue to revise and reformulate our plans and strategies.

Working with cravings and urges. As clients pay more careful attention to the role of substances or other problematic behaviors in their lives, they are invited to "unwrap the urge" to develop an awareness of how cravings present themselves and how they relate to them. Clients frequently report that they are unaware of a craving or they may not use that term to describe the experience. Cravings often lead to action and clients are encouraged to try to sit with an urge before taking action in an attempt to "unwrap" them by practicing mindfulness to better understand the multiple meanings and gather information about what important needs are being met through use (Tatarsky 2007). Questions like, "what happens in your body when you notice a craving, what thoughts and emotions accompany it, does it feel inevitable to act on it?" can be useful. If it is early in the treatment process, we may not have any expectations about change as we are still gathering data and trying to understand what contributes to urges and use. With continued use, we can explore how it feels to take in a substance or engage in a certain behavior and observe the impact of these choices over time. Clients often benefit from being reminded that change does not occur in a linear fashion and it takes considerable time and effort for change to be maintained over time.

Cultivating curiosity about how one reacts to cravings can also be very useful. Cravings are a valuable source of information about the complex interaction of cognitive, biological, and affective processes associated with substance use. Adopting a mindfulness approach, with its emphasis on acceptance and acknowledging the transitory and impermanent nature of our experiences, may offer an alternative path for managing cravings. Often, clients describe cravings and urge to use substances in a negative light and many view cravings as something that one must "battle" with. What they may not realize is that by focusing one's attention on cravings and adopting a negative stance toward them, they inadvertently prolong their duration and possibly increase the intensity of how they are experienced. Instead, we can suggest that cravings contain important data and that we have the capacity to stop, slow down, and observe them without acting on them. We can also propose that the presence of a craving does not necessitate action. Of course, this takes time and practice. Once we have a sense of the information contained in a craving, we can then consider how we would like to respond to it.

By shifting the narrative of cravings as "bad" or "unwanted" and beginning to welcome them with compassionate curiosity (as consistent with the goals of many forms of meditation), we can consider alternative responses that may be the pathway toward healing and growth (Tatarsky 2007). By adopting this accepting and nonjudgmental stance toward cravings, we can reduce the intensity of the reaction and clients can access other resources to respond skillfully in the moment rather than reacting based on aversion or desire. It is also an opportunity to help boost self-efficacy and demonstrate that they can tolerate their experiences by adjusting how they relate to them. Mindfulness allows us to "turn the volume down" on a craving so we can slow down, approach it with openness, interest, and integrate a different response. If we overly attach to a craving and have a harsh reaction, this increases distress and suffering. Alternatively, if we accept that a craving will occur, we can shift our awareness toward it with curiosity and learn when it would be more useful to shift our attention away from it if the intensity is too great.

Accepting ambivalence. The change process is complex and clients vary in terms of their readiness and commitment to change. It is important to include an ongoing exploration of feelings of ambivalence and fear about change. As we begin to develop and implement strategies for change, clients may experience uncertainty and apprehension about change (Rothschild 2015). All parts of the client are invited to join the conversation and actively inquire about whether there is a self-state who is committed to continuing to use who may not be "on board" as we develop plans for change (Rothschild 2015; Tatarsky 2007). By accepting the ambivalence and conflict between the "inner critic" who has the potential to viciously attack following instances of use, and the aspects of the self that might rebel against change goals through continued excessive and risky use, we can disengage from this bind and help clients develop self-reflective capacities (Tatarsky 2003, 2007). We can move out of a possible enactment where a client feels as though only the "pro-change" aspect of him/herself is allowed to be present in the room and instead allow space for the "pro-use" part who may be committed to continued use. A clue that this might be unfolding is when a client enthusiastically makes plans for stopping use and in the next session, reports an escalation in use. Rather than reinforcing this split and colluding with the part that is in favor of change, we can shift to an exploration of the feelings associated with change and engage in a dialogue with the aspect of the self that is invested in continuing to use. This may also include going through a decisional balance where clients identify the pros and cons of changing and not changing. Only by partnering with all aspects of the client's experience can we move forward in developing a change plan that feels reasonable and sustainable (Rothschild 2015; Tatarsky 2007).

Goal setting. As we gain a sense of the nature of their substance use and possible barriers regarding change, clients can begin to consider the ideal relationship they wish to have with a certain substance or behavior based on their values such as increasing self-care, focusing on health, improving relationships, and increasing pleasurable activities (Tatarsky 2007). We start slowly and develop small goals that we negotiate together based on the client's observation of what they would like to change and how they envision that substance playing a role (or not) in their lives. Again, a common misconception about harm reduction psychotherapy is that abstinence is not considered as a goal. This is not the case and many clients who initially pursue moderation or reduced used as a goal eventually decide that abstinence is the safest and most optimal choice for them.

When developing goals for reducing substance use or other behaviors, we are very specific in how we construct the treatment plan. With some clients, an initial goal may be to maximize the benefits of the substance while minimizing the consequences. This may be difficult for family members and others to understand and support; however, harm reduction principles encourage us to "meet clients where they are" and that means some clients are not ready, willing, or able to stop using, but benefit from ongoing discussions about the risks and benefits of use along with a consideration of safe use practices to minimize harm (Denning and Little 2012). Specifically, we can explore the circumstances under which use is acceptable and situations where a different response is warranted. We might decide that using a substance to manage a certain emotion is no longer an acceptable option and, develop together a menu of options to try during instances of increased urges to use (Tatarsky and Kellogg 2010). If a client has a goal of reducing her marijuana use, for instance, we identify the circumstances, thoughts, emotions, behaviors, and somatic sensations that precede a craving to use marijuana. The client may say that she has a craving to use when she is feeling anxious, has racing thoughts about the work she has to do the next day, feels her heart racing and has tension in her shoulders and neck. The client might then acknowledge the presence of a "pro-use" thought, "if I smoke some weed now, I will feel relaxed and I won't have to worry about what I need to do tomorrow." By applying mindfulness and being able to step back and observe these various processes, the client can then pause and make a choice. She might greet that craving with acceptance and shift to feeling compassion for herself in the moment and might say, "I know I really want to use right now, but let me take a few breaths, try to do a body scan and then see how I feel—I can always decide to use later, but for now, let me see if I can work with this." During times like this, clients are encouraged to "surf the urge" or "ride the wave" (see Appendix 4) and use the image of waves and incorporate breath as a metaphorical surfboard (Bowen et al. 2014).

Trauma. Considering the prevalence of trauma among those with substance use issues, it is important to have a framework for conceptualizing trauma and incorporating psychoeducation about trauma in our work. According to Herman (1992, p. 197), "helplessness and isolation are the core experiences of psychological trauma. Empowerment and reconnection are the core experiences of recovery." Complex trauma impacts one's capacities to adapt, experience a sense of control, connection, and meaning. Symptoms of trauma typically fall under three broad categories and include hyperarousal (e.g., exaggerated startle, autonomic reactivity), intrusion (e.g., flashbacks, images, somatic memories), and constriction (e.g., detachment, dissociation, altered sense of reality). Herman (1992) outlined the stages for the healing process which consist of helping survivors establish a sense of safety through the development of more adaptive ways to self-soothe, decreasing risky behaviors such as self-injury and problematic substance use, and detaching from unsafe circumstances and people. Seeking Safety (Najavits 2002), a treatment program for survivors of trauma with substance use issues is focused on establishing safety through the development of coping skills and psychoeducation about trauma and substance use. Remembrance and mourning is the next stage and includes a gradual processing of the memories and feelings associated with trauma once more adaptive self-soothing capacities have been established. Finally, the reconnection stage addresses the next phase of the survivor's life that includes building a new identity, expanding connections to others and feeling more empowered (Herman 1992).

It is recommended that we be cautious when incorporating mindfulness with survivors of trauma so that we are sensitive to their varying capacities to tolerate being present with uncomfortable bodily sensations, emotions, images, and thoughts. Pacing is important and offering a rationale for why mindfulness might be useful is also especially critical. I often begin by helping clients practice mindfully attending to external objects and engage their sensory systems before moving inward to attend to thoughts, sensations, and feelings in the body (see Appendix 5). As clients develop mindfulness skills, they learn how to attend to their present-moment experiences and shift away from the content and reaction to a stance of being curious about her experiences and reactions. Instead of getting caught in the story and re-experiencing intense fear reactions, clients can develop the capacity to expand their attention in order to describe and observe the experience without engaging in a cascade of fear-based thoughts and emotions stemming from trauma (Ogden et al. 2006).

Case Example

I first met Vanessa when I was working at an outpatient clinic for women with substance use issues and histories of trauma. She was in her mid 50s at the time and had been in treatment at the clinic for two years before I began working with her. Vanessa is a lesbian-identified African-American woman, who grew up in the Harlem section of Manhattan. She initially presented as experiencing symptoms of depression due to profound feelings of grief over her grandson who had been murdered two years prior to her entering treatment and the deaths of two of her children to complications from AIDS and substance use several years before that. She was skeptical that she could be helped given the extensive traumas she had endured and was reluctant to address her use of marijuana, cocaine, and alcohol as she could not imagine a life without substances and did not wish to pursue abstinence. She was very attached to her previous therapist who had left the clinic and was apprehensive about engaging in treatment with me.

Vanessa shared that her mother had issues with alcohol and substances so she was raised by both her mother and grandmother and would spend time at each of their homes as a child. Vanessa described her early life as having little structure or stability. Vanessa witnessed physical violence between her mother and her boyfriends and was also the victim of repeated instances of childhood sexual abuse. Vanessa began to drink alcohol around the age of 12 and also began to smoke marijuana at that time. When she was 14, she became pregnant and her mother kicked her out of their home. Vanessa then moved in with her grandmother, who helped raise her daughter. She reported that she would frequently run away and stay in abandoned buildings with friends where she would drink and use substances, eventually leading to her use of crack-cocaine and heroin. Vanessa did not graduate from high school and later gave birth to a son who was also raised by family members.

Many years of Vanessa's life were a blur to her. She said that she often felt "ugly" and uncomfortable in her body. She engaged in sex work to pay for alcohol and drugs and was subject to physical violence and sexual assaults during that time as well. Heroin helped her to detach from her surroundings and numb herself. She made the decision to stop using heroin and crack-cocaine when she woke up one day in an abandoned building with other substance users and she said to herself, "what am I doing here? I need to get out of here." She left and moved back in with her mother, who at that time had been raising her daughter and son. Vanessa stopped using heroin on her own, although she reported that the withdrawal process was one of the most painful experiences of her life. She vowed to never use heroin again and maintained that commitment. However, Vanessa continued to drink alcohol and smoke marijuana on a daily basis and reported that she and her daughter experienced a strained and tumultuous relationship as a result. Due to symptoms of hypervigilance and increased arousal, Vanessa admitted to having a fierce temper and feeling as though she constantly had to defend herself. Following the deaths of her daughter and son to AIDS years later, Vanessa described how alcohol would allow her to retreat and detach from her feelings of sadness, anger, and loneliness. Certain anniversaries were particularly painful for her and she would binge drink during those dates and began using powder cocaine again several times a week after the deaths of her children. She attempted to help raise her grandchildren and had tried to limit her substance use unsuccessfully.

Over time, Vanessa found a loving and supportive partner whom she married. Her partner, Ann, was someone who Vanessa knew from her neighborhood. They developed mutual feelings of attraction to one another and were very committed to their relationship. As part of our work together, I had the chance to meet Ann and see how she and Vanessa interacted with each other. I witnessed a tender and caring side of Vanessa. Despite the many years they had been together, she never fully felt like she deserved such a stable and loving partner. She continued to carry an identity as someone who was "dirty," "bad," and "unloveable." Sexual intimacy was also difficult due to her history of trauma and would sometimes result in using cocaine as a way to feel more sexually engaged with Ann.

When Vanessa would speak of her past and the losses she experienced, she displayed intense feelings of sadness and would become practically nonverbal from crying so intensely. We began to slowly put words to her feelings and identify where she felt them in her body. We also explored her thoughts and reactions to intense emotions and how she had been impacted by the multiple traumas she experienced. We reflected on how using marijuana, alcohol, and cocaine offered her freedom from uncomfortable feelings and allowed her to feel more at ease in her body. Vanessa smoked marijuana throughout the day, every day and had for several years, however her use of alcohol and cocaine was mostly limited to the weekends. Sometimes Vanessa would binge, particularly during times that reminded her of those who she had lost.

Together we discussed her experiences as a woman of color and how she had been affected by racism and prejudice throughout her life. I inquired about her feelings working with a younger white woman from a privileged background and our relationship ended up being a focal point of our work together. There were several incidents that occurred during our work together where she felt slighted by others and attributed it to racism or discrimination. I always made space for us to talk about these interactions and encouraged her to describe her experiences so I could better understand her. I also shared my feelings of sadness and frustration that she had to deal with these experiences as it was not something I had ever experienced as a white woman navigating the world. It was clear that we both had strong feelings of warmth and concern for one another. She sometimes asked me questions about my personal life and we discussed our relationships with our dogs, which was a source of connection and allowed us to share how our dogs offered us unconditional love and support during times of stress. Vanessa would occasionally bring me a piece of cake following a birthday celebration as she knew how much I loved sweets. We would also talk about recipes and how food and family celebrations were so important to her. She appreciated that I was able to "let my guard down" and "be real" with her. Had I been more with withholding and distant, I imagine that she would have not stayed in treatment with me. Through careful self-disclosure, our bond grew.

Vanessa's initial goal was to reduce her use of cocaine and we set specific limits about when and how much to use along with helping her develop other coping skills. She said cocaine helped her to feel relaxed and she would often use it alone to unwind in her bedroom in conjunction with smoking marijuana. We practiced grounding and self-soothing skills (see Appendix 5) that focused on breathing techniques and shifting her attention to what she noticed around her (e.g., colors, shapes, scents). I gave her a small stone as an object for contemplation that we used when we practiced together. She kept that stone with her at all times. Once Vanessa was better able to regulate her emotions and manage intense feelings of distress, we began to practice mindfulness together and started by doing brief body scans. We discussed the importance of practicing on a regular basis so she developed a routine each morning and evening that consisted of doing focused breathing exercises and short body scans. I taught her how to practice the 3-minute breathing space (Segal et al. 2002), which was a "portable" practice that she could use whenever she wanted to throughout the day. The 3-minute breathing space is a precursor to the SOBER Breathing Space (see Appendix 1), which at that time, I had not yet been introduced to.

By learning how to settle her emotions and feel more grounded in her body, Vanessa slowly began to reduce her cocaine use. We tracked it and over the course of our four years working together, she reduced her use from approximately 2–3 times per week to 1 time per month. Since she had high blood pressure, we discussed how cocaine could compromise her health which served to further motivate her desire to reduce her use. Vanessa's alcohol use also greatly decreased although she continues to enjoy alcohol moderately on social occasions but no longer binged during difficult anniversaries. Mindfulness practices gave her space to experience her feelings, acknowledge the layers of reactivity, and then choose how to respond. We created moderation goals for alcohol use that included making sure she ate before she drank, that she had plenty of water, and paced her intake of alcohol. We developed other rituals for those more difficult anniversaries where she would have previously binged, included lighting candles, saying prayers, and connecting with family. Interestingly, despite her reluctance to formally address her marijuana use, she also noticed that she had fewer cravings to smoke marijuana and was able to limit her use to once in the daytime and once in the evening. She also began to entertain the idea of working toward going through a day without any marijuana use. We were both pleasantly surprised by this development and I encouraged her to experiment with a day of abstinence, which she eventually did.

Conclusion

My work with Vanessa is an example of the power of a harm reduction approach and how we can gradually work together with clients to build positive change. Given her extensive trauma history and complex bereavement issues, I first focused on helping her develop grounding skills based on the work of Najavits (2002; see Appendix 5) and gave her space to process her memories and feelings about these experiences once she was able to. I educated her about trauma and the symptoms she was experiencing so she could be prepared for them. We experimented with different techniques for managing intrusive images, feelings of agitation, hyperarousal, numbing, and dissociation. We also worked on developing a "window of tolerance" so she could speak about her experiences and process them without feeling overly flooded (hyperaroused) or dissociative and numb (Herman 1992; Siegal as cited in Ogden et al. 2006). As we moved through the stages of healing from trauma and she found that she could care for herself without relying exclusively on substances, Vanessa was able to mourn her losses and articulate the impact of the multiple traumas she endured (Herman 1992). She established a better connection to her partner, felt more at ease with others, and more comfortable about her role in the world.

Mindfulness was an important aspect of our work together and we regularly practiced in our sessions together. We began by focusing Vanessa's awareness on the sensations of her breath and we gradually moved inward so she could be present with difficult emotions and build awareness of the ways in which she was narrating her experiences. Helping her increase the capacity to mindfully attend to her experiences nonjudgmentally allowed us to explore and process the intense emotions she feared and also enhanced her ability to engage other ways of self-soothing in the moment. Vanessa reported feeling more grounded in her body and more confident in her ability to manage feeling overwhelmed. Through her own experiences with practicing mindfulness, goals about changing her relationship to substances emerged along with a commitment to greater self-care. From there, we developed safe use plans and she was gradually able to reduce her substance use. All of this occurred in a safe therapeutic space, where I was open to her changing needs and adjusted my stance based on what she needed in the moment rather than focusing on predetermined treatment goals.

Appendix 1: SOBER Breathing Space (Bowen et al. 2010)

This is a practice you can do almost anywhere and at anytime. This is an especially useful practice to try during times of increased stress or in high-risk situations. When things in ourselves or in our environment trigger us, we tend to go into automatic pilot mode, which can result in reactions and behaviors that are not in our best interest. This is a technique that can be used to help us step out of that automatic mode and become more aware and mindful of our actions.

STOP: Stop, slow down, and check in with what is happening, this is the first step in shifting out of automatic pilot.
OBSERVE: Observe the sensations in the body. Observe any emotions, moods, thoughts, or judgments you are having. Just notice as much as you can about your experience.
BREATH: Gather your attention and bring it to your breath.
EXPAND: Expand your awareness to include the rest of your body, your experience, and the situation, seeing if you can gently hold it all in awareness.
RESPOND: Respond (vs. react) mindfully, with awareness of what is truly needed in the situation and how you can best take care of yourself. Whatever is happening in your mind and body, you still have a choice in how your respond.

Appendix 2: Harm Reduction and Mindfulness Resources

Harm Reduction Resources

Alternatives Addiction Treatment (Los Angeles, CA): http://addictionalternatives.com
The Center for Optimal Living (NYC): www.centerforoptimalliving.com
The Center for Harm Reduction Therapy (San Francisco, CA): www.harmreductiontherapy.org
HAMS, Harm Reduction for Alcohol: www.hamsnetwork.org
Harm Reduction Coalition: www.harmreduction.org
Moderation Management: http://moderation.org
Practical Recovery (San Diego, CA): www.practicalrecovery.com
SMART Recovery: www.smartrecovery.org.

Mindfulness Resources

Mindfulness-based cognitive therapy: http://mbct.com
Mindfulness-based relapse prevention: www.mindfulrp.com
Jenifer Talley's website with meditation downloads: www.jenifertalley.com/practice
Tara Brach's website: www.tarabrach.com
Jill Satterfield, Vajra Yoga + Meditation: http://vajrayoga.com
UCLA Mindful Awareness Research Center: http://marc.ucla.edu.

Appendix 3: Checking-in Practice

This practice can be done as part of a formal sitting practice and can also be used throughout the day as a way to gather your awareness and observe your experiences. The intention of this practice is to help you slow down and note what is happening in the mind, body, heart, and breath. As you notice your experiences and sensations in the body, try to greet them with openness, curiosity, and compassion. Try to welcome your experiences without judgment.

Let us pause for a few moments and acknowledge what is here now:

- What is the quality of your breath? Where do you notice your breath?
- How does your body feel in this moment? Try a brief body scan starting with the crown of the head and observe sensations in your body. What posture is your body in right now? Can you feel the weight of your body in the chair, on the floor? Can you observe where your body is making contact with the fabric of your clothes, with the seat that you are on or the ground beneath you? Do you notice the temperature of the air on your skin?
- What types of thoughts do you notice? How are you narrating this moment? Are there critical thoughts? Worry thoughts? See if you can observe your thoughts without attaching judgment to them.
- How is your heart feeling? What emotions are here now?
- Allow your awareness to rest on your breath again and observe the sensations of your breath. If you get distracted, simply begin again with the next breath. If you find it difficult to focus on breath, try to experiment with counting your breath each time you exhale and when you reach 5, start over. You can also practice counting how long it takes to inhale and exhale without manipulating it—just notice how long each of your breaths are.

What was it like for you to slow down and check in with yourself?

Appendix 4: Urge Surfing Practice (Adapted from Bowen et al. 2010)

For this practice, you will imagine a situation where you find yourself struggling to manage an intense urge or craving to use a substance or engage in a behavior that might be problematic for you. Select a scenario that is not too overwhelming and that is of moderate intensity to start with.

This practice will guide you through the process and will help you stay with your experience without reacting in habitual ways. Please remember that you are doing your best and that the intention is to greet all your experiences with kindness, curiosity, openness, and compassion. If the practice feels too intense, you can always open your eyes, notice your surroundings, and observe the position of your body and the connection to your seat and/or chair.

Once you have selected the scenario you wish to practice with, take a few moments to really imagine yourself there. Perhaps close your eyes and allow yourself to feel the experience more fully. How you are feeling? What thoughts are here? Note sensations in your body, the emotions you are observing, and how your breath is.

Try to imagine the scenario up until the point where you might have previously responded to with reactivity and without full awareness. See if you can pause and stay here for a moment without reacting. How does it feel to stay with and notice the experience without reacting? What do you observe? Can you stay with the experience and be gentle with yourself? What about this feels intolerable? What sensations do you notice in the body? What emotions are you feeling? How are you thinking about this experience?

Remember that you can always pause and open your eyes if this is feeling too overwhelming. You may shift to just observing the sensations of your breath before deciding to return to the practice.

Observe how it feels to be with this urge or craving—can you feel it without resisting it or judging it? How does it feel to not engage in the behavior and continue to observe the experience? Can you explore what else is here? What you might truly need or want in this moment? Is there a longing for something? What are you seeking? See if you can gently observe this with curiosity and kindness.

If the craving feels intense, you may begin to image that it is like a wave in the ocean. Imagine the size of the wave, its color, its size. Imagine that you are now riding that wave using your breath as a surfboard that allows you to stay steady. Try to keep your balance by focusing on your breath as you ride out the intensity of the wave. See if you can be with these feelings and intensity using your breath to help you.

Perhaps you are noticing that you can be with this craving and this intensity without reacting to it or wishing it would go away. You are watching how the craving rises and falls, how it shifts with time and as you move your focus to your breath.

Take your time to gently let go of this scenario and return your attention to your breath and to your surroundings. Perhaps observe the sounds in the room, the shapes and colors you see and observe the position of your body. You may take a few deep breaths and make gentle movements with the body, if you would like.

Appendix 5: Grounding and Focusing on Five Senses (Adapted from Najavits 2002; Linehan 1993; Marra 2004)

At times, it is useful to practice grounding and orienting to the present moment. You can try this practice when you are feeling overwhelmed, have difficulty shifting your focus away from a disturbing memory, intense emotions, or a strong craving to engage in a behavior you feel is problematic for you. During times of increased distress, we might struggle to soothe ourselves in adaptive ways and you may try some of these practices to see if they help you navigate difficult situations with more ease. Some people find it helpful to focus on their surroundings and notice the five senses during times of increased distress and reactivity. This practice is focused on moving your awareness to what is external rather than focusing inward.

Suggestions for Practice

- You should begin to experiment with these practices when you are not feeling overly distressed or overwhelmed. It takes time to learn these practices and identify which ones feel most useful to you.
- You can practice this anytime and anywhere. It is recommended that you keep your eyes open and be aware of your surroundings.
- Try to rate how you are feeling before and after the practice using a scale of 1–10.
- Remember to maintain your focus on the present moment and if you mind wanders to the past or future, gently try to bring your attention back to the present.
- Avoid judging yourself as you practice. You may feel distracted and you may struggle to engage with this practice. Try to be patient and adopt an attitude of kindness toward yourself and your experiences.
- The intention of this practice is to help you accept the moment and engage in safer ways of coping with discomfort and distress.

Focusing on the Five Senses

Gently and with a playful attitude, see if you can move your awareness to your senses and what you are observing around you.

Vision: What can I look at that will make me feel good things?
Hearing: What is pleasing to the ear? What can I listen to that soothes me?
Smell: What aromas make me feel at ease?
Taste: What can I eat and savor that is pleasing to me?
Touch: What can I touch that will invoke feelings that are different from what I am experiencing right now?

Grounding Practices

- Observe and describe your present environment in detail—what colors, shapes, and textures do you see? Where are you in right now? What position or posture is your body in?
- Carry a special object with you that you can focus on such as a small stone, lotion, mints, a picture, or a certain song you can listen to.
- Count to a certain number such as 10 or 20 and then start again.
- Notice how your feet are making contact with the floor—perhaps press your feet downward so you can feel the connection to the ground beneath you.
- Stretch your arms, legs, move your head from side to side, do a gentle twist in your seat.
- Practice mindfully walking and observing the movement of each leg/foot as you walk along with the sights, sounds, smells around you.
- Observe your breath and count each time you inhale and exhale. Perhaps pair a certain word with each in-breath and out-breath such as "soften," "soothe," "release" or any other word that you would like to use. Notice how the body gently moves with each breath.

- Imagine a safe place—it can be a place you have been to before or a place that you create for yourself in your mind. Using your senses, try to imagine yourself in that safe space and observe how it feels to be there. How is your breath?
- Say a self-soothing statement to yourself like, "this will pass," "may I be at ease," "I will be okay," "this is feeling won't last forever."

References

American Psychiatric Association. (2013). *Diagnostic and statistical manual of mental disorders* (5th ed.). Washington, D.C.: American Psychiatric Publishing.

Back, S.E., Contini, R. & Brady, K.T. (2006). Substance abuse in women: Does gender matter? Psychiatric Times. Retrieved from http://www.psychiatrictimes.com/substance-use-disorder/substance-abuse-women-does-gender-matter.

Binswanger, I. A., Redmond, N., Steiner, J. F., & Hicks, L. S. (2012). Health disparities and the criminal justice system: An agenda for further research and action. *Journal of Urban Health, 89*(1), 98–107.

Bowen, S., Chawla, N., & Marlatt, G. A. (2010). *Mindfulness-based relapse prevention for addictive behaviors: A clinician's guide*. New York, NY: Guilford Press.

Bowen, S., Witkiewitz, K., Clifasefi, S. L., Grow, J., Chawla, N., Hsu, S. H., et al. (2014). Relative efficacy of mindfulness-based relapse prevention, standard relapse prevention, and treatment as usual for substance use disorders: A randomized clinical trial. *JAMA Psychiatry, 71*(5), 547–556.

Brewer, J. A., Bowen, S., Smith, J. T., Marlatt, G. A., & Potenza, M. N. (2010). Applying mindfulness-based treatments to co-occurring disorders: What can we learn from the brain? *Addiction, 105,* 1698–1706.

Brewer, J. A., Elwafi, H. M., & Davis, J. H. (2013). Craving to quit: psychological models and neurobiological mechanisms of mindfulness training as treatment for addictions. *Psychology of Addictive Behaviors, 27*(2), 366–379.

Brown, K. W., Ryan, R. M., & Crewsell, D. J. (2007). Mindfulness: Theoretical foundations and evidence for its salutary effects. *Psychological Inquiry, 18*(4), 211–237.

Broyles, L. M., Binswanger, I. A., Jenkins, J. A., Finnell, D. S., Faseru, B., Cavaiola, A., et al. (2014). Confronting inadvertent stigma and pejorative language in addiction scholarship: A recognition and response. *Substance Abuse, 35,* 217–221.

Davis, A. K., & Rosenberg, H. (2013). Acceptance of non-abstinence goals by addiction professionals in the United States. *Psychology of Addictive Behaviors, 27*(4), 1102–1109.

Denning, P., & Little, J. (2012). *Practicing harm reduction psychotherapy: An alternative approach to addictions* (2nd ed.). New York: The Guilford Press.

Dube, S. R., Dong, M., Chapman, D. P., Giles, W. H., Anda, R. F., & Felitti, V. J. (2003). Childhood abuse, neglect, and household dysfunction and the risk of illicit drug use: The adverse childhood experiences. *Pediatrics, 111*(3), 564–572.

Greenfield, S. F., Back, S. E., Lawson, K., & Brady, K. T. (2010). Substance abuse in women. *Psychiatric Clinics of North America, 33*(2), 339–355.

Hart, C. (2014). *High price: A neuroscientist's journey of discovery that challenges everything you know about drugs and society*. New York: Harper Perennial.

Herman, J. L. (1992). *Trauma and recovery*. New York: Basic Books.

Hsu, S. H., Collins, S. E., & Marlatt, G. A. (2013). Examining psychometric properties of distress tolerance and its moderation of mindfulness-based relapse prevention effects on alcohol and other drug use outcomes. *Addictive Behaviors, 38,* 1852–1858.

Kabat-Zinn, J. (1990). *Full catastrophe living*. New York: Bantam Dell.

Kaskutas, L. A. (2009). Alcoholics anonymous effectiveness: Faith meets science. *Journal of Addictive Diseases, 28*(2), 145–157.

Khantzian, E.J. (1985). The self-medication hypothesis of addictive disorders: focus on heroin and cocaine dependence. American Journal of Psychiatry, 142(11), 1259–1264.

Khantzian, E. J., & Albanese, M. J. (2008). *Understanding addiction as self-medication: Finding hope behind the pain*. Lanham, MD: Rowman & Littlefield Publishers Inc.

Larimer, M., Palmer, R. S., & Marlatt, G. A. (1999). Relapse prevention: An overview of Marlatt's cognitive-behavioral model. *Alcohol Res Health, 23*(2), 151–160.

Linehan, M. (1993). *Skills training manual for treating borderline personality disorder*. New York: The Guilford Press.

Linehan, M. (2014). *DBT skills training manual* (2nd ed.). New York: The Guilford Press.

Marlatt, G. A., & Gordon, J. R. (1985). *Relapse prevention: Maintenance strategies in the treatment of addictive behaviors*. New York, NY: Guilford Press.

Marlatt, G. A., Larimer, M. E., & Witkiewitz, K. (2012). *Harm reduction: Pragmatic strategies for managing high risk behaviors* (2nd ed.). New York: Guilford Press.

Marlatt, G. A., & Witkiewitz, K. (2005). Relapse prevention for alcohol and drug problems. In G. A. Marlatt & D. M. Donovan (Eds.), *Relapse prevention: Maintenance strategies in the treatment of addictive behaviors* (2nd ed., pp. 1–44). New York: Guilford.

Marra, T. (2004). *Depressed and anxious: The DBT workbook for overcoming depression and anxiety*. California: New Harbinger.

Maté, G. (2010). *In the realm of hungry ghosts: Close encounters with addiction*. Berkeley, CA: North Atlantic Books.

McCauley, J. L., Killeen, T., Gros, D. F., Brady, K. T., Back, S. T., & Johnson, R. H. (2012). Posttraumatic stress disorder and co-occurring substance use disorders: Advances in assessment and treatment. *Clinical Psychology, 9*(3), 283–304.

Miller, W., & Rollnick, S. (2013). *Motivational interviewing: Preparing people to change* (3rd ed.). New York: The Guilford Press.

Murphy, S. L., & Khantzian, E. J. (1995). Addiction as "self-medication" disorder: Application of ego psychology to the treatment of substance abuse. In A. Washton (Ed.), *Psychotherapy and substance abuse* (pp. 161–175). New York: Guilford.

Najavits, L. (2002). *Seeking safety: A treatment manual for PTSD and substance abuse*. New York: The Guilford Press.

Ogden, P., Minton, K., & Pain, C. (2006). *Trauma and the body: A sensorimotor approach to psychotherapy*. New York: W.W. Norton & Company.

Pietrzak, R. H., Goldstein, R. B., Southwick, S. M., & Grant, B. F. (2011). Prevalence and Axis I comorbidity of full and partial posttraumatic stress disorder in the United States: Results from wave 2 of the National Epidemiologic Survey on Alcohol and Related Conditions. *Journal of Anxiety Disorders, 25*(3), 456–465.

Prochaska, J. O., DiClemente, C. C., & Norcross, J. C. (1992). In search of how people change: Applications to addictive behaviors. *American Psychologist, 47*(9), 1102–1114.

Rotgers, F., Kern, M. F., & Hoeltzel, R. (2002). *Responsible drinking: A moderation management approach for problem drinkers*. Oakland, CA: New Harbinger.

Rothschild, D. (2010). Partners in treatment: Relational psychoanalysis and harm reduction therapy. *Journal of Clinical Psychology. In Session, 66*(2), 136–149.

Rothschild, D. (2015). Working together: Integrating relational psychoanalysis and traditional substance use treatment in harm reduction therapy. In J. Bresler & K. Starr (Eds.), *Relational psychoanalysis and psychotherapy integration: An evolving synergy* (pp. 161–179). New York: Routledge.

Ruglass, L. M., Lopez-Castro, T., Cheref, S., Papini, S., & Hien, D. (2014). At the crossroads: The intersection of substance use disorders, anxiety disorders, and posttraumatic stress disorder. *Current Psychiatry Reports, 16,* 505.

Segal, Z. V., Williams, J., & Teasdale, J. D. (2002). *Mindfulness-based cognitive therapy for depression*. New York: Guilford Press.

Tatarsky, A. (2003). Harm reduction psychotherapy: Extending the reach of traditional substance use treatment. *Journal of Substance Abuse Treatment, 25,* 249–256.

Tatarsky, A. (2007). *Harm reduction psychotherapy*. Lanham, MD: Rowman & Littlefield Publishers Inc.

Tatarsky, A., & Kellogg, S. (2010). Integrative harm reduction psychotherapy: A case of substance use, multiple trauma, and suicidality. *Journal of Clinical Psychology. In Session, 66*(2), 123–135.

Van Amsterdam, J., & van den Brink, W. (2013). Reduced-risk drinking as a viable treatment goal in problematic alcohol use and alcohol dependence. *Journal of Psychopharmacology, 27*(11), 987–997.

Washton, A. M., & Zweben, J. (2008). *Treating alcohol and drug problems in psychotherapy practice: Doing what works*. New York: The Guilford Press.

Witkiewitz, K., Greenfield, B. L., & Bowen, S. (2013). Mindfulness-based relapse prevention with racial and ethnic minority women. *Addictive Behaviors, 38,* 2821–2824.

Witkiewitz, K., Lustyk, M. K., & Bowen, S. (2012). Re-Training the addicted brain: A review of hypothesized neurobiological mechanisms of mindfulness-based relapse prevention. *Psychology of Addictive Behaviors, 27,* 351–365.

Witkiewitz, K., & Marlatt, G. A. (2006). Overview of harm reduction treatments for alcohol problems. *International Journal of Drug Policy, 17,* 285–294.

Wurmser, L. (1993). Psychodynamics in compulsive drug use. In J. D. Levin & R. H. Weiss (Eds.), *The dynamics and treatment of alcoholism: Essential papers* (pp. 176–206). Northvale, NJ: Jason Aronson Inc.

Zgierska, A., Rabago, D., Chawla, N., Kushner, K., Koehler, R., & Marlatt, G. A. (2009). Mindfulness meditation for substance-use disorders: A systematic review. *Substance Abuse, 30,* 266–294.

Chapter 10
Beginning with the Modality: Learned Helpfulness in Mindful Group Work with Individuals with Serious Mental Illness

Rebecca Strauss

> I learned to go to a place of comfort (no pain) in my body, to breathe and concentrate on my breath. I came in feeling ashamed and in physical pain. Now I feel relaxed.—Mindfulness group member

> The part of my body that felt good was able to flow into the part of my body that felt pain. —Mindfulness group member

Introduction

Serious mental illness comes with psychosocial implications that are much farther reaching than symptom management of thoughts, fantasies, and impulsive behaviors. Individuals who live with such diagnoses are often confronted with a weakened self-structure due to a history of trauma and neglect, thwarted development, or an environment of chaos and despair. The subjective experience of one with serious mental illness is often complicated by the social stigma of having such illness, low self-esteem, difficulties in self-regulation that lead to unmanageable emotions, disruptive behaviors, and inflexible thoughts of being unique in their suffering.

As mindfulness interventions become more mainstream in clinical social work, exploring these cognitive practices with individuals diagnosed with serious mental illness may provide a bridge to recovery that instills clients with hope, empowerment, and resilience. As clients learn to cultivate internal awareness, in the present moment, without a sense of self, social, or moral judgment, they may experience a willingness to accept life as it unfolds, with greater curiosity and more adaptive response behaviors. Research supports the hypothesis that mindfulness practices, in particular mindfulness meditation, essentially train the mind and change the structure and functions of the brain. In doing so, they provide a concrete process for building

R. Strauss (✉)
Turning Point Behavioral Health Care Center, Skokie, IL, USA
e-mail: rjs0825@gmail.com

T.B. Northcut (ed.), *Cultivating Mindfulness in Clinical Social Work*,
Essential Clinical Social Work Series, DOI 10.1007/978-3-319-43842-9_10

skills that may positively impact recovery and the quality of one's life (Begley 2008; Treadway and Lazar 2010). In this way, regular mindfulness practices instill a sense of ***learned helpfulness***, provided by one's increased capacity to observe what is happening internally first, and respond in ways that feel more helpful.

In this chapter, focus will be given to highlighting a mindfulness meditation practice facilitated weekly in a psychosocial rehabilitation (PSR) group setting with individuals with serious and persistent mental illness. Special considerations will include the possibility of strengthening the self through mindfulness skills, a brief review of current research supporting these practices, a discussion of limitations, and the need for clinicians to experience mindfulness practices on some level before offering them in direct practice settings.

Serious and Persistent Mental Illness

> I need help badly to get out of these thoughts so I can be present instead of somewhere else.—Mindfulness group member

> Being non-judgmental with myself helps me cope with my paranoia.—Mindfulness group member

The burden of mental illness extends far beyond symptomology. In 2014, approximately 18% of adults in the United States, or roughly 43.6 million Americans, experienced some form of mental illness (Samhsa 2014). Of this population, approximately 4.1%, or approximately 9.8 million individuals were reported to have a serious mental illness such as Schizophrenia, Major Depression Disorder (MDD), Posttraumatic Stress Disorder (PTSD) or Bipolar Disorder (Samhsa 2014). Individuals living with such diagnoses are often associated with high resource utilization, increased psychiatric hospitalization, increased risk of chronic medical conditions, and die on average 25 years earlier than those without such diagnoses (Colton and Manderscheid 2006). They have higher comorbidity rates than the general population (Samhsa 2014; DiClemente et al. 2008) and experience a higher drop out rate at the student level (U.S. Department of Education 2006). Furthermore, a history of one or more psychiatric disorders is indicated in more than 90% of those who die by suicide (American Association of Suicidology 2012).

Mental illness is defined as "all diagnosable mental disorders or health conditions that are characterized by alterations in thinking, mood, or behavior, or some combination thereof, associated with distress and/or impaired functioning" (U.S. Department of Health and Human Services 1999). Those diagnosed with *severe and persistent* mental illness are significantly functionally impaired by the illness for an indefinite period of time. They may present with positive symptoms of psychoses such as hallucinations or delusions, disorganized speech, bizarre behaviors and impaired judgment, and/or negative symptoms such as extreme dependency, social withdrawal, poverty of speech, inability to experience pleasure (anhedonia), restricted affect, and deficits in attention or behavioral control.

As with any diagnoses, those living with serious mental illness present with symptoms on the continuum in terms of frequency, severity, and overall impact on emotional, behavioral, and interpersonal functioning. One of the biggest hurdles in living with persistent mental illness is the significant uncertainty associated with the illness. Severity of symptoms fluctuates and is often impacted by external stressors such as co-occurring behaviors, medication side effects, or issues related to non-compliance. For some, limited access to financial, transportation, social, healthcare, and other supportive resources create additional barriers to recovery. Problems are compounded by a felt sense of stigma associated with such diagnoses, often leading to social isolation, rejection, and a persistent sense of hopelessness (Perry 2011).

Unbridled uncertainty and anxiety threatens the individual's sense of self, amplifying one's potential for depression, isolation, emptiness, loss of agency, and sense of helplessness (Garret and Weisman 2001). Adjusting to mental illness thus requires the development of coping skills that are available and accessible for myriad presenting problems. The clinician's role is to help clients realistically assess and accept their illness, connect with a more cohesive sense of self, and introduce skills that will facilitate readjustment and adaptation in their everyday environment.

The Mindfulness Perspective—A Great Equalizer

> I focus on sitting up straight, breathing, and the present moment. My posture has improved. My muscles are stronger. I have more energy.—Mindfulness group member

> I feel less anxiety by focusing on the present instead of the past. It feels safer.—Mindfulness group member

Meditation has been a part of Eastern spiritual traditions for thousands of years, with the purpose to bringing the practitioner to "states of deeper connection to something larger than the self, ultimately leading to enlightenment (Segalla 2003, p. 788)." More recently, Western medicine, including the realm of psychotherapy, has evolved with a greater appreciation for integrating secular mindfulness practices in the healing of mind and body (Kabat-Zinn 2009; Begley 2008; Germer et al. 2005). Research is helping considerably to build acceptance of mindfulness practices in mainstream living. Findings support the hypothesis that regular meditation practices have the potential to lead to enduring changes in the structure and function of the brain related to reduced suffering and improved well-being (Lazar 2005; Treadway and Lazar 2010; Ricard et al. 2014). Mindfulness training is a central component of Dialectical Behavior Therapy (Linehan 1993a, b), Mindfulness-based Cognitive Therapy (Teasdale et al. 1995), and a core practice in the stress reduction and relaxation program known as Mindfulness-Based Stress Reduction (Kabat-Zinn 1982). The mindfulness field is discussed pervasively in news and social media

(Harris 2014), and has been quietly incorporated into corporate life at General Mills, Aetna, BlackRock Financial, and Google (Gelles 2015; Rathbone 2013). At some point, mental exercises like those practiced in mindfulness meditation may be regarded the same way as physical exercise is thought of today. Instead of strength and agility training for the body, mindfulness exercises might be practiced regularly to promote strength and agility training for the mind.

By tending to one's inner experience, a skill that is cultivated in mindfulness practices, we have the potential to access a dimension of the self often ignored in the more traditional models of engagement (Segalla 2003). Mindfulness interventions within group settings bring a special focus to building awareness of what happens in the here and now, internally and interpersonally. They *provide a safe and supportive space* in which to process and learn from these experiences with others. Group members engage in a conscious observation of the self through breathing exercises, guided meditations, synchronized movement with the breath, or observed stillness from the perspective of openness, curiosity, acceptance, and nonjudgment. The attention and awareness that is cultivated helps one notice thoughts and feelings as they emerge, and highlights the temporary nature of these subjective states as having a beginning, middle, and end. From a mental health perspective, mindfulness practices are introduced to train one's attention on the moment-to-moment experience and use this awareness to manage uncertainty or distress with greater flexibility. For example, when one begins to notice they are angered or distressed by a particular situation, the task becomes one of working skillfully with the bare experience of distress by practicing "an alternative inner response (Fulton 2013, p. 212)." Through one's mindful attention to the experience of anger that is neither shaming nor judging, one may be able to develop the skill to observe and respond more thoughtfully, rather than react in patterned ways that have historically made matters worse.

Many individuals with chronic mental illness face additional complications related to comorbid physical illness, intellectual disabilities, transportation difficulties, unstable housing, limited financial means, and social supports. Once learned, mindfulness practices are free and accessible to anyone; all one needs for practice is their body, breath, and mind. From this perspective, mindfulness practices are *a great equalizer*, minimizing the gap between socioeconomic levels, intellectual capacity, academic and occupational achievements. When clients have the opportunity to learn mindfulness practices through group or individual work, they have an opportunity to enhance their own recovery through greater empowerment and self-efficacy, true hallmarks of best clinical social work practice.

Psychosocial Rehabilitation (PSR) Groups

> I feel like I keep learning something new about meditation each week. Trying to breathe from the belly takes practice and it does make a difference in how I feel.—Mindfulness group member

> I liked the 5/6 breathing meditation in group today. I am happy to have new tools to help me calm down during panic.—Mindfulness group member

Just as in direct service with individuals, the social work perspective as seen in groups is informed by assessing client strengths and vulnerabilities, goals and objectives, capacity and motivation, and the subtleties of presenting symptoms. The person-centered approach is supported in group work with individuals with serious mental illness by creating a therapeutic space of potential, engaging clients in skill-building or processing opportunities that lead to greater self and social intelligence.

In contrast to groups of a therapeutic nature that rely on the interactions of the group members to guide each other toward a "corrective emotional experience" (Yalom 1995), psychosocial rehabilitation (PSR) groups are skills-based groups that are issue-specific. They have a higher level of leader direction, and a more structured protocol that emphasizes skills-acquisition. PSR groups are facilitated with adults 18 years and older, who are diagnosed with a serious mental illness that significantly impacts their social, emotional, and occupational functioning (Department of Human Services (DHS) 2015). They differ from traditional group therapy in that the group leader functions as a trainer, teaching skills for managing symptoms, problem solving and coping, socializing, improving concentration and attention to tasks, following directions, planning and organizing, and establishing or modifying activities of daily living. The PSR group experience involves mastery of these skills through psycho-education, modeling relevant skills, peer collaboration, opportunities to give and receive feedback, and the real time witnessing of alternate perceptions and response behaviors of others in the group. Many clients in PSR programs have co-occurring physical illnesses and intellectual disabilities, adding ongoing layers of challenge to their recovery. Although the capacities of PSR group members vary on the continuum, the individual groups are designed to help participants develop the necessary skills to live as independently as possible, manage their mental illness with as little intervention as possible, and to achieve functional, social, educational, and vocational goals (DHS 2015).

Therapeutic Factors in Psychosocial Rehabilitation (PSR) Group-Work

> I found the group difficult today because of my feelings of sadness. I am thankful though, to be in a space where my emotions are not judged.—Mindfulness group member

> This group gives me peace and comfort. It helps me to relax. My mind is filled with fear, anxiety, being upset and very unorganized. This group makes me feel more positive.—Mindfulness Group Member

Therapeutic factors exist that are central to the change process in traditional group therapy settings. According to Yalom (1995), instillation of hope, universality, imparting information, altruism, a recapitulation of the primary family group, development of socializing techniques, imitative behavior, interpersonal learning, catharsis, existential factors, and group cohesiveness are all factors that occur within group experiences in a nonlinear fashion. Their relevance varies from group to group and from individual to individual (Yalom 1995). Age, diagnosis, and symptom presentation, the length of time in treatment, the client's level of social, emotional, and cognitive functioning, their motivation and capacity to change, and closely held spiritual and/or cultural beliefs all have the potential to influence one's experience of therapeutic factors and treatment outcome in traditional group work.

Yalom (1995) described cohesiveness, or the feeling of being connected to the group, as the primary curative group factor in group therapy. Even though PSR groups are facilitated primarily for skills-acquisition purposes, group members have a unique opportunity to witness changes in one's self and in others when a strong sense of connection or cohesiveness is cultivated in the group setting. When perceived as a safe and supportive environment, research suggests that psychosocial group modalities promote improved functioning in cognitive processing, social skills, and interpersonal communication (Yalom 1995; Ahmed and Goldman 1994; Luk 2011).

For clients with severe mental illness, participation in PSR groups is often their first experience of social connectedness in an environment of mutual understanding and support. For others, the mere act of joining a group setting may begin to address lifelong implicit feelings of shame and being alone in one's struggles. Having provided effective skills training, the astute facilitator may witness an expansion of hope that emerges within group members as capacity builds, as greater self and social awareness develops, and as a shared experience emerges in knowing one's problems are not unique. From a treatment perspective, the facilitator's goal is that relevant life skills are initially learned and practiced in the group setting, and eventually internalized and practiced in the client's natural setting, leading them to greater independence and stability in living.

Mindfulness in PSR Groups

> It was hard to send kindness to myself during the meditation. I'm not used to being kind to myself, but it's something I'm willing to work towards. I think it takes practice.—Mindfulness group member

> I was very anxious at the start and more relaxed at the end. I like breathing into the body as a whole. Thank you.—Mindfulness group member

Facilitating a PSR group for individuals with myriad psychiatric symptoms and traumatic developmental histories can be challenging for many reasons. As human beings, our negotiation between creating a strong sense of self and experiencing self with others is a relevant challenge for many individuals (Segalla 2003). Symptoms of mental illness become realistic barriers to one's ability to connect with others in meaningful ways. They often prevent one's capacity to learn and practice skills that are necessary for healthy, adaptive living. Difficulties with reality testing, inflexible thinking, feelings of being a burden to others, persistent paranoia, insufficient finances and other supportive services, and periodic psychiatric hospitalizations are often client experiences that facilitators must navigate carefully in the skills-building realm of any PSR group.

Mindfulness practices speak to cultivating the power of letting go of the past (its already done), the future (it has not happened yet), and staying grounded in the present (what is happening right now). It is the same message for anyone, regardless of the individual's personal struggles or levels of success. The *great equalizer* perspective, as mentioned earlier in this chapter, works in favor of mindfulness practices in groups for clients with serious mental illness. So often, their perspective of self is mired in shame and difference, stigma and separation from what is perceived as "normal." Very often balancing thoughts that counter engrained and negative thinking patterns are very difficult to imagine, let alone embrace. These unique attention-building practices invite a sense of normalcy for individuals who feel the ongoing stigma associated with their illness. In many ways, their goals of finding calm under pressure, building self-awareness, managing stress, navigating pain and suffering, embracing life's uncertainties, or tolerating extreme emotions can be experienced by many, regardless of one's position in life. Many learn to feel the body change from tense to calm, notice when negative thoughts emerge, find relief in recognizing thought patterns come and go, or begin to relate to pain and distress in a new and different way. Others may practice with no goals or objectives in mind, other than to experience moments of stillness and calm in daily living. Whatever one's intention, mindfulness practices that occur in a group setting shift the focus away from recovery of the self, to recovery of the *self with others*, strengthening feelings of being connected rather than isolated and alone in one's struggles.

Clients who are motivated and committed to making change are most likely to benefit from mindfulness practices (Germer et al. 2005). The vulnerable populations served by clinical social workers often struggle with myriad psychiatric issues related to their diagnoses, including lack of motivation, impaired cognitive functioning, and limited overall functioning. Early experiences with mindfulness meditation can be frustrating, rather than relaxing, as one struggles with staying awake, binding anxiety, or harnessing racing thoughts. Consequently, introduction to contemplative practices may need to be more gradual to allow for the client's experiential component to be felt and processed, with the attitudes of nonjudgment and acceptance central to their understanding (Turner 2008).

Case Study: Mindfulness Meditation PSR Group

> Group was calming today. Acceptance is something I am working on myself, so the practice of acceptance in today's meditation was relevant to my needs.—Mindfulness group member

> I felt the stress and worry about future job and housing things change with 3 little words, 'just this moment.' I have to remember that!—Mindfulness group member

The following case study describes a PSR group, Mindfulness Meditation, as facilitated at a private, nonprofit, community mental health center in a multicultural and multiracial urban setting in the Midwestern United States. The agency provides individual therapy, PSR and group therapy, case management, and psychiatric services to children, adolescent, and adult populations. Due to functional and/or socioeconomic status, most clients at this agency receive government entitlements that provide insurance coverage for their mental health care. Anyone receiving PSR group services must demonstrate "medical necessity" for these services, as defined by an individual state's Department of Mental Health. Although it is beyond the scope of this chapter to identify the full range of requirements for meeting medical necessity, individuals must demonstrate a level of care score, as determined by a LOCUS assessment (DHS 2010), of 17 or below and a have a clinical need for skills-building groups that will enhance progress toward recovery goals and objectives.

At the agency involved, clients register for PSR groups during a registration period that lasts 2 weeks prior to the start of each term; each term lasts approximately 16 weeks. Each client is required to sign a PSR agreement stating that they have reviewed the rules and regulations for group participation, including attendance and confidentiality statements. Most PSR groups are not closed, however they are limited to a maximum of 15 participants. Special considerations are provided for adding new members *during the term* if the cohesion or the safety of the group process will not be in jeopardy.

Due to the experiential nature of mindfulness practices, it is suggested that clinicians personally experience contemplative practices on some level before teaching them to others (Kabat-Zinn 2003; Baer 2003). In this case study, both facilitators of the Mindfulness Meditation group have personal experience with mindfulness practices, including a daily formal meditation practice and informal moment-to-moment awareness training. Each term, the facilitators establish a weekly schedule of mindfulness-related attitudes or skills to teach, along with prepared meditations that reflect the content of each session and allow for the experiential portion.

The Group Sequence

The Mindfulness Meditation group is approximately 50 min and meets once per week. Soft music is often playing as group members filter in and find their seats. There is no music playing during the group unless it is a part of the formal meditation practice. Due to space limitations, the participants sit on chairs that are arranged in an oval fashion, rather than circular, with everyone visible. The room is well-lit and quiet. Facilitators sit on opposite ends of the room to observe the group process and be better able to address any challenges that may occur during the session.

Each session begins with a three-minute centering exercise to help group members transition into the contemplative process and invite access to their internal states. This is followed by a brief check-in where group members use *one word* to describe whatever is present for them in that moment. The group leaders present information on mindfulness attitudes or practices for approximately 20 min, and follow with a 20-minute guided mindfulness meditation related to the session's focus. Each group concludes with time for processing subjective experiences, always invited from the perspective of curiosity and nonjudgment.

At the end of session, group members are asked to provide feedback on their experience by answering one of the following questions: (1) Did you have any reactions to anything addressed in the group today? (2) Did you learn a new skill? (3) How will what we covered today apply in your life outside of this agency (work, relationships, family)? (4) What were your feelings in group today? This feedback loop is documented in official progress notes and used to help facilitators address any unspoken conflicts or concerns and ultimately, provide a supportive learning environment for all participants.

The "Mindfulness Pause"

The following is an example of the three-minute centering exercise used to help group members transition into the meditation group. During the first minute, members get centered on their breath. In the second minute, they are invited to focus on the self, noticing what they are experiencing physically, mentally, or emotionally. During the last minute they are invited to focus on the group as a whole. The purpose of the internal/external focus is to invite both *self-awareness and connection* in the confines of the group setting. The facilitators frame the brief meditation the same way each week:

> Please find your meditation posture [pause], sitting up nice and tall, in a dignified way but not too stiff, both feet on the floor, hands resting comfortably in your lap. [pause] If you are comfortable doing so, gently close your eyes. If you're not comfortable closing your eyes, just drop your gaze to the floor to harness any visual distractions. [pause]
>
> Now as best you can, begin to take a few deep breaths, inhaling through the nose, and exhaling through the mouth [facilitator models breathing]. With each inhalation, invite relaxation in; with each exhalation, imagine softening and letting go. [pause] Take a few moments to notice *any thoughts or feelings that are present for you*, right now. [pause] Observe them with curiosity, openness, and a willingness to be with what is... [pause] When you are ready, allow yourself to become aware of the presence of others in this room. Notice any *feeling of connection* to the group as a whole... [pause] And if you do not feel a sense of connection, let that be present, too. There is no right or wrong experience.. just your experience. [pause] Imagine extending yourself to those *present and absent* from group today. [pause] Experience the *shared energy* of everyone present in this space, right now. [pause] Continue to feel your whole body breathing, feeling connection to yourself and perhaps, to others in this group. [pause] When you are ready, slowly open your eyes, and come back.

Mindfulness Skills-Building Content

Mindfulness embodies the moment-to-moment awareness of one's inner world. It is a state of mind that is cultivated by paying attention to things in a nonjudgmental, open, and curious way (Kabat-Zinn 2009). The formal mindfulness practice of meditation explores the nature of the mind, providing a way to train awareness and attention on one's subjective mental and physical states from the first person perspective. By developing the ability to focus attention on one's internal world, individuals may be able to resculpt neural pathways in ways that lead to greater self-awareness and self-regulation (Siegel 2011), producing a variety of outcomes ranging from being a little more relaxed and less anxious, to coping more effectively with chronic pain and other sources of distress (Davidson and Kaszniak 2015). These benefits of meditation coincide with recent neuroscientific findings supporting the notion that the adult brain has the capacity to transform with new experience (Ricard et al. 2014). But change never just happens; one has to be exposed to the skills that support change and have the opportunity to practice these skills in a safe and supportive environment.

Although the curriculum for the Mindfulness Meditation group varies each term, the first two sessions introduce group members to what it means to be present, how to sit with dignity, and how to breathe with intention. Later sessions might explore mindful eating, the process of loving kindness, applications for chronic pain, and developing a home practice. Further didactic content is provided on the potential conceptual and practical pitfalls that one might experience as their mindfulness meditation skills unfold. Group leaders inform clients of the spiritual origins of meditation, and reinforce that this meditation group is presented in a secular way, without any need to align with a particular faith or sense of spirituality. Most importantly, group members are reminded that mindfulness meditation is a skill that requires repeated practice in all sorts of conditions to access the benefits when they need them most.

In the learning process, group leaders assume from the start that as long as participants are breathing, there is more right with them than wrong with them, no matter how ill or hopeless they may feel (Kabat-Zinn 2009). The group leaders stress that the attitude one brings to the practice of paying attention is crucial to calming the mind, relaxing the body, or seeing things more clearly. This awareness requires *only* that one notice things as they are without any need to change. One of the ways this is addressed is by teaching the following attitudinal foundations of mindfulness practice (Kabat-Zinn 2009).

1. Non-judging

When individuals practice paying attention to their inner experience in a very deliberate way (ex: the inhales and exhales of their breath, thoughts, and/or physical sensations), it is common to discover they are constantly generating judgments about their experience. Leaders help group members understand that constant judgments make it difficult to find any peace from within.

They reinforce that their only task is to *be aware of* what is happening internally, without any need to judge, change, or act on the judgments in any way.

2. Patience

Group leaders present patience as a type of inner wisdom, and encourage group members to "allow things to unfold in their own time." The facilitators stress that individuals be patient with themselves as mastery of any skill requires practice and repetition. When thoughts or feelings of impatience come up, group leaders suggest that individuals recognize that these thoughts or feelings are their reality, unfolding in that particular moment. Patience is particularly helpful when thoughts repeatedly return to a painful past or linger in future fears. It can help group members accept their wandering minds without getting caught up in the stories that create more suffering.

3. Beginner's Mind

"The richness of the present moment is the richness of life itself (Kabat-Zinn 2009, p. 35)." The group leaders encourage participants to be willing to practice as if it was their first time, without expectations of how it should be or how it was last week. Leaders reinforce that a beginner's mind attitude invites members to participate more fully in the present, without expectations from past experience or preconceived thoughts and opinions.

4. Trust

The notion of trust is often a challenging concept for individuals with a diagnosis of serious mental illness. So often their lives have been mired in chaos, trauma, or impaired cognitive functioning that genuine trust in self or others has never been experienced. Group leaders introduce trust from the perspective of honoring one's self, paying attention to one's intuition, and what feels right in that moment.

5. Non-striving

Non-striving is introduced and explored from the perspective of *what it is not*. Most group members can understand that they often do things for a purpose. An example might be their goal of attending the Meditation group to learn how to manage anxiety or stress more effectively. Even though the meditation takes practice, non-striving is about practicing without any goal whatsoever, other than tending to each moment-to-moment experience. It is essentially a "non-doing" experience (Kabat-Zinn 2009) and participants are invited to simply allow any part of their experience, just as it is. Although non-striving can be difficult to conceptualize, group members have reported that it can be very freeing to "just be," without any need to do anything.

6. Acceptance

The concept of acceptance is presented from the perspective of accepting things as they are, *right now*; it does not mean agreement, passivity, or that one needs to abandon their own principles or values. Group leaders stress that acceptance establishes a baseline from which to see things as they really are and if desired, make changes from this point of greater honesty and clarity. Group leaders also reinforce the impermanence of each moment, taking each one as they come and go, with an openness to being with whatever is present.

7. Letting Go

Letting go, or nonattachment to outcome, is fundamental to a mindfulness practice. Group leaders encourage members to notice whatever comes up during the meditation practice, acknowledge thoughts or feelings that the mind seems to want to hold on to, and let them go. Letting go is a way of accepting things as they are, without grasping for the pleasant or pushing away the unpleasant. Group leaders are explicit in their guided meditations, "When thoughts start to take you away from the present moment, notice where they took you, and kindly, bring your attention back to your breath."

The Mindfulness Experience

The two group leaders take turns facilitating each week. One guides the meditation, and the other participates and observes the dynamics of the group. In most meditations, group members are directed to "anchor their attention on the inhales and exhales of their breath." Group members are reminded that they are always breathing; they just do not have to pay attention to their breath because the body is designed to do this automatically. Facilitators reinforce that "nothing is closer to the present moment, than the inhales and exhales of one's breath." Group members are instructed to notice when thoughts take them somewhere else, observe these thoughts, and kindly redirect their attention back to their breath, with a sense of openness, curiosity, and nonjudgment.

For some clients, tending to the breath is very difficult as they have never consciously paid attention to their breath before, or their pattern of breathing is so shallow that it takes greater effort to actually feel the breath in their body. Additionally, individuals with serious mental illness often have unresolved trauma that is easily triggered with directed attention on parts of the body, the breath, or with the eyes closed. For this reason, group leaders use invitatory language that gives participants the freedom to choose how they will experience the meditation. For example, options are given for the eyes to be open or closed, or to use alternate anchors of attention such as finding a neutral place on the body (ex: hands or feet) to focus on during the meditation that feel more comfortable and safe. Periodic pauses are also placed throughout the guided meditation to allow group members to settle into physical stillness, give time to notice thoughts that emerge, or redirect themselves back to the inhales and exhales of their breath in a nonjudgmental way. For some individuals, especially those with active paranoia or ruminative thinking habits, too much time alone with their thoughts can be emotionally dysregulating.

Consequently, the amount of time spent in a “meditation pause” will range from as brief as a few breaths, to no more than five minutes, with facilitators carefully tending to any explicit signs of discomfort by those in the group.

Limitations

> I felt angry before group… backed up… I felt like shouting out during the quiet! Then I thought it wouldn’t get a good reaction. I let go and meditated to calmness.—Mindfulness group member

> I need help badly to get out of these thoughts. Thank you for giving us the opportunity to focus on the here and now.—Mindfulness group member

Despite the apparent usefulness of mindfulness for all individuals in all types of settings, there are situations or times when certain criteria should be met or important limitations may make it difficult to find mindfulness beneficial. For example, mindfulness interventions in individual or group therapy settings need to be introduced within a therapeutic alliance that is felt as safe, secure, and with the client’s best interest in mind. Careful assessment for active psychosis, unresolved trauma, and cultural or spiritual beliefs that may negatively impact the client experience is necessary to determine whether or not mindfulness-related interventions are clinically appropriate. When actively engaging the body’s resources in therapy, even the smallest, most gentle direction may have profound impact on the therapeutic experience. Many individuals, including those at the therapist level, are not often aware of what is going on inside their bodies and how they feel beneath the surface. To pause, breathe deeply, and pay attention to *how it feels* may be enough to trigger a history of shame that is stored at the core of their being.

In the case presented, the majority of clients who receive agency services have a diagnosis of serious mental illness such as MDD, Bipolar Disorder, Schizophrenia, or PTSD. Assessment for appropriateness for groups is completed at the time of group registration by agency clinicians who are trained and designated members of the PSR/Groups Team. Meditation practices must be provided with careful attention to the psychological states of the participant as the internal focus can precipitate psychosis or release a destabilizing flood of painful affect for some individuals with serious and persistent mental illness (McGee 2008). When appropriate, accommodations are thoughtfully provided to allow for greater participation among the client population. In these circumstances group leaders consult with the individual’s providers (psychotherapist, case manager, or psychiatrist) to clarify any clinical concerns or possible limitations. For example, an exception could be made to allow an individual to register for the Mindfulness Meditation PSR group with history of auditory hallucinations, who is currently delusional, however with full capacity to follow the content of the group.

A significant component of serious mental illness is that one’s degree of impairment and frequency of symptoms are often unpredictable. With this in mind, challenges to appropriateness might occur *during the PSR term*, when a client becomes overly symptomatic in ways that prevent their ability to stay focused. Further challenges to appropriateness occur when a participant becomes actively delusional or presents with new psychotic behaviors that prevent the ability to reality test. For others, personality traits may simply prevent one from focusing on their internal experience without dysregulation, leading to constant disruptions that negatively impact the cohesiveness of the group. Options must be provided to empower clients with a choice in practicing the way they feel most comfortable, and in giving them options for *what to do* if they begin to feel unsafe for any reason. At other times, the decision is made that an individual is no longer appropriate and they are asked to withdraw. Coordination of care among all providers is necessary during these instances to assure a safe and clinically supported transition out of group.

A facilitator's skill level may pose a limitation for leading a contemplative group. The clarity and self-awareness that comes with mindfulness practices cannot be implicitly known without experience. For this reason, and for the purpose of providing clinical social work services with competence, mindfulness practices need to be experienced on some level before one explores teaching these contemplative practices to others in a direct practice setting (Kabat-Zinn 2003; Baer 2003). In addition, group leaders must have a thorough working knowledge of group dynamics to understand how dependency issues, group affiliation, as well as the individual diagnostic symptomatology may be influencing the group process (Dobkin et al. 2011; Williams et al. 2008). With a certain degree of experience, facilitators can have confidence and comfort with experiencing their own vulnerabilities, anticipating difficulties certain conditions or group members may have to negotiate, and the self-knowledge which identifies how and when they may overidentify with group members or resist feeling connected to each member and their unique diagnostic constellation.

Finally, mindfulness practices have their own inherent limitations. It is not widely known what type of meditation practice are most helpful, what component of the mindfulness is most effective, who might benefit most, or how long benefits from a mindfulness practice will last (Davidson and Kaszniak 2015; Treadway and Lazar 2010). Much remains to be known about the impact of mindfulness practices on the quality of life for those who struggle with serious mental illness. Although research in mindfulness practices is moving at a profound pace, there is still more uncertainty versus certainty about the benefits of mindfulness practices and how one best utilizes them in the field of mental health.

Conclusion

> After today's meditation, as I opened my eyes, I felt very ALERT and everything felt so fresh.—Mindfulness group member

> I liked the meditation today even though it was a challenge. I find it hard to be loving and kind to myself. I can be compassionate with others but hard on myself.—Mindfulness group member

Clients often enter PSR groups with thoughts that they are alone in their struggles. Group modalities provide a platform for experiencing relief in knowing that others share the same feelings of shame, guilt, inadequacy, fear, or other challenging life experiences (Yalom 1995). In the aforementioned case, the group leader verbally invites group members to notice what they are thinking and how they are feeling, without judgment, with a sense of openness, and curiosity. Using invitatory language and encouraging clients to "practice choice" are important facilitator skills to cultivate. They derive from an empathic stance and may work to build cohesion at the group level, and empowerment at the individual level. Invitatory language, as the name implies, invites participants to *explore their own capacity* to engage in the guided mindfulness practice, whether it be focusing on a specific thought pattern, physical movement, or breathing exercise. By beginning with phrases such as, "now, as you are ready," or "if this feels right," the group leader creates a verbal landscape inviting clients to stay grounded in the present by paying attention to how they feel, both physically and mentally. Invitatory language encourages group members to validate their felt sense of comfort or discomfort, without judgment, and to choose how to proceed based on their self-assessment. Careful attention is given to holding a safe and supportive environment for all group members. When necessary, group leaders must address disruptive client behaviors in the here and now, in collaboration with other care providers, and/or through formal supervision.

Opportunities for interpersonal processing often tease out common experiences among participants that are unsettling and difficult. For example, a new member's experience in the meditation group was one of frustration because her mind kept wandering, making it difficult to harness her attention on her breath. She noted that this added to her overall feelings of inadequacy in and outside of group. The facilitator invited other members to share their similar experiences, and normalized their "mental wandering" as something everyone does. The nature of such contemplative practices also invite a level of processing that is more internally directed, specifically to help clients cultivate greater self-awareness. Facilitator comments such as, "take a moment to notice what you are thinking or feeling, right now," allows space for the practice of taking a conscious pause. Learning how to pause skillfully may be useful in helping one regulate moods or change patterned, reactive behaviors to more thoughtful, response behaviors.

Group leaders regularly reinforce that mindfulness is a skill that takes time and practice to develop, just as an Olympic marathon runner must run or a concert pianist must play the piano to earn expertise status in their field. Group leaders remind participants that mindfulness meditation is the training of one's attention, on what they are experiencing in the moment, with a sense of openness, curiosity, and acceptance. Further discussion includes that acceptance does not necessarily mean approval; it refers more to an acknowledgment or acceptance of how things are right now. In cultivating an internal sense of acceptance as things are, right now, one connects with a new baseline from where the process of change can begin.

The group leaders in the highlighted case provide formal instruction on mindfulness attitudes, possible benefits of developing mindfulness skills, and the ways in which individuals can incorporate mindfulness practices in daily living. Special emphasis is placed on the fact that once learned, mindfulness practices are free of charge and only require one's body, breath, and mind for skillful use. Group leaders remind participants that these skills can be practiced for any amount of time, including a momentary pause, for 5 minutes, or longer. For some, hope springs from the witnessing of more seasoned members who have made progress in integrating mindfulness in ways that make a positive difference in their lives outside of the agency setting. Therapeutic space is always allowed for processing the mindfulness exercises and encouraging suggestions from group members when appropriate. For example, it is common in the early stage of group that one or more members express difficulty noticing or feeling their breath. In response to one's concern, another group member demonstrated how to feel the breath by resting both hands on her lower belly, and feeling the belly rise and fall with each inhale and exhale. Time was allowed for the entire group to "feel their breath move through their body" in this manner. This individual expressed pride in being a "helpful influence," and the other member expressed his gratitude at learning something that made him "feel more capable" in the group.

As stated earlier, PSR groups are highly directed, with co-facilitators leading didactic and experiential learning. The leaders work with members to identify ways they can use mindfulness skills in life outside of the agency setting, with friends and family members, at work or other social environments. After two terms in this PSR group, one member noted on a positive outcome she experienced during a family conflict. By noticing her thoughts and feelings as they emerged she was able to respond in a way that made things better, rather than making things worse. The client reported, "By pausing, I became aware that I was getting angry. By pausing, I was able to control my anger and I ended up getting the help I needed from my sister without the drama."

The "learned helplessness" hypothesis (Abramson et al. 1978) suggests that mental illnesses may persist from a real or perceived absence of control over the outcome of a situation. For individuals with serious and pervasive mental illness, whose livelihood is closely connected to federal entitlement, the outlook may feel grim, the stigma attached to their illness may be real, and they may not try to improve their situation because the past has taught them they are helpless. Perhaps mindfulness practices can be an antidote to learned helplessness by giving clients a new language, of sort, to reflect on personal experience with openness, rather than judgment or harsh criticism. By learning concrete skills that help one stay grounded in present, instead of ruminating in the past or worrying about the future, perhaps one will experience a new level of control in how their life unfolds. By being given the opportunity to learn and integrate mindfulness practices in a safe and supportive group, perhaps individuals can develop new skills to respond to life challenges with "learned helpfulness" and greater adaptability in their natural setting.

References

Abramson, L., Seligman, M., & Teasdale, J. (1978). Learned helplessness in humans: Critique and reformulation. *Journal of Abnormal Psychology, 87*(1), 49–74.

Ahmed, M., & Goldman, J. (1994). Cognitive rehabilitation of adults with severe and persistent mental illness: A group model. *Community Mental Health Journal, 30*(4), 385–393.

American Association of Suicidology. (2012). *Suicide in the USA based on 2010 data.* Washington, D.C.: American Association of Suicidology.

Baer, R. (2003). Mindfulness training as a clinical intervention: A conceptual and empirical review. *Clinical Psychology: Science and Practice, 10*(2), 125–143.

Begley, S. (2008). *Train your mind. Change your brain.* New York, NY: Random House.

Colton, C., & Manderscheid, R. (2006). Congruencies in increased mortality rates, years of potential life lost, and causes of death among public mental health clients in eight states. *Preventing Chronic Disease, 3*(2), 1–14.

Davidson, R., & Kaszniak, A. (2015). Conceptual and methodological issues in research on mindfulness and meditation. *American Psychologist, 70*(7), 581–592.

Department of Human Services, State of IL. (2010). *LOCUS Assessment*, retrieved online at http://www.dhs.state.il.us/OneNetLibrary/27896/documents/By_Division/MentalHealth/FY2011/Locus2010/LOCUS2010.pdf

Department of Human Services, State of IL. (2015). *Rule 132 59 ILAC, Medicaid Community Mental Health Services Program, Part of Section 132.150 Treatment Services, Psychosocial Rehabilitation Service,* retrieved online at http://www.dhs.state.il.us/page.aspx?item=56754

DiClemente, C., Nidecker, M., & Bellack, A. (2008). Motivation and the stages of change among individuals with severe mental illness and substance abuse disorders. *Journal of Substance Abuse Treatment, 34,* 25–35.

Dobkin, P. L., Irving, J. A., & Amar, S. (2011). For whom may participation in a mindfulness-based stress reduction program be contraindicated? *Mindfulness, 3*(1), 44–50.

Fulton, P. (2013). Contributions and challenges to clinical practice from Buddhist psychology. *Clinical Social Work Journal, 42*(3), 208–217.

Garret, C., & Weisman, M. (2001). A self-psychological perspective on chronic illness. *Clinical Social Work Journal, 29*(2), 119–132.

Gelles, D. (2015). Amid the chattering of the global elite, a silent interlude. *The New York Times.* Retrieved online from http://dealbook.nytimes.com/2015/01/21/amid-the-chattering-of-the-global-elite-a-silent-interlude/

Germer, C., Siegel, R., & Fulton, P. (2005). *Mindfulness and psychotherapy.* New York, NY: Guilford Press.

Harris, D. (2014). *10% Happier: How I tamed the voice in my head, reduced stress without losing my edge, and found self-help that actually works–A true story.* New York, NY: Harper Collins Publishers.

Kabat-Zinn, J. (1982). An outpatient program in behavioral medicine for chronic pain patients based on the practice of mindfulness meditation: Theoretical considerations and preliminary results. *General Hospital Psychiatry, 4*(1), 33–47.

Kabat-Zinn, J. (2003). Mindfulness-based interventions in context: Past, present, and future. *Clinical Psychology: Science and Practice, 10*(2), 144–156. -

Kabat-Zinn, J. (2009). *Full catastrophe living. Using the wisdom of your body and mind to face stress, pain, and illness* (15th ed.). New York, NY: Bantam Dell.

Lazar, S. (2005). Mindfulness research. In C. Germer, R. Siegel, & P. Fulton (Eds.), *Mindfulness and psychotherapy* (pp. 220–238). New York, NY: Guilford Press.

Linehan, M. (1993a). *Cognitive behavioral treatment of borderline personality disorder.* New York, NY: Guilford Press.

Linehan, M. (1993b). *Skills training manual for treating borderline personality disorder.* New York, NY: Guilford Press.

Luk, A. (2011). Investigating the long-term effects of a psychiatric rehabilitation programme for persons with serious mental illness in the community: A follow up study. *Journal of Clinical Nursing, 20,* 2712–2720.

McGee, M. (2008). Meditation and psychiatry. *Psychiatry, 5*(1), 28–41. Retrieved online from http://www.ncbi.nlm.nih.gov/pmc/articles/PMC2719544/

Perry, B. (2011). The labeling paradox: Stigma, the sick role, and social networks in mental illness. *Journal of Health and Social Behavior, 52*(4), 460–477.

Rathbone, J. (2013). Zen and the art of management. *Financial Times.* Retrieved online from http://www.ft.com/intl/cms/s/2/32e0b9b4-1c5f-11e3-8894-00144feab7de.html#axzz41hGkKVop

Ricard, M., Lutz, A., & Davidson, R. (2014). Neuroscience reveals the secrets of meditation's benefits. *Scientific American.* Retrieved online from http://www.scientificamerican.com/article/neuroscience-reveals-the-secrets-of-meditation-s-benefits/

Segalla, R. (2003). Meditation and group psychotherapy. *Psychoanalytic Inquiry, 23*(5), 784–799.

Siegel, D. (2011). *Mindsight. The new science of personal transformation.* New York, NY: Bantam Books.

Substance Abuse and Mental Health Services Administration (Samhsa). (2014). *Mental health issues among adults and adolescents.* Retrieved online at http://www.samhsa.gov/disorders

Teasdale, J., Segal, Z., & Williams, J. (1995). How does cognitive therapy prevent depressive relapse and why should attentional control (mindfulness) training help? *Behaviour Research and Therapy, 33,* 25–29.

Treadway, M., & Lazar, S. (2010). Meditation and neuroplasticity: Using mindfulness to change the brain. In Ruth A. Baer (Ed.), *Assessing mindfulness and acceptance processes in clients* (pp. 185–205). Oakland, CA: New Harbinger.

Turner, K. (2008). Mindfulness: The present moment in clinical social work. *Clinical Social Work Journal, 37,* 95–103.

U.S. Department of Education. (2006). *Twenty-eighth annual report to Congress on the implementation of the Individuals with Disabilities Education Act*, Vol. 2. Washington, D.C.

U.S. Department of Health and Human Services. (1999, December). *Mental health: A report of the surgeon general.* Rockville, Md.: DHHS.

Williams, J. M. G., Russell, J., & Russell, D. (2008). Mindfulness-based cognitive therapy: Further issues in current evidence and future research. *Journal of Consulting and Clinical Psychology, 76,* 524–529.

Yalom, I. (1995). *The theory and practice of group psychotherapy.* New York, NY: Basic Books.

Chapter 11
Beginning with the Larger Social System: Mindfulness and Restorative Justice

Connie Sheehan

Tell me and I forget, teach me and I may remember, involve me and I learn.

Benjamin Franklin

Introduction

Mindfulness and Restorative Justice (RJ) share in common an ancient way of addressing contemporary issues of conflict and pain. Each draws attention to lived experiences, feelings of being judged, and self-judgment while underscoring the potential for change. As a participant and participant–observer in both practices, I am often struck how often I hear participants report 'life-changing' experiences as a result of their involvement with mindfulness and RJ. As a clinician and a social worker, the two practices seem to reinforce what our profession has long emphasized: starting where the client is, and the importance of understanding how the biopsychosocial-spiritual context can shape and transform lives. The literature on mindfulness and its many permutations and applications is vast, however, Restorative Justice is only in the early stages of examining "best practices" and "outcomes." This chapter attempts to begin a conversation about the alchemy and intersection of these two important practices.

Key Concepts

Mindfulness

Mindfulness, specifically Mindfulness-Based Stress Reduction (MBSR) first entered the mainstream in the late 1970s with Jon Kabat Zinn developing the

C. Sheehan (✉)
Department of Social Work, DePaul University, Chicago, IL, USA
e-mail: CSHEEHA6@depaul.edu

T.B. Northcut (ed.), *Cultivating Mindfulness in Clinical Social Work*,
Essential Clinical Social Work Series, DOI 10.1007/978-3-319-43842-9_11

secular 10-week program (later reduced to an 8-week program) for those interested in the benefits of meditation to help with chronic illness and pain (Kabat-Zinn 1994). Interestingly both RJ and mindfulness are ancient practices of healing though they may not always have been named specifically as such. The term mindfulness, to many a contemporary term, was however, first introduced by author Davids when he translated the Buddhist term *sati*—a word that some early translators referred to as "remembrance" or "memory" (Gethin 2001, p. 264). Remembering can be viewed as having two related effects. One aspect of remembering is the importance of reminding oneself to stay in the "present experience with acceptance" (Germer 2013, p. 7; Pollak et al. 2014). Remembrance can also be interpreted as "coming back to oneself". Everyday thoughts, whether daydreaming, excessive worry, or cognitive distortions of some kind, can fragment our sense of self. By remembering to stay in the present, we are freed from the troublesome thoughts that interfere with maintaining a sense of internal cohesion.

Restorative Justice and Social Work

Restorative Justice is a theory of justice that addresses repairing harm caused by crime and includes, when possible, multiple stakeholders who take part in repairing that crime. RJ takes into consideration the needs of the victim, community, and offender to repair the harm done by crime. RJ emerged in North America in the early to mid-1970s (Daly and Immarigeon 1998) with varying degrees of reception. It has emerged in many forms from schools, juvenile courts, community, and workplace disputes. RJ can be considered a social movement or perhaps a humanistic way to repair harm to victims of crime. Generally, RJ refers to repairing harm to all the stakeholders of a crime, which includes victim, *and* offender amongst other related stakeholders. Daly and Immarigeon refer to the "ruptured social bonds resulting from crime" (Daly and Immarigeon 1998, p. 22). There are many RJ practices (e.g., victim–offender mediation; family group conferencing, and talking circles). For the purpose of this chapter, we will limit our discussion to talking circles. One way of repairing harm caused by crime is the RJ practice of sitting in a healing or talking circle. Multiple stakeholders may be invited to sit in circle; victim, offender, community members, lawyers, judges, police officers, family members to name a few. Sitting in a "talking circle" in order to restore community and solve issues is possibly as ancient as human civilization.

As a social worker with a focus on complex trauma and forensic social work, exploring multifaceted ways of healing has long been essential to my practice. To that end over several years, I completed several yoga teacher trainings as well as Jon Kabat-Zinn's Mindfulness-Based Stress Reduction (MBSR) teacher training. During that time of better understanding our mind–body connection, I became very interested in Dan Siegel's Interpersonal Neurobiology work (e.g., Siegel 2001, 2006, 2007) and completed the entire series of that training. Coupled with extensive RJ training with Mark Umbreit at University of Minnesota and subsequent facilitator training in Chicago, I began to see how the mind–body connection through mindfulness, specifically Mindfulness-Based Stress Reduction (MBSR) could improve the outcomes of RJ in general and talking circles specifically. Mindfulness informs and supports RJ, allowing it to optimally function.

Mindfulness—the Process Enhancing Presence and Resonance

The Oxford Dictionary (2015) defines mindfulness as "the quality or state of being conscious or aware of something." Mindfulness as defined by Kabat-Zinn (1990) is simply "moment to moment awareness" (p. 2). Later Kabat-Zinn expands that definition to, "paying attention on purpose, in the present moment, and nonjudgmentally, to the unfolding of experience moment to moment". Mindfulness-Based Stress Reduction is a skillful means by which to practice mindful awareness. Taught in an 8-week format, MBSR combines meditation, cultivating awareness of thoughts, feelings, images, and our attachment or aversion to varying states of being.

In intervention settings, mindfulness skills can be taught to prepare people to be reflective and therefore more capable of self-regulation, particularly in instances where individuals have been avoiding the consideration of events that produce internal negative reactions. Mindfulness skills can be used to decrease anxiety or fear in confronting these stressors. Davis and Hayes describe the use of mindfulness in reducing stress around conflict thereby enabling resolution and contributing to more effective communication. The practice of mindfulness in RJ practices may be particularly valuable since these conditions often entail conflict, emotional distress, mistrust, and problems in communication. Contemplative neuroscience is emerging and beginning to show us more concretely what happens in the brain and body when we practice mindfulness. To that point, one small pilot study by Himmelstein et al. found after a 10-week mindfulness-based intervention with incarcerated adolescents there was a significant decrease in perceived stress and a significant increase in healthy self-regulation.

Presence

An aspect of mindful awareness, *presence* is an emotional, cognitive, and physiological state cultivated by living in the present moment. By being present, we redirect our tendency to try to control our circumstances by reliving our past and fretting over the future, to staying in the "here and now." By being aware of and living in the present moment, we can regulate cognitions and affective and physiological responses to that which is actually happening and be with "what is."

The magnitude of psychological and mental health issues that plague significant numbers of individuals, especially those caught up in the criminal justice system, bears this out; humans often react to frustrated efforts to control with depression, anxiety, fear, anger, and denial, and violence, and these often manifest negatively in physiologic terms. Recognizing our essential lack of control and learning to acknowledge and accept this fact is central to mindful living and to maintaining a state of "presence," which then leaves room for tolerance and patience, resisting the instinct to control the conditions or the situation.

Resonance

While resonance or 'feeling felt' with another is linked to the experience of empathy, it becomes a natural outgrowth of mindfulness. As an individual stays in the moment, he or she is able to perceive the facial or bodily expression of another and resonates with it (Siegel 2001). This goes beyond the process of attunement alone which might best be described as *feeling* another whereas empathy approaches a feeling of *knowing* the other. This resonating internal state is often the result of attuned communication. In restorative talking circles, there is an emphasis on the importance of speaking from the heart and deep respectful listening, which are key aspects of attuning to self and other and creating a sense of resonance. In that way, restorative practices, which encourage resonance and presence utilize important aspects of the process of mindfulness which enables the healthy integration of victim, offender, and the stakeholding community.

Restorative Justice

Restorative processes seek to bring perpetrators, victims, and care providers (police officers, criminal justice workers, community service professionals, and social workers) together as stakeholders in acknowledging the harm caused by the harming or criminal behavior and finding ways for the offender to take responsibility and participate in the victim and community healing. The RJ process helps create the potential for something meaningful and positive to be made out of an otherwise negative situation (Latimer et al. 2005). The underlying presumption of RJ is that at least some perpetrators and victims of criminal acts are interested in rectifying the harm that is engendered by these acts as a step toward healing and overcoming the negative outcomes of crime by bringing offenders, victims, and care providers together. Certainly, this is not a viewpoint shared by everyone, particularly those who are engaged in the criminal justice system. The philosophy of punishment for the crime can make it difficult to determine if there is room for restoration in the community affected by the offenses or crimes committed.

Mindfulness may be a vital component in cultivating the ability in both the offender and the victim to "turn toward" (as Jon Kabat Zinn describes it) painful parts of self and past harm. In Ireland, mindfulness practices are brought into jails for those who are preparing reentry into the community. Brewer maintains that to break any harmful habit we need to mindfully move from knowledge to wisdom with curiosity. With this perspective, The Centre for Mindfulness Ireland facilitates an 8-week MBSR Programme at Shelton Abbey Open Prison. This restorative approach provides skillful means, guidance, and practiced planning for incarcerated persons to successfully return to the stressors of life outside the prison walls (personal communication, Irish social worker John Peelo).

Sherman et al. argue that for RJ to be realized, the victim must participate in the process and be given a voice in determining how to address the repercussions of the violation. It is not difficult to imagine that participating and facing one's offender may be a daunting task. Often, automatic fear or stress responses take over when in such a situation. The application of mindfulness practice in this familiar scenario could open the pathway for restorative communication between the stakeholders, particularly within talking circles.

The Talking Circle

The talking circle (sometimes called peace circles or healing circles) emerged out of Native American tribal practice (Pranis 2005). Members of the tribe sat together in a circle and the conversation went round in turn with a talking piece as a respectful way for each member to have the opportunity to express themselves until a consensus was reached across the entire group on a subject up for consideration.

There are some basic guidelines for effective circle discussion such as the "keeper" or facilitator who explains the circle's intention and meaning of the object serving as the talking stick. The leader begins with a process question designed to encourage discussion, be it for education or restorative purposes. The keeper participates as a circle member while also holding sacred space for all. The keeper often models a response to the first question so that the other members of the group understand the type of disclosures and sharing that will be most productive. It is made clear that no one is obligated to speak and the talking piece will pass around again in the case that a member would like to speak after passing. Once they have the talking stick in hand, if they choose not to speak a member can simply pass it on to the person on their left. Often, talking circles allow for an expression of personal storytelling and revealing of emotion in a ritualized safe and predictable setting. This setting may be the only safe space for some individuals to express their shame, anger, and fear in an open and nonjudgmental way.

Circle processes are central to RJ practice and may benefit from an integration of intentional mindfulness practices. Walker and Greening (2010) discussed how RJ circles are designed to support victims of violent crime who may find that even once their perpetrator is tried and convicted, the justice system process has left them feeling exhausted and unheard. Similarly, mindful informed restorative circles may support the families, victims, community, and offenders in regulating feelings, anxieties, and concerns associated with the criminal justice system. The critical function of healing circles is to allow those suffering to have their pain heard and felt by the others in the circle.

The following outline that this author has created and used effectively may serve as a guide equally well in RJ talking circles, Victim Offender Mediation (VOM) and Family Group Conferencing (FGC):

- Brief clarification of mindfulness
- Mindful Breathing/Grounding Exercise
- Check in
- Opening Topic
- Mini Mindful Meditations
- Questions/Concerns
- Mini Mindful Exercise
- Discussion/Solution
- Mini Mindful Contemplations
- Honorable Closing.

The facilitator in this case could open the circle with a grounding exercise such as a guided body scan or another guided imagery of peace and/or openness. She could also ask participants prior, during, and after the practices to simply spend a bit of quiet time alone and perhaps engage in one-minute meditations. It is not necessary to use the language of mindfulness or meditation—the instructions can be as simple as noticing one's breathing or silently repeating a word such as 'peace', 'harmony' or a loving 'it's ok'. The facilitator could also start with an invitation for all parties to come into the present moment, to be present as a human being. To be present to the sense of what is fair or just, present to the respect of process and perhaps a sense of compassion.

The invitation of presence (i.e., an ability to stay in the 'here and now') may take a good 5 to 10 min asking participants to listen with total attention to one another. The facilitator may want to encourage a posture that embodies presence, dignity, and respect For some, this may be the beginning of body awareness and will require basic instruction, discussion of what that posture may feel like from person to person, and finally guided practice to best feel comfortable in this posture. A usual posture is sitting tall and maintaining awareness of the breath moving in and out of one's body, including the rate, depth, and quality of breath and whether it shifts as each person listens and speaks. The practitioner monitors the participants' body language (engagement via eye contact or appearance of alertness; slow and regular breathing, minimal fidgeting or distractedness) and when it seems members are at the risk of disengagement, she may suggest taking momentary breaks to focus on breathing or to engage in a body scan encouraging awareness and inhibiting the tendency of our minds to "fill in the blanks" or jump to conclusions before the whole story is told. The practitioner supports suspension of judgment and witnessing full awareness moment to moment.

Often when we set an intention of peace or restoration, we orient the mind toward equanimity versus fear and upset. Bringing mindfulness and becoming gently aware of the body is available to everyone regardless of culture, ethnicity, and socioeconomic status. By being in our bodies, we can check in with our reactions that often spring from physiological discomfort or at times our negative thinking. Presence in the body also helps make room to detect when ill feelings are being avoided, or when we are more committed to being "right" then listening and receiving information.

Cultivating qualities of mindfulness often includes a sense of kindness and care. A suggestion of focusing on the dignity of each stakeholder may be useful: that each person not be defined by their actions alone, but instead as a whole person. The RJ process asks for responsibilities and co-created consequences for actions, but in a respectful way.

Heaversedge and Halliwell make the excellent point that there is "nothing exclusively Eastern about bringing mindfulness to the body" and that to "reinhabit" the body is part of a rehabilitation (p. 55). And, I would add, to restore the spirit, reconnect to self and others as a result, feeling more "whole" and integrated. The facilitator or keeper could close the circle or series of circles with the suggestion that the mindfulness be practiced going forth allowing the members to retain the sense of resolution, understanding, and connection by integrating the practice into their daily life.

Case Illustration

A young African-American male breaks into his neighbor's home, a white Chicago police sergeant. He ransacks the living room, kitchen, and bedrooms. The victim reports missing an iPhone, jewelry of deep sentimental value, and various food items. The young man is caught trying to sell the phone at a pawn shop, the police are called, and the young man is arrested. The police sergeant is livid because one of the rings the minor stole was the only memento he had from his father. Witnessing the effectiveness of restorative practices in the community, the victim requested a restorative circle with local clergy, a circle keeper, a family member of the offender, as well as a victim family member. Guidelines are established with all stakeholders agreeing to how they will keep the circle safe and respectful.

After several rounds with the talking piece, the stakeholders build a sense of safety and trust. The victim reveals in the round of 'what he needs from this circle' that he just wants to understand what happened and to explain face-to-face how important his father's jewelry is to him. He tears up when speaking of how disrespected, angry, and ultimately sad he felt when he discovered that the last remembrance of his father was stolen from him. He told a story of how he would sometimes stroke his father's ring when he needed guidance or was losing his way and that not only the ring was taken from him but that sense of connection to his father's wisdom.

During one round stakeholders were asked what caused them to feel deep pain, the young man revealed that his father abandoned the family a few years prior. He went on to reveal that he had stolen the items to buy a new pair of designer shoes. His mother refused to spend that much of the family income on a single pair of shoes. He revealed he felt shame, sadness, and anger that his father is not present to help buy him gym shoes and be a part of his life; as they listened, members of the circle swallowed audibly and seemed to wince in pain as they considered the young man. The police officer, still angry, shares the story of his father dying when he was about the same age as the minor offender. As he speaks, he coughs and chokes up, disclosing he actually resonates with the young man in the pain and loss of his father. The young man fights back tears while the officers speaks and when it is his turn he cries and says that he is so sorry he took a keepsake that had so much emotional value. As the talking piece is passed with the question of what is needed to heal, the young man says that he wants to do something to payback the victim's kindness. The sergeant asks if it would be alright if he can mentor the young man so that he might have a father figure in his life, perhaps bringing a bit of his own father back through their interactions. In this way, the talking circle helps heal the harm and is reparative in victim, offender, and community.

Given the complexities of current criminal activity, the above example may give the impression that a talking circle is a solution for merely minor offenses. Indeed, RJ is often used in juvenile court with cases that are relatively minor. In such straightforward nonviolent crimes the solution may seem simple, even sweet. The struggle many have with conceiving RJ use is in addressing more severe crimes, which include violence. These crimes are sometimes vicious and at times the result of multilayered issues. RJ is not a panacea for all crimes committed, nor does it absolve the perpetrator of violence of the legal repercussions of his or her actions. However, RJ has the possibility of acknowledging societal inequality to access of resources, structural inequalities, including long-standing institutional racism and other forms of deep disrespect. Human harm and human healing is profoundly personal and nuanced, which can be addressed sometimes for the first time in a restorative setting.

We see in this particular example that a skilled facilitator is called for—one who both a police officer and minority youth can feel has their best interests in mind and can metaphorically make the circle a safe space for disclosures. The story of the officer or that of the youth is compelling and rife with potential emotional reactivity. Each could easily captivate the keeper in losing a sense of equanimity and becoming caught up in right and wrongdoing. This restoration is about a new understanding of self and other. Like so many restorative cases it is about understanding that in the end we are one and the same. We may have different ways of expression and different backgrounds but our suffering is the same. A skilled practitioner understands this but the fully unanswered question is, what makes for a good practitioner? Rather than leaving skilled facilitation to chance or the lure of a charismatic personality there are systematic ways of developing skillful mindful awareness, thereby creating a higher quality of facilitation. RJ facilitation training which also focuses on cultivating a regular mindfulness practice would be one way of strengthening such facilitation.

Implications for Practice

Social workers who work in RJ capacities can apply their understanding of mindfulness to their own experiences in guiding others toward mindful integration of their multilayered experiences. Professionals can readily practice mindfulness to assess how their own physiological, emotional, and cognitive processes may be impacted by their clients and how these, in turn, impact their clients. Trained professionals are in a position to determine how their limbic and somatic realities are affected by their own perceptions. In other words, remaining mindfully aware of our own physical states as social workers and restorative practitioners is an essential piece of becoming attuned and understanding interpersonal relationships (Siegel 2006). Further exploration and research is needed to have a deeper understanding of how to responsibly and effectively bring mindful practices into RJ. Both models rightfully emphasize the stance of participants engaging in the process voluntarily and authentically.

Future Directions

There is much research needed in the area of RJ and other holistic ways to approach victims, offenders, and employees of the system. Connection or disconnection from a sense of purpose or humanity is an oft-heard complaint from those in the criminal justice system. Healing circles, specifically, mindfully informed healing circles may address that disconnection and build upon the few small studies by using larger samples and more specific samples such as co-worker or interdepartmental circle and youth or worker circles. Intentionally integrating mindfulness would elucidate the most effective use of mindfulness within the RJ system. Given evidence-based practices are being touted as the gold standard in criminal justice (Maruna and LeBel 2010), larger studies of the effect of mindfulness embedded in RJ on healthy and sustainable change are in dire need. Healthy change in talking circles can be considered transformative or even transcendence. However, transformation, transcendence, and even "healthy integration" in circles are elusive concepts that could be refined and reinterpreted in ways that would be more "justice system friendly." Using plain language of the sometimes heady and esoteric concepts of mindfulness and RJ and looking more thoroughly at the intersection of mindfulness and talking circles and the well-researched evidence-based mindfulness studies would be an excellent foundation for future studies.

Conclusion

Offering the integration of mindful practices within RJ is not a simple objective. It is unlikely we can measure what is working and more likely we can point to what is not. It is a curious concept to imagine a person will report being "restored" to pre-harm levels, as we can never truly return to a previous moment or time. Inevitably victims and offenders have suffered and/or grown as a result of the injury or harm. My basic proposal for advocating practices of mindfulness within RJ is to suggest that mindfulness practices may be a way of skillfully guiding participants to recognize, tolerate, and articulate the harms and accompanying suffering common to all, and specifically within the talking circle.

Having illustrated that RJ may be served by the integration of intentional mindfulness practices, it is my contention that we are shaped by experience and that through mindfully informed RJ, positive experiences can be promoted which in turn can result in prosocial behavior. Conceptualizing RJ as an opportunity to introduce and integrate mindfulness practices may not only reward the victim and offender, but also the stakeholders including the facilitators and court personnel. This model veers from blame and shame and instead considers self-regulation, and an environment that encourages connection, compassion, and new possibilities of healing.

Zehr and Mika (1998) emphasized that while there may be no single agreed upon definition of RJ, there are critical essential elements used to define RJ and restorative practices. He emphasizes, however, that these elements are "dynamic in response to changing needs, changing relationships and cultural values" (p. 51). My proposal argues that practices of mindfulness are already at play in RJ and yet, can be cultivated in a more formal way to enhance restorative practices and address the changing needs of our communities. The interpersonal focus on healing within RJ speaks to the usefulness of mindfulness practices. When facing an accuser (victim) the offender may essentially be facing the worst parts of him or herself or the worst behavioral manifestations of self. Mindfully turning toward one's suffering in an open, compassionate manner may expedite and enrich the RJ process.

Kabat-Zinn (2011) stated that the quality of MBSR as an intervention is only as good as the MBSR instructor and his or her understanding of what is required to deliver a truly mindfulness-based programme (p. 281). The very same can be said of a RJ facilitator, and social worker. Social work, with its focus on social justice and biopsychospiritual perspective, is in a unique position to lead the movement of integrating mindfully informed approaches to RJ practice. We have increasing evidence supporting the notion that brains do not perform well under threat, adversity, and in poverty (Blair and Raver 2012). For those who have lived in chronic conditions of adversity, violence, or poverty, the functions that most serve us in promoting well-being become compromised. These functions include difficulty in the ability to delay gratification, an increased learned helplessness, greater psychological distress, and reduced working memory. These impairments add up to increased stress physiology, and trouble with self-regulation. The functions most likely to fail those with the greatest need are the functions cultivated in mindfully informed RJ practices. Given the expense and energy that is given to our criminal justice system, it is worth inquiring whether these mindfulness and restorative practices may have a positive impact on victims, offenders and all stakeholders well-being, as well as the capacity for effectively and efficiently improving our current system.

References

Arrien, A. (1993). *The four fold way*. New York: HarperCollins.

Blair, C., & Raver, C. C. (2012). Child development in the context of adversity. *American Psychologist, 67*(4), 309–319.

Brooks, D. (2015, May 22). Building spiritual capital. *The New York Times*. Retrieved from http://www.nytimes.com/2015/05/22/opinion/david-brooks-building-spiritual-capital.html.

Daly, K., & Immarigeon, R. (1998). The past, present, and future of restorative justice: Some critical reflections. *Contemporary Justice Review, 1*(1), 21–25.

Fortune, D., Thompson, J., Pedlar, A., & Yuen, F. (2010). Social justice and women leaving prison: Beyond punishment and exclusion. *Contemporary Justice Review, 13*(1), 19–33.

Germer, C. (2013). Mindfulness: What is it? What does it matter? In C. K. Germer, R. D. Siegel, & P. Fulton (Eds.), *Mindfulness and psychotherapy* (2nd ed., p. 3–35). New York: Guilford Press.

Gethin, R. (2001). On some definitions of mindfulness. *Contemporary Buddhism, 12*(1), 263–279.

Gilbert, M. J. (2010). Approved protocols: Restorative justice San Antonio pilot project. UTSA, Office of Community and Restorative Justice. Retrieved on March 10, 2012 http://copp.utsa.edu/assets/uploads/centers_and_institutes/Protocol_Final_Approved_-_Modified_2.pdf.

Goleman, D. (2013). *Primal leadership: Unleashing the power of emotional intelligence*. Boston, MA: Harvard Business Review Press.

Himelstein, S., Hastings, A., Shapiro, S., & Heery, M. (2012). Mindfulness training for self-regulation and stress with incarcerated youth. *Probation Journal, 59*(2), 151–165.

Hurley, M. (2009). Restorative practices in institutional settings and at release: Victim wrap around programs. *Federal Probation, 73*(1), 16–22.

Kabat-Zinn, J. (1990). *Full catastrophe living: Using the wisdom of your body and mind to face stress, pain, and illness*. New York: Bantom Dell.

Kabat-Zinn, J. (1994). *Mindfulness meditation for everyday life*. New York: Hyperion.

Kabat-Zinn, J. (2011). Some reflections on the origins of MBSR, skillful means, and the trouble with maps. *Contemporary Buddhism, 12*(1), 281–306.

Kitchen, S. E. (2013). Restoring the professor and the students: A circle process and contemplative practices in a restorative justice seminar. *Contemporary Justice Review, 16*(1), 28–42. doi:10.1080/10282580.2013.769307.

Latimer, J., Dowden, C., & Muise, D. (2005). The effectiveness of restorative justice practices: A meta-analysis. *The Prison Journal, 85*(2), 127–144.

Maruna, S., & LeBel, T. P. (2010). The desistance paradigm in correctional practice. In F. McNeill, P. Raynor, & C. Trotter (Eds.), *Offender supervision: New directions in theory research and practice*. Cullompton: Willan.

Mawby, R. C., & Worrall, A. (2011). "They were very threatening about do-gooding bastards": Probation's changing relationships with the police and prison services in England and Wales. *European Journal of Probation, 3*(3), 78–94.

Meyer, J. F., Paul, R. C., & Grant, D. R. (2009). Peacekeepers turned peacemakers: Police as mediators. *Contemporary Justice Review, 12*(3), 331–344.

Pollak, S., Pedulla, T., & Siegel, R. (2014). *Sitting together: Essential skills for mindfulness-based psychotherapy*. NY: Guilford.

Pranis, K. (2005). *The little book of circle process*. Intercourse, PA: Good Books.

Raynor, P., & Robinson, G. (2009). Why help offenders? Arguments for rehabilitation as a penal strategy. *European Journal of Probation, 1*(1), 3–20.

Schwalbe, C. S., & Maschi, T. (2009). Investigating probation strategies with juvenile offenders: The influence of officers' attitudes and youth characteristics. *Law and Human Behavior, 33*(5), 357–367.

Schwartz, S. (2005). Life skills project. *Journal of Correctional Education, 56*(2), 115–123.

Schwartz, S., Hennessey, M., & Levitas, L. (2003). Restorative justice and the transformation of jails: An urban sheriff's case study in reducing violence. *Police Practice & Research, 4*(4), 399–410.

Siegel, D. J. (2001). Toward an interpersonal neurobiology of the developing mind: Attachment relationships, "mindsight", and neural integration. *Infant Mental Health Journal, 22*(1–2), 67–94.

Siegel, D. J. (2006, April/May). An interpersonal neurobiology approach to psychotherapy: Awareness, mirror neurons, and neural plasticity in the development of well-being. *Psychiatric Annals*.

Siegel, D. J. (2007). *Reflection on the mindful brain: A brief overview: Adapted from the mindful brain: Reflection and attunement in the cultivation of well-being*. New York: WW Norton.

Teasdale, J., & Chaskalson, M. (2011). How does mindfulness transform suffering? II: The transformation of dukkha. *Contemporary Buddhism, 12*(1), 103–124.

Umbreit, M. S., Coates, R. B., & Vos, B. (2007). Restorative justice dialogue: A multi-dimensional, evidence-based practice theory. *Contemporary Justice Review, 10*(1), 23–41.

Walker, L., & Greening, R. (2010). Huikahi restorative circles: A public health approach for reentry planning. *Federal Probation, 74*(1), 43–47.

Wolf, P. R., & Rickard, J. A. (2003). Talking circles: A Native American approach to experiential learning. *Journal of Multicultural Counseling & Development, 31*(1), 39–43.

Zehr, H., & Mika, H. (1998). Fundamental concepts of restorative justice. *Contemporary Justice Review, 1*(1), 49–55.

Chapter 12
On the Road to Mindfulness: Concluding Thoughts

Terry B. Northcut

> Western philosophy since Descartes believed that humans have a faculty of reason (cognition, mind) that is separate from and independent of what we do with our bodies. Reason is independent of perception and bodily movement. It's what makes us uniquely human and distinguishes us from other animals…. (Today) the evidence from cognitive science, especially neuroscience, is that there is no fully autonomous faculty of reason separate from bodily capacities, such as movement and perception. The evidence supports, rather, an evolutionary view in which reason (mind) uses and grows out of such bodily capacities. Philosophy in the flesh even postulates that mind is itself a bodily function. This gives us a radically different view of what mind is and what the human is. (Senn 2016)

Cultivating mindfulness in clinical social work practice can be challenging but extremely rewarding for clients and clinicians. Authors in this text share with us their accounts of how mindfulness has provided a forum to reunite mind and body in unique positive ways to better meet personal and professional needs. Despite their different voices and experiences, a number of themes emerged. Each author emphasized the importance of some kind of personal practice and/or the need to understand the limits of his or her personal knowledge when choosing to apply mindfulness concepts and practices with clients in a variety of contexts. Likewise, mindfulness practices were tailored to individual and group needs over any form of allegiance to a particular intervention. Case examples demonstrated that clients or practitioners experienced a great deal of relief by incorporating mindfulness into their treatment or practice in terms of improved management of symptoms and respite from relentless racing thoughts and often unruly emotions. Of critical importance was the utilization of mindfulness within a therapeutic relationship as an embedded, relational practice. What may have been a surprise for some readers is that mindfulness was not universally suggested for every person at all times over the course of the treatment. Negative thoughts and feelings can emerge with the increased attention to the moment generated in mindfulness practice. However, therapeutic relationships, groups, or talking circles can provide the necessary monitoring to ensure the titration of this practice in accordance with biopsychoso-

T.B. Northcut (✉)
School of Social Work, Loyola University of Chicago, Chicago, IL, USA
e-mail: tnorthc@luc.edu

T.B. Northcut (ed.), *Cultivating Mindfulness in Clinical Social Work*,
Essential Clinical Social Work Series, DOI 10.1007/978-3-319-43842-9_12

cialspiritual supports or stresses. With attuned ongoing assessment, mindfulness can provide relief for many symptoms and systems.

Mindfulness can also be a great leveler; meaning that it is accessible for any person regardless of race, ethnicity, culture, age, or economic class. For example, while not specifically discussed in this text, children in school settings, incarcerated youth, and communities have also benefited from different types of mindfulness programs (Goodman 2005; Himmelstein et al. 2012, etc.). Research continues to be positive and promising for a range of ages and settings.

Nevertheless, when assessing for the appropriateness of mindfulness as an adjunct to treatment, it is still essential to consider what it may mean to clients to do so. In our zeal to promote the benefits of what may be our choice for their treatment, clients sometimes suffer the consequences and may hesitate to say if they do not have the same comfort or passion for our methodology that we do. Jenifer Talley (Chap. 9) uses a clinical illustration which discussed a client who was not able or interested in a traditional AA program but was more suited to a risk reduction framework that allowed for the timely introduction of mindfulness skills. With mindfulness in particular, clients' prior negative experience must be factored into the exploration and assessment process. In addition, clients may prefer a type of contemplative practice that fits better with their religious or spiritual beliefs. This is perhaps the best mindfulness has to offer clinical social work; a flexibility that can meet client needs when the clinician is tuned into those needs, either explicitly or implicitly via his or her own practice.

In terms of future research, there are a number of directions that can do much to facilitate a more precise and perhaps wider application of mindfulness. One major area that is currently under investigation is the identification of particular components evident in mindfulness practices. We already have early results that suggest mindfulness increases self-compassion and an ability to direct one's attention to the present moment (Whitesman and Mash 2015). We also know that mindfulness has a positive impact on reducing stress levels and enhancing continued good health as cited in this text. Future research is needed to broaden those findings to determine if mindfulness can consistently increase health seeking behaviors and reduce high-risk behaviors to prevent mind/body difficulties. With increasing costs in medical care and uncertain political commitment to national health care (including mental health), any intervention which can reduce risk and enhance resiliencies is of critical value.

An additional promising area warranting continued study is the use of mindfulness in diverse countries and with a wide variety of cultural groups; not, however, to encourage broad generalizations or reinforce biases about "other" groups. What is more compelling is the more nuanced way in which mindfulness training can possibly enhance an ability to be present with differences between clinicians and clients. As we accept our own thoughts with compassion, we also can feel curious and compassionate about the persons around us. Edwards (2016) discusses mindful "discerning attention" (p. 216) as a means to develop cultural intelligence through awareness, attention, and remembering. As she quotes Kabat-Zinn (1990), mindfulness entails "cultivating and refining our innate capacity for paying attention and for a deep, penetrative seeing/sensing of interconnectedness of apparently separate aspects of experience, many of which tend to hover beneath our ordinary level of awareness regarding both inner and outer experience" (p. 15; cited in Edwards 2016, p. 216). As Natalie Beck (Chap. 4) explained, there are neurological reasons that mindfulness can facilitate "neural integration and flexible self-regulation" (Siegel 2007, p. 132). In its simplest form, when a bridge is built between physiological, cognitive, and emotional areas of brain, more effective use of the prefrontal cortex is possible which in turn allows us to tolerate uncertainty and discomfort that can result when working with clients, particularly if clients are perceived as being different than us. Mindfulness can smooth the edges of that difference by facilitating a process in which we feel more connected to, rather than different from others, whether we are in a classroom, therapeutic session, the criminal justice system, or negotiating macro-practice. Connie Sheehan (Chap. 11) demonstrated the use of talking circles that mindfully engage seemingly unlikely collaborators in a mindfulness process; a juvenile offender and the victim of the crime. Whether in our own communities or on a broader societal level, we are becoming even more diverse and need all the tools at our disposal which can enhance our ability to more effectively listen to each other even when we vehemently disagree.

The use of a facilitating partnership as Winnicott might have termed it (Applegate and Bonovitz 1995) may be helpful to conceptualize the relational process of mindfulness that is often overlooked or minimized. Historically, mindfulness was not practiced or taught without being grounded in an ongoing teacher–student relationship that helped negotiate the unknown and unpredictable thoughts and feelings that can emerge during its repetition. Michael Rogan (Chap. 6) showed how he provides a relationship in the individual monitoring he does with each participant as they move through the training in mindfulness for clinicians. Even training in Mindfulness-Based Stress Reduction or similar programs with predetermined protocols need facilitating partnerships that provide the emotional and cognitive scaffolding to negotiate the ups and downs of beginning mindful practice. Rogan provided numerous examples of clinicians with differing experiences which shaped how they learned mindfulness.

When working with perceived differences, clinicians often have difficulty tolerating their own assumptions, attributions, and anxieties about clients or colleagues as not being politically correct or reflecting ideal social work values. However, ignoring or not acknowledging these biases does far more damage and is often transmitted unconsciously to the other anyway. Natalie Beck (Chap. 4) found mindfulness allowed her to tolerate rapidly fluctuating intense affective states when interacting with her outpatient mental health group. When the groups were supplemented with interventions from a trained mindfulness therapist, all participants' emotional regulations were enhanced, including the therapist's. We block the potential for clients to acknowledge their own biases if we are communicating an inability to sit with discomfort and close it off from even our own awareness. Mindfulness can be useful to detect and respond compassionately to those thoughts or feelings as they emerge within us or in others. Supervision has historically been the most helpful tool to cope with countertransference reactions when practicing clinically. The addition of mindfulness does not eliminate the need for quality supervision. However, the addition of a thoughtful mindfulness intervention can enhance everyone's ability to stay in the moment without reverting to typical patterns of behavior such as intellectualizing or attributing any interpersonal difficulties solely to clients' thoughts and feelings.

Relational-cultural theory (RCT) developed by Jordan et al. (1991) challenged the notion of a highly differentiated self. Believing instead that we can only understand and grow in the context of a relational matrix advances our ability to take advantage of interventions such as mindfulness that support our ongoing efforts to "get along". Karen Horney described our very human reactions to others as moving toward a relationship, moving against a relationship, and a moving away from a relationship (1945); the common denominator being we act, react, and orient ourselves based on our relationships. The critical point is that regardless of background and regardless of our professional or personal lens, we all interact and react to each other in a process that would benefit from increased thoughtfulness. From a theological or spiritual perspective, we are nourished by connections as identified by Martin Buber as I-Thou relationships. Brooks (2016) in an unusual editorial in the NYTimes related to the combativeness and isolation present in our current political environment, reminds us of Buber's ideas. He states

> I-Thou relationships…are personal, direct, dialogical — nothing is held back. A Thou relationship exists when two or more people are totally immersed in their situation, when deep calls to deep, when they are offering up themselves and embracing the other in some total, unselfconscious way, when they are involved in mutual animated describing….Buber argued that it's nonsensical to think of the self in isolation. The I only exists in relation to some other…(However) You can't intentionally command I-Thou moments into being. You can only be open to them and provide fertile soil….These moments don't last. It is the "exalted melancholy of our fate" that Thou moments always fade …. But a world has been built during such intense moments. A binding cord has been strengthened. The person who has experienced the I-Thou has been thickened and comes closer to wholeness. (Brooks 2016)

There is much in our technologically advanced world that pulls us apart from each other. One only needs to be confronted by teenagers at the dinner table, engrossed in their smartphones, to understand how technology unwinds the social threads that bind us all together. Mindfulness strengthens the ability to tolerate connecting with ourselves and ultimately clients in a way that meets them in the moment. This is perhaps one of the greatest gifts we can give and receive as clinicians. If mindfulness could be incorporated into the training of clinicians of all kinds we may be able to enhance the ability to learn empathy. "Although the importance of empathy for the psychotherapy relationship is well established (Norcross 2001), there is relatively little evidence that it can be taught to psychotherapists to improve their performance. There is however, a growing corpus of literature on the use of meditation and mindfulness to cultivate empathy." (Morgan and Morgan 2005, p. 82) What poses a more challenging research question for the future is to link the empathy developed out of mindfulness to a positive outcome from the therapeutic relationship. What kinds of skills or wisdom does mindfulness cultivate that can enhance our relationships to ourselves, each other, and even globally? Certainly, mindfulness has demonstrated promise in effecting change at the micro-, mezzo-, and macro-levels of social work practice.

Enhanced empathy calls for us to relax, mentally, spiritually, and physically in order to "let one's self go into the other person with a willingness to be changed in the process" (May 1967, p. 97). Salzburg (1995) describes empathy as a "cohesive factor" because it connects us to our own feelings and to those of others. Our experience of shared humanity increases our ability to feel our way into an "other" to facilitate "moments of meeting." Susan Lord's meditative dialogue (Chap. 8) demonstrated the benefits of co-meditation to couples. Relational joining is not only something we practice or teach with clients; all who participate are collaborating in being mutually attentive. Mindfully engaging individuals or systems does not abdicate our professional responsibility to be focused on the experience of our clients, however it allows us to broaden and extend our ability to move beyond our own self and relational images and move into compassionate equanimity (Surrey 2005).

The critical component of compassion can be seen to stem from "unflinching empathy" according to Marotta (2003); an ability to tolerate what thoughts and feelings may occur in the moment in all participants. This ability to share compassion, not in a way that circumvents the therapeutic, teaching, or advisory role, rather allows for a "psychological metabolic process" (p. 112) in which meaning can be made as it is experienced. Whether as an administrator, researcher, clinician, or teacher, as Peterson, Zajakowski Uhll, and Grossman (Chap. 5) described, mindfulness enables an embodied reflectiveness in the moment. There is a frequent, popular misunderstanding about Buddhist mindfulness that the goal is a separation or detachment from self and others. In contrast, Mukerji (2016) makes the case that compassion is intimate equanimity—not detachment or being a spectator on one's own life or the suffering of others. Rather the Buddhist path is meeting pain and suffering with intimacy, but not being the victim of that experience. Equanimity allows us to move beyond the present moment into the next moment, but does not circumvent attention to the moment itself.

Concluding Thoughts

Mindfulness assumes the mind and body are integrated and are powerful factors in resiliency, an assumption that is not a historical given in western societies. Robin Carnes' (Chap. 7) Warriors at Ease program demonstrates the degree to which the mind and body have to be reunited to help veterans or survivors of Complex trauma. With the assistance of a relationship, mindfulness can facilitate learned helpfulness as Rebecca Strauss (Chap. 10) suggests with her groups. Participants in Carnes' groups responded to the enormous effort she put into making the group space safe for reconciling opposites. Likewise Strauss' training helped clients feel much less helpless despite their often debilitating and stigmatizing mental conditions. Utilizing mindfulness moves us toward a better synthesis of the mind/body duality that has permeated western health and mental health care.

Pine (1990) uses an interesting illustration about the advantage of being stranded on a desert island with a set of tools rather than with a finished house. While the complete house provides immediate shelter, it does not allow us to have the equipment we need for future tasks or projects that would enable us to function better and meet environmental challenges. In a similar way, mindfulness is an important tool that builds foundations of many houses by assisting us in future interactions and negotiations in the world. In true paradoxical fashion, mindfulness is a product as mentioned in Chap. 3, as well as a process that allows us to experience the present in a meaningful, accepting, and compassionate manner that in turn effects change in ever widening circles of impact in our social environment.

References

Applegate, J. S., & Bonovitz, J. M. (1995). *The facilitating partnership: A Winnicottian approach for social workers and other helping professionals*. Lanham, MD: Jason Aronson/Rowman & Littlefield.

Brooks, D. (2016, November 1). Read Buber, Not the Polls. *New York Times*. http://www.nytimes.com/2016/11/01/opinion/read-buber-not-the-polls.html?smprod=nytcore-ipad&smid=nytcore-ipad-share&_r=1

Edwards, J. B. (2016). Cultural intelligence for clinical social work practice. *Clinical Social Work Journal, 44,* 211–220.

Goodman, T. A. (2005). Working with children: Beginner's Mind. In C. K. Germer, R. D. Siegel, & P. R. Fulton (Eds.), *Mindfulness and Psychotherapy* (pp. 197–219). NY: Guilford.

Himelstein, S., Hastings, A., Shapiro, S., & Heery, M. (2012). Mindfulness training for self-regulation and stress with incarcerated youth. *Probation Journal, 59*(2), 151–165.

Horney, K. (1945). *Our inner conflicts: A constructive theory of neurosis*. NY: Norton.

Jordan, J., Kaplan, A., Miller, J. B., Stiver, I., & Surrey, J. (1991). *Women's growth in connection: Writings from the Stone Center*. Harvard, MA: Harvard University Press.

Kabat-Zinn, J. (1990). *Full catastrophe living: Using the wisdom of your body and mind to face stress, pain and illness*. NY: Delacourte.

Marotta, S. (2003). Unflinching empathy: Counselors and tortured refugees. *Journal of Consulting and Development, 81,* 111–114.

May, R. (1967). *The art of counseling*. NY: Abingdon Press.

Morgan, W. D., & Morgan, S. T. (2005). Cultivating attention and empathy. In C. K. Germer, R. D. Siegel, & P. R. Fulton (Eds.), *Mindfulness and Psychotherapy* (pp. 73–90). NY: Guilford.

Mukerji, S. (2016). *Acceptance and mindfulness in reducing burnout among helping professionals.* Unpublished paper, Loyola University of Chicago School of Social Work, Chicago, IL.

Norcross, J. (Ed.) (2001). Empirically supported therapy relationships: Summary report of the Division 29 Task Force. *Psychotherapy*, 38(4), 345–356.

Pine, F. (1990). *Drive, ego, object & self: A synthesis for clinical work.* NY: Basic Books.

Salzburg, S. (1995). *Lovingkindness: The revolutionary art of happiness*. Boston, MA: Shambhala.

Senn, F. (2016, October). *The Self-inquirer news and notes for the Grateful Yoga Inquirer*, 19.

Siegel, D. J. (2007). *The mindful brain: Reflection and attunement in the cultivation of well-being*. New York: W. W. Norton & Company.

Surrey, J. L. (2005). Relational psychotherapy, relational mindfulness. In C. K. Germer, R. D. Siegel, & P. R. Fulton (Eds.), *Mindfulness and Psychotherapy* (pp. 91–112). NY: Guilford.

Whitesman, S., & Mash, R. (2015). Examining the effects of a mindfulness-based professional training module on mindfulness, perceived stress, self-compassion and self-determination. *African Journal of Health Professions Education, 7*(2), 220–223.

Appendix

Different Forms and Types of Mindfulness

Beck, C. (1989). *Everyday Zen: Love and work.* San Francisco: Harper SanFrancisco.

Brach, T. (2003). *Radical acceptance: Embracing your life with the heart of a Buddha*. New York: Bantam/Dell.

Chodron, P. (1997). *When things fall apart: Heart advice for difficult times*. Boston: Shambhala.

Chodron, P. (2009). *Taking the leap: Freeing ourselves from old habits and fears.* Boston: Shambhala.

Dalai Lama. (2001). *An open heart: Practicing compassion in everyday life.* New York: Little Brown.

Dalai Lama & Cutler, H. (1998). *The art of happiness: A handbook for living*. New York: Riverhead Books.

Goldstein, J. (1993). *Insight meditation: The practice of freedom.* Boston: Shambhala.

Goldstein, J. & Kornfield, J. (1987). *Seeking the heart of wisdom.* Boston: Shambhala.

Goleman, D. (2003). *Destructive emotions: How can we overcome them?* New York: Bantam/Dell.

Gunaratana, B. (2002). *Mindfulness in plain English.* Somerville, MA: Wisdom.

Hanh, T. N. (1999). *The miracle of mindfulness* (2nd ed.). Boston: Beacon Press.

Hanh, T. N. (1991). *Peace in every step: The path to mindfulness in everyday life.* New York: Bantam.

T.B. Northcut (ed.), *Cultivating Mindfulness in Clinical Social Work*,
Essential Clinical Social Work Series, DOI 10.1007/978-3-319-43842-9

Helminski, K. E. (1992). *Living presence: A Sufi way to mindfulness and the essential self.* New York: Tarcher/Perigree Books.

Kabat-Zinn, J. (1994). *Wherever you go there you are: Mindfulness meditation in everyday life.* New York: Hyperion.

Keating, T. (2006). *Open mind, open heart: The contemplative dimension of the Gospel.* New York: Continuum International Group.

Kornfield, J. (1993). *A path with heart: A guide through the perils and promises of spiritual life.* New York: Bantam.

Kornfield, J. (2008). *The wise heart: A guide to the universal teachings of Buddhist psychology.* New York: Bantam.

Lama Surya Das. (1998). *Awakening the Buddha within: Tibetan wisdom for the western world.* New York: Doubleday.

Lew, A. (2005). *Be still and get going: A Jewish meditation practice for real life.* Boston: Little, Brown.

Peninngton, M. B. (1982). *Centering prayer: Renewing an ancient Christian prayer form.* Garden City, NY: Image Books.

Rosenberg, L. (2004). *Breath by breath: The liberating practice of insight meditation.* Boston: Shambhala.

Salzberg, S. (1995). *Lovingkindness: The revolutionary art of happiness.* Boston: Shambhala.

Salzberg, S. (2011). *Real happiness: The power of meditation.* New York: Workman.

Smith, J. (Ed.). (1998). *Breath sweeps mind: A first guide to meditation practice.* New York: Riverhead Books.

Suzuki, S. (1973). *Zen mind, beginner's mind.* New York: Weatherhill.

Clinical Books

Aronson, H. (2004). *Buddhist practice on Western ground: Reconciling Eastern ideals and Western psychology.* Boston: Shambhala.

Bien, T. (2006). *Mindful therapy: A guide for therapists and helping professionals.* Boston: Wisdom Publications.

Brantley, J. (2007). *Calming your anxious mind: How mindfulness and compassion can free you from anxiety* (2nd ed.). Oakland, CA: New Harbinger.

Epstein, M. (2004). *Thoughts without a thinker: Psychotherapy from a Buddhist perspective*. New York: Perseus Publishing.

Forsyth, J., & Eifert, G. (2008). *The mindfulness and acceptance workbook for anxiety*. Oakland, CA: New Harbinger.

Germer, C. K. (2009). *The mindful path to self-compassion: Freeing yourself from destructive thoughts and emotions*. New York: Guilford Press.

Germer C. K., & Siegel, R. D. (Eds.). (2012). *Wisdom and compassion in psychotherapy: Deepening mindfulness in clinical practice*. New York: Guilford Press.

Germer, C. K., Siegel, R. D., & Fulton, P. R. (Eds.). (2013). *Mindfulness and psychotherapy* (2nd ed.). New York: Guilford Press.

Hayes, S. C., Follette, V. M., & Linehan, M. M., (Eds.). (2004). *Mindfulness and acceptance: Expanding the cognitive-behavioral tradition*. New York: Guilford Press.

Hayes, S., & Smith, S. (2005). *Get out of your mind and into your life: The new acceptance and commitment therapy*. Oakland, CA: New Harbinger.

Hayes, S. C., Strosahl, K. D., & Wilson, K. G. (1999). *Acceptance and commitment therapy: An experiential approach to behavior change*. New York: Guilford Press.

Kabat-Zinn, J. (1990). *Full catastrophe living: Using the wisdom of your body and mind to face stress, pain, and illness*. New York: Dell.

Kabat-Zinn, J. (2005). *Coming to our senses: Healing ourselves and the world through mindfulness*. New York: Hyperion.

Linehan, M. M. (1993). *Cognitive-behavioral treatment if borderline personality disorder*. New York: Guilford Press.

Linehan, M. M. (1993). *Skills training manual for treating borderline personality disorder*. New York: Guilford Press.

Magid, B. (2002). *Ordinary mind: Exploring the common ground of Zen and psychotherapy*. Boston: Wisdom Publications.

Molino, A. E. (1998). *The couch and the tree*. New York: North Point Press.

Neff, K. D. (2011). *Self-compassion: Stop beating yourself up and leave insecurity behind*. New York: William Morrow.

Orsillo, S. M., & Roemer, L. (2011). *The mindful way through anxiety: Break free from chronic worry and redeem your life*. New York: Guilford Press.

Peltz, L. (2013). *The mindful path to addiction recovery: A practical guide to regaining control over your life*. Boston: Shambhala.

Segal, Z. V., Williams, J. M. G., & Teasdale, J. D. (2012). *Mindfulness-based cognitive therapy for depression* (2nd ed.). New York: Guilford Press.

Siegel, D. J. (2010). *The mindful therapist: A clinician's guide to midnight and neural integration*. New York: W. W. Norton.

Siegel, R. D. (2010). *The mindfulness solution: Everyday practices for everyday problems*. New York: Guilford Press.

Shapiro, D. H., & Astin, J. (1998). *Control therapy: An integrated approach to psychotherapy, health, and healing*. New York: Wiley.

Stahl, B., & Goldstein, E. (2010). *A mindfulness-based stress reduction workbook*. Oakland, CA: New Harbinger.

Strosahl, K., & Robinson, P. (2008). *The mindfulness and acceptance workbook for depression*. Oakland, CA: New Harbinger.

Thera, N. (1973). *The heart of Buddhist meditation: Satipatthna: A handbook of mental training based on the Buddha's way of mindfulness*. New York: Weiser Books.

Walsh, R., & Vaughan, F. (Eds.). (1993). *Paths beyond ego*. Los Angeles: Tarcher.

Williams, J. M. G., Teasdale, J. D., Segal, Z. V., & Kabat-Zinn, J. (2007). *The mindful way through depression: Freeing yourself from chronic unhappiness*. New York: Guilford Press.

Buddhist Psychology

Batchelor, S. (1997). *Buddhism without beliefs*. New York: Riverhead Books.

Bodhi, B. (Ed.). (1999). *A comprehensive manual of Abhidhamma*. Seattle: Buddhist Publication Society.

Fleischman, P. (1999). *Karma and chaos: New and collected essays on vipassana meditation*. Seattle: Vipassana.

Johansson, R. (1979). *The dynamic psychology of early Buddhism*. New York: Humanities Press.

Kalupahana, D. (1987). *The principles of Buddhist psychology*. Albany: State University of New York Press.

Nyanaponika, T. (1996). *The heart of Buddhist meditation*. Boston: Weiser Books.

Rahula, W. (1986). *What the Buddha taught*. New York: Grove Press.

Websites

Mindful Awareness:

Mindful Awareness Research Center at the University of California, Los Angeles
www.marc.ucla.edu

Mindfulness-Based Stress Reduction:

UMass Medical School
Center for Mindfulness in Medicine, Health Care, and Society
55 Lake Avenue North
Worcester, MA 01655
www.umassmed.edu/cfm

Mindfulness-Based Stress Reduction and Mindfulness-Based Cognitive Therapy:

Prifysgol Bangor University
Centre for Mindfulness Research and Practice
Bangor, Gwynedd, LL57 2DG
United Kingdom
www.bangor.ac.uk/mindfulness

Acceptance and Commitment Therapy:

www.contextualpsychology.org/act
Dialectical Behavior Therapy:

www.behavioraltech.org

Mindfulness-Based Cognitive Therapy:

www.mbct.com

Mindfulness-Based Relapse Prevention:

www.depts.washington.edu/abrc/mbrp

Mindfulness-Based Symptom Management:

www.ottawamindfulnessclinic.com

Mindfulness-Based Eating Awareness Training:

www.tcme.org

The Institute for Meditation and Psychotherapy:

www.meditationandpsychotherapy.org

The Back Sense program for mindfulness-oriented treatment of chronic pain:

www.backsense.org

University of Calgary MBSR

http://www.mindfulnesscalgary.ca

Center for Contemplative Mind in Society
www.contemplativemind.org

Mind & Life Institute
www.mindandlife.org

Audiovisual materials
www.soundstrue.com
Tara Brach: www.tarabrach.com
Jack Kornfield: www.jackkornfield.com
Sharon Salzburg: www.sharonsalzberg.com
Thich Nhat Hanh: www.iamhome.org, www.plumvillage.org
Pema Chödrön: www.shambhala.org/teachers/pema
Dalai Lama: www.dalailama.com
Lama Surya Das: www.dzogchen.org
Father William Menninger: www.contemplativeprayer.net

Buddhist journal (US)
www.tricycle.com

Thich Nhat Hanh & Buddhist links
www.iamhome.org

Index

T.B. Northcut (ed.), *Cultivating Mindfulness in Clinical Social Work*,
Essential Clinical Social Work Series, DOI 10.1007/978-3-319-43842-9

The manufacturer's authorised representative in the EU is Springer
Nature Customer Service Centre GmbH, Europaplatz 3, 69115 Heidelberg,
Germany. If you have any concerns regarding our products, please
contact ProductSafety@springernature.com

Printed and bound by CPI Group (UK) Ltd, Croydon, CR0 4YY
25/09/2026
02222869-0007